CLASSIC
COLORADO
SKI DESCENTS

Jenn,

Enjoy the

Snow — I see
a hut trip in
our future :)

— Jon

The author making turns high on Snowmass (14,092'). Hagerman Peak and the Maroon Bells serve as a stunning backdrop in the Elk Range. Photo by Tara Nichols

COLORADO
MOUNTAIN CLUB
GUIDEBOOK

CLASSIC
COLORADO
SKI DESCENTS

JON KEDROWSKI, PH.D.

The Colorado Mountain Club Press
Golden, Colorado

Classic Colorado Ski Descents

PUBLISHED BY

The Colorado Mountain Club Press
710 10th Street, Suite 200, Golden, CO 80401
303-996-2743   email: cmcpress@cmc.org
website: http://www.cmc.org

Contacting the publisher: We would appreciate it if readers would alert us to any errors or outdated information by contacting us at the address above.

Jon Kedrowski: photographer unless noted otherwise
Takeshi Takahashi: designer
Jodi Jennings: copyeditor
Clyde Soles: publisher

Cover photo: Roger Carter rips down the southwest face of Columbia (14,073') in the Sawatch with Mount Yale (14,196') in the distance. Photo by Jon Kedrowski

DISTRIBUTED TO THE BOOK TRADE BY:

Mountaineers Books
1001 SW Klickitat Way, Suite 201, Seattle, WA 98134, 800-553-4453,
www.mountaineersbooks.org

We gratefully acknowledge the financial support of the people of Colorado through the Scientific and Cultural Facilities District of greater metropolitan Denver for our publishing activities.

TOPOGRAPHIC MAPS are created with CalTopo.com software.

ISBN 978-1-937052-38-6

Contents

CHAPTER 1   FRONT RANGE

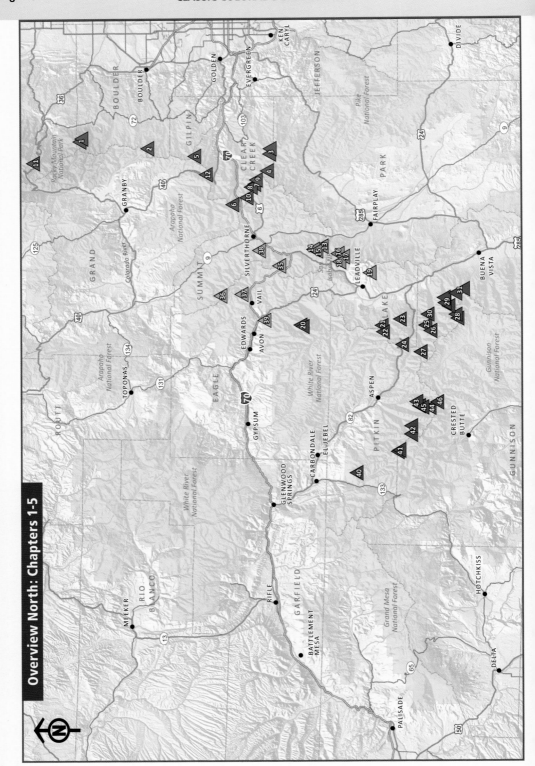

Overview North: Chapters 1-5

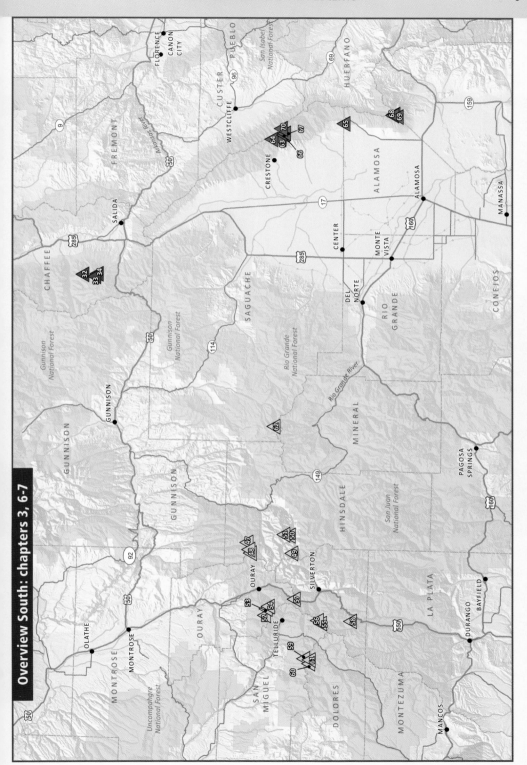

Overview South: chapters 3, 6-7

A gorgeous morning in the Holy Cross Wilderness en route to skiing the famous Holy Cross.
Photo by Brad Burgtorf

Foreword

In 2006, my first winter in Colorado, I remember getting kinks in my neck while riding the Pallavicini chairlift at Arapahoe Basin, straining to look back across the valley in awe at skiers painting fresh tracks down "The Professor"—a popular 2,000 foot backcountry line that descends from a bowl from near the top of Loveland Pass towards the resort's parking lot. I knew immediately that that was the type of skiing I had to experience.

The next fall, I bought a pair of AT skis and bindings, all the necessary avalanche gear, signed up for an avi course, and booked my first backcountry ski weekend at Margy's Hut, a 10th Mountain Division cabin outside of Aspen. At the time, it was the most money I'd ever spent outside of buying my car. Looking back, it was one of the best investments of my life.

I skinned into Margy's Hut wondering if there'd be enough snow to ski, but after a record setting storm rolled in that weekend, one that closed the Denver airport and the greater metro area for days, we skied powder that was so good it would be years before I would experience anything like it again.

In the ten seasons since, my skin tracks have taken me places—both literally and figuratively—I could never have dreamed of going. The pursuit at times can be hard to rationalize. I've sobbed, suffered, froze, gotten lost, been humbled, and failed more times than I'd like to admit. I've skied snow so unforgiving, in gale force winds that seemed to blow thoughts right out of your head, and experienced moments that had me swearing to never clip into bindings again... only to find myself planning the next outing from a micro-brewery that same evening.

What I love most about Colorado backcountry skiing are its endless possibilities. Once beyond the chairlift, there are thousands of ski descents like "The Professor" throughout the state. And our diverse mountain ranges, long seasons and reliable snowfall mean that you can find one all to yourself for most of the year—and every so often if you're lucky, experience the kind of snow that will keep you chasing perfect lines for decades to come.

But there's no need to strain your neck, Jon gives you the perfect headstart in this guidebook.

See you out there,

Brad Burgtorf, skier and outdoor explorer
July 2017

Enjoying a sunrise in the San Juans.

Acknowledgments

I have the honor of giving credit where credit is due on yet another exciting adventure and book—this time here in Colorado. Without my friends, family, and business partners, this would have never been possible.

I want to thank many of my ski partners over the years that have helped motivate me to ski and to capture content and photos: Torrey Udall, Austin Porzak, Scott Benge, John Fielder, Brad Burgtorf, Connor Drumm, Tara Nichols, Steve House, Chris Tomer, Anna Marie Migl, Mike Lewis, Ryan and Ashley Belanger, Eric Sangueza, Roger Carter, Garrett Eggers, Ted Mahon, and Chris Davenport. I'm so grateful for additional Folks contributed their photos as well: Andrew Warkentin, Calen Orlowski, Dennis Humphrey, Jason Gebauer, Jordan White, and Ben Conners.

My publisher was the amazing Clyde Soles. I also appreciate the hard work of designer Takeshi Tokahashi, and copy editor Jody Jennings. Thanks also to Sarah Gorecki, my former editor, who also had a hand in editing this manuscript and helping conceive the idea of doing a guidebook and beginning this great adventure. To Rebecca Finkel, my long time trusted designer, your role in my books never goes unnoticed. Also, Sarah Jenniges – your work on the overview maps and other advice on map editing is always appreciated. To the Colorado Mountain Club Press and Executive Director Scott Robson: thanks so much for giving all my fun books a chance. To some of my sponsors over the years: Enerplex, Zeal Optics, MountnGo, GoScope, Skratch Labs, Kästle Skis, Silver Oak, Honey Stinger, Mountain Hardwear, Lifeproof, Four Points and the Steadman Clinic: thanks so much for supporting all of my ski days out there to gather the information I needed to produce this book.

Thanks to my family: my parents Bob and Barb, my brother Jared and his family (Michelle, Kash, and Kaden), my sister Krista and her husband Zack, and my brother Robbe and his family. Now everyone knows what the heck I was always doing climbing and skiing all these peaks! Enjoy.

If there is anyone else I might have forgotten along the way, thank you and come ski with me!

Introduction

Skiing is a sport in Colorado that has been around for over a century. Rather than recreationalists, our first skiers were explorers, dating back to Enos Mills in 1904. Mills traveled into the Colorado backcountry as a "Colorado Snow Observer," collecting weather and snowfall data on a pair of skis that would more than likely be impossible for us modern day ski mountaineers to put on our feet much less use to carve turns (especially without using stiff plastic boots, which weren't even invented until 1957). Our skiers in the mid-1900s were those from the 10th Mountain Division of the US Army, who trained and skied in the backcountry above Camp Hale near Vail. These were truly our first backcountry ski pioneers.

Perhaps our most influential ski mountaineer of today is the legendary Lou Dawson. Lou was the first to ski from the top of Colorado's official 54 14ers. His feat lasted from 1978 to 1991. After he accomplished this goal, he continued to ski peaks all over Colorado. Many other backcountry skiers emerged in the early 2000s to find recreation in the mountains, following Dawson's footsteps.

Fast-forward to the past decade of skiing here in Colorado. Our ski resorts are becoming more crowded, and making first tracks is always a challenging post-storm prospect. Many people desire to stay fit and to seek out powder and solitude on our mountains; they love to earn their own turns and feel the incredible satisfaction of standing on top of a peak or remote backcountry line taking in the views before carving their own first tracks. Enos Mills, the 10th Mountain Division soldiers, or even Lou Dawson would have never imagined that backcountry skiing could have come this far in Colorado. Over 100 years later, with ultralight gear, state of the art bindings, and skis that can get into any terrain, today's backcountry skiers can travel into any location and ski down nearly anything.

This book is for everyone who desires the Colorado backcountry skiing experience. While I have outlined and selected some of my favorite backcountry locations as well as peaks and lines to ski, I suggest even more options for creating your own adventures. Enjoy making your own turns throughout our great State of Colorado! Perhaps I'll see you on the next summit.

Jon Kedrowski, May 2017

How to Use this Guide

SKI DESCENT ROUTE CLASSIFICATION

In the sections of this book that discuss the **DESCENTS** as well as **"ALTERNA-TIVES,"** the routes are classified as:

Easy Slopes ● Terrain that includes wide-open snow slopes, minimal crevassed terrain on glaciers, and steepness less than 25 degrees. This also includes logging roads, access roads, or snowcat roads. Avalanche danger is low.

Intermediate ■ Terrain that includes wide couloirs, minor gullies, moderately crevassed terrain on glaciers, and steepness between 25 and 35 degrees. This also includes four-wheel-drive roads, hillsides that have dispersed trees, glades, or moderately forested terrain. Avalanche danger is generally moderate.

Expert/Advanced ◆ Terrain that includes couloirs, gullies, heavily crevassed terrain on glaciers, and steepness between 35 and 50 degrees. This also includes hillsides with complex terrain and thicker forests. Avalanche danger can be high.

Expert/Extreme ◆◆ Terrain that includes steep narrow couloirs, deep gullies, cornices, extremely crevassed terrain on glaciers, and steepness greater than 50 degrees. Cliffs and the ability to ski off of cliffs and cornices may be mandatory, as well as the ability to rappel down where necessary. Tree skiing is required and vegetation in forests may be very steep, thick, and extremely difficult to navigate and ski. Avalanche Danger can be extreme.

DESCENTS are recommended ski lines that are described in detail for this guide. **ALTERNATIVES (marked as EC on Maps)** are ski lines that are often considered more difficult but can be very rewarding for the skier who decides they want to put in extra effort and exploration to ski and explore options that the author has chosen to place on a map but may not have described the ski route or line in explicit detail.

CLIMBING CLASSIFICATIONS

When a climbing route is described in this guide, the following descriptions are used:

A: Snow steepness ratings

Easy	0–30 degrees
Moderate	30–45 degrees
Steep	45–60 degrees
Very Steep	60–80 degrees
Vertical	80–90 degrees

B: Rock Ratings

The climbing difficulty of the routes listed in this guide is classified under the Yosemite Decimal System (YDS).

Class 1—Trail hiking or any hiking across open country that is no more difficult than walking on a maintained trail. The parking lot at the trailhead is easy Class 1, groomed ski trails are midrange Class 1, and some of the big step-ups on the rocks, such as those near the top of the Barr Trail of Pikes Peak, are difficult Class 1.

Class 2—Steep trail and/or climber's trail hiking or off-trail hiking. Class 2 usually means bushwhacking or hiking on a talus or loose rock slope. You are not yet using handholds for upward movement. Occasionally, the rating Class 2+ is used for a pseudo-scrambling route where you will use your hands but do not need to search hard for handholds. Most people are able to downclimb Class 2+ terrain facing out and without the use of hands, while using superb balance and careful stepping.

Class 3—The easiest climbing (not hiking) category. People usually call this "scrambling." You are beginning to look for and use handholds for upward movement.

Basic climbing techniques are used, which are noticeably beyond the level of any walking movements. Although you must use handholds, you don't have to look hard to find them. Occasionally putting your hand down for balance while crossing a talus slope does not qualify as Class 3; this is still Class 2. About half of the people feel the need to face in toward the rock while downclimbing Class 3.

Class 4—This level of climbing is within the realm of "technical climbing." You are not just using handholds; you have to search for, select, and test them. You are beginning to use muscle groups not involved with hiking, those of the upper body and abdominals in particular. Movement at Class 4 is more focused, thoughtful, and slower.

Many people prefer to rappel down a serious Class 4 pitch that is exposed rather than to downclimb it. Many Class 3 routes in California would be rated Class 4 in Colorado.

Class 5—Technical climbing and nothing less. You are now using a variety of climbing techniques, not just cling holds. Movements may involve stemming with your legs, cross-pressure with your arms, pressing down on handholds as you pass them, edging on small holds, smearing, chimneying, jamming, and heel hooks. A lack of flexibility will be noticeable and can hinder movement, and any movement at Class 5 totally occupies the mind of the individual. Most people choose to rappel down Class 5 pitches.

Class 5 climbing described within the YDS:

Class	Description
5.0–5.7	Easy for experienced climbers; where most climbers begin. Two or three great handholds/footholds are present for upward movement using the four extremities.
5.8–5.9	Where most weekend climbers become comfortable; employs the specific skills of rock climbing, such as jamming, liebacks, and mantels. One or two good handholds/footholds are present for upward movement using the four extremities.
5.10	A dedicated weekend climber may attain this level; strong fingers and great footwork are necessary, only one good handhold/foothold per four extremities for upward movement.
5.11–5.15	The realm of true experts; demands much training and natural ability, and often, repeated working of a route utilizing very few handholds of solid grip, many times zero handholds at all per four extremities.

The Basics

Do you want to ski in Colorado's backcountry and safely enjoy your adventure? Here's what I've learned after many years of backcountry ski mountaineering:

The most important variable to consider is the weather. Before packing a single bag, be sure you understand the weather and avalanche forecasts inside and out. Equally as important, educate yourself on mountain meteorology as well as avalanche safety. Being able to diagnose the weather you see unfolding in the field as well as the type of snow conditions can save your life. This kind of wisdom will help you decide whether to attack the summit or turn around and go home. Consult local weather experts for information, or attend personalized mountain meteorology workshops. Don't forget those valuable avalanche safety courses as well.

Know the mountain geography, specifically the route topography. Research the peak and know the escape routes if bad weather rolls in. Knowing the route will also give you a good estimate of how long it will take you to reach the summit and how you can ski down. Keep in mind you'll only be as fast as your heaviest pack and slowest group member. Understanding topography can also help you select the route safest from avalanche danger. Terrain selection is often the most critical factor in managing risk in the mountains.

Increase your fitness and acclimatization ahead of time. Efficiency is a key piece of the puzzle, and if you're in great shape you can move faster and feel better. Sleep in a high mountain town or backcountry hut first, then increase the elevation gradually to backcountry experiences on 12ers or 13ers to further acclimatize. As you climb and ski bigger objectives, you'll want to have the stamina, speed, and fitness to escape almost any situation that comes up.

Lighten your load. The more weight you carry, the slower you will move. Heavy weight also increases fatigue.

> **Bare essentials:** I am a bare-minimalist during most of my travels, but it's up to you to experiment to see what you can survive without. My bare essentials are my whippet/ice axe, an ultralight hoozdy down jacket, waterproof jacket, and pants (which also act as wind breakers), water reservoir, headlamp, energy bars, hat, gloves, cameras, sunscreen, sunglasses, toilet paper, lighter, ultraviolet water purifier, and pre-packed pizza (among other snacks and food for the backcountry). If you are headed for a hut trip or winter camping you'll need to add a –15 to 15°F down ultralight sleeping bag

(depending on how cold you get), a sleeping pad, an ultralight one-to-three person tent, and maybe an additional ultralight bivy sack.

Stoves: Don't forget your stove either, as it might come in handy to melt snow for water! On multi-day peaks or hut trips, a stove is sometimes needed, and if I do carry one, it's a very small and light MSR PocketRocket.

Avalanche gear: In avalanche terrain, a beacon, probe, and shovel are essential, and an avalanche inflatable bag is nice, but remember that they won't prevent you from being caught in an avalanche; they will only help you find and dig others out. A beacon will also facilitate your own rescue, should you be caught in an avalanche. Make sure your probe extends to a long enough distance (15 feet or more), otherwise it will be useless if your companions are buried!

Ski equipment: My preferred light weight ski equipment consists of the Kästle TX90 or TX98 length 177 and 187 touring line with Dynafit Radical bindings and Scarpa Maestrale touring boots.

Know your limits. You'll want to climb and ski the peaks in this guide in traditional alpine style before attempting overnight camping as well. Cold winters make backcountry camping tough. Hut trips in Colorado are becoming very popular with the 10th Mountain Division Hut System (www.huts.org) and other hut options (see the appendix). Over time you can learn to ski difficult terrain and to assess avalanche conditions in the field, which will make your trips very rewarding.

Before you leave on a ski trip, browse websites for avalanche information and reports. Start easy and build from there. After guiding numerous groups up 14ers, volcanoes, and other peaks throughout the world, including everywhere in Colorado, I've found that it's often one of the most difficult things hikers, skiers, and boarders have ever done.

Select your team carefully and conserve your energy in the backcountry. Traveling in small groups of less than five people is usually the safest practice in the mountains. Too many people tends to slow things down, and if you are skiing a relatively narrow objective or small mountain face, managing slough or other objective hazards with more than five people can be a chore. I honestly prefer a party of two to four for maximum enjoyment, unless the objective hazards are minimal. But I also have a few rules within groups when it comes to setting skin tracks and helping to conserve energy on big objectives:

Sunrise on the Front Range as a storm rolls in.
Photo by Chris Tomer

Make the youngest and strongest members break trail and set the skin track, but don't be afraid to rotate through to keep everyone fresh to reach your summits in a timely, efficient manner.

Always stop to rest with the group and evaluate terrain in safe zones that are out of the way of avalanche paths and rockfall zones. Some of the locations described in this book (i.e., Loveland Pass, Uneva Peak on Vail Pass, or Meadow Mountain near Vail) are ideal locations for setting a skin track and using it over and over during multiple runs that day. If you see someone hiking up your skin track, especially a snowboarder or snowshoer, give them a stern warning that you worked hard to put that skin track in.

But most of all, have fun!

The Ten Essentials

Within the basic gear items mentioned above, increase your survival chances in extreme environments by always carrying items from this list.

1. Navigation
2. Sun protection
3. Insulation
4. Illumination
5. First-aid Supplies
6. Fire
7. Repair kit and tools
8. Nutrition
9. Hydration
10. Emergency Shelter

Backcountry ski equipment

With an explosion of brands and types of gear becoming available in the world of backcountry skiing it can be hard to keep it all straight. Over the last decade the skis, boots, and bindings have all seen significant modifications, mainly to shave off weight while allowing us to ski and tour nearly everywhere.

SKIS

The two most important factors to take into account when choosing a new alpine touring ski are where you will be skiing and how you will be skiing.

Will you be touring to access chest-deep powder in the San Juans, or to make June turns on firm snow on Longs Peak on the Front Range? Likewise, do you want to start racing up the mountain in record time or just enjoy the solitude of the mountains with a couple of buddies at your leisure? Will you be dropping every cornice you see, or do you prefer to keep your skis down on the couloir below you as you carve turns? Once you are clear about what kind of skiing you will be doing, you can better evaluate your options in terms of width, length, shape, and weight.

Width: Choose a ski width that matches your skiing style. For long spring or summer tours where you will not be encountering too much deep snow, choose a ski with a waist width in the 70–90mm range. The narrower the ski, the lighter and more nimble it will be when making kick turns on your ascent, but performance in deeper or variable snow will be affected.

On the other side of the touring spectrum, choose a ski width between 90–115mm if you like catching air and expect to be skiing variable conditions or powder. You will sacrifice some weight, but wider skis provide more stability in rough conditions, and of course, superior float in the deep stuff.

Shape and Profile: Ski shape and profile are just as important as ski width. When it comes to the profile of touring-specific skis, the two most common styles are traditional camber and a hybrid profile. The latter usually features a rockered tip (also referred to as early-rise tip) with camber underfoot and a flat tail.

Traditional, full-camber profiles are generally found in the narrower touring skis that are used for hard-packed snow conditions. This type of profile provides the most contact with the snow, which in turn provides more grip on the uphill and powerful turn initiation and edge hold on the descent.

As ski width increases, we generally begin to see the hybrid ski profile. A rockered tip allows the ski to plane better in powder and blast through variable crud, while the camber underfoot and flat tail still allows for good snow contact and edge control on the downhill.

The one ski profile that isn't seen too often in the touring world is full rocker. Not that it can't be done, but aside from not holding climbing skins all that well, fully rockered skis make minimal contact with the snow, sacrificing grip on the uphill and making kick-turns a little more difficult if you are not an experienced uphill traveler. However, if you don't mind a little slippage and inefficiency on the track and expect to be hitting deep snow on the way down, it may be the way to go.

Length: The length of an alpine touring ski shouldn't differ too much from what you typically use for skiing. However, if you plan on racing or doing more uphill than downhill travel, you may want to choose a ski on the shorter side. This will allow for easier kick-turns and reduce ski weight—but high-speed downhill performance will be affected.

Construction: The construction of alpine touring skis is really what sets them apart from the norm. Materials like carbon fiber, paulownia, beech, poplar, and bamboo are often used to lighten the skis, which helps with taking thousands of steps uphill with weight on your back. The heavier your ski setup, the more quickly you will tire out, possibly ending your ski day prematurely.

Lightweight construction, however, requires a small tradeoff for ski performance because these skis often lack some of the damp, chatter-free characteristics that are helpful for hard and variable snow conditions. Therefore, don't automatically choose the lightest ski you can find. Instead, choose a ski offering the width and shape that aligns with your ski style, and look for other ways to lighten your setup, such as using lighter boots or bindings.

But as with all rules, there are exceptions; there are a handful of brands such as Black Diamond, Kästle, and Dynafit that offer top performance on both ascents and descents, in exchange for a somewhat higher sticker price.

Tips and Tails: Another element to take into account is the shape of the tip and tail and the presence of company-specific skin attachment systems. Because ski touring requires the use of climbing skins, which attach to your ski's bases via the tip and tail to gain uphill grip, choosing a ski that allows for easy and secure skin attachment is key.

BOOTS

Alpine touring (AT) boots are different from alpine ski boots. AT boots are designed for both downhill skiing and ascension using climbing skins, while alpine boots are primarily downhill-oriented. AT boots have a supportive ski mode for skiing downhill, plus a flexible unlocked or "walk" mode that lets your ankle and lower leg flex forward and back for skinning and bootpacking uphill. AT boots usually have a curved (rockered) and lugged rubber sole like a hiking boot that gives improved grip on slippery surfaces and lets you walk more naturally. They also focus on lightness and are increasingly made with lightweight materials like carbon fiber to save weight without sacrificing performance.

Stiffness can be an issue with AT boots. Any boot's stiffness will usually decrease with use. Some new AT boot designs come close to or surpass alpine boots in stiffness and downhill performance while adding a walking hinge and lugged sole. These boots are suitable for strong and experienced skiers who intend to charge hard in the backcountry and plan to include air and speed in their touring. With advances in touring boot technology, these boots can be much lighter than similarly stiff alpine models and have excellent cuff mobility for touring. Consider crampon compatibility with your ski boots; this is important to your ability to make smooth transitions before climbing up a steep couloir or when taking crampons off before clicking in to skis.

BINDINGS

AT bindings come in a variety of brands and are made to match boots that generally have compatible toe-pins. The combination of bindings and boots allows the user to travel easier in two ways: skinning (cross-country uphill with skins on the bottom of the skis for traction), or keeping the boot in walk mode to walk or climb. The right setup makes for easy transitions: once a ski mountaineer reaches his or her summit destination, pulling skins off, rotating heel pieces, and tightening boots to make them stiffer around the lower leg and ankle takes a few minutes at most. For an excellent summary of backcountry ski bindings and their evolution, visit the online museum at www.wildsnow.com/backcountry-skiing-history/binding-museum-backcountry-skiing.

Though I mentioned the exact equipment I tend to use, my best advice for you is go to a local rental shop and demo some gear. You can also demo backcountry ski gear at industry-sponsored events.

Super light AT gear makes accessing steep and isolated terrain in the San Juan Range much easier.
Photo by Eric Sangueza

ICE AX AND CRAMPONS

Carrying an ice axe and crampons is also a personal decision based on terrain selection and difficulty of your ski descent and climbing objective combined with seasonal snow conditions. For example, you might not need crampons even if the couloir you are climbing is 40 degrees, but the snow is punchy or powdery, allowing for good steps. If the snow is icier, your ice axe might come in handy, but if the slope is moderately steep but powdery, a tool called a whippet might be a better choice for you. A whippet is an adjustable ski pole with an ice axe on the end. I prefer whippets for moderate couloirs where you need to stand taller but then I also have the security of my ax for traversing or climbing relatively steep terrain or tricky climbing sections. In addition to traditional crampons, 'ski-crampons' are great tools that can be quickly attached to your skis and used while skinning up on top of the frozen and consolidated snowpack, particularly in April, May, or June when it hasn't snowed for days. Consider using ski-crampons on moderately steep snow that is still not steep enough for a full-on boot pack and when you are headed up early to ski corn snow in the warmth of the morning sun.

Meteorology: Regional Weather and Climate

During an average year, the Colorado mountains receive anywhere from 250 to 750 inches of snow. Most of the snow falls between November and May in the higher elevations and areas near timberline (12,000 feet). Generally, in May, the change of seasons produces high pressure that combines with warm and long days that will settle the snowpack and make it ideal for skiing and backcountry travel. In spring, the high pressure can settle in for days, providing warm, stable weather, which becomes more prolonged by summer's arrival in late June. Because the seasons are changing, bad weather days can also occur, when it can still rain in the valleys below 9,000 feet and snow, especially at higher elevations, for days at a time. In 2015, Colorado's high country above 10,000 feet saw upwards of 48 inches of snow during May. The highest peaks, especially at and above timberline, benefited from the snow, while mountain towns in the valleys only saw rain. Big upslope snow storms commonly hit the Front Range during May, providing the sticky snow coverage (along with lack of wind) needed for skiing many peaks that only be navigated for a month or two each year.

At lower elevations, the distinct continental dry climate lends itself to evergreen, conifer, and aspen forests. It's a good rule of thumb to remember that the higher elevations (with tundra vegetation above the timberline) not only receive the lion's share of the seasonal snowfall, but can also experience intense blizzards and strong winds at any time of year. April and May are the best months to ski Colorado's mountains, but the weather can mimic summer with pleasant, warm days, or winter, with extremely cold temperatures and jet stream-fed winds.

The orographic (rain shadow) effect also plays a significant role in weather and highland climate in the Colorado mountains. There is generally less snowfall and overall precipitation east of the Continental Divide, and the eastern aspects of the Front Range generally receive less precipitation than the windward and wetter sides of the Divide (with the exception of upslope springtime snow events on the Front Range peaks). For the same reason, there is typically more snowfall in the southern mountains like the San Juans, or the central Elk Range, versus the Sangre de Cristos. Even the Sawatch or Gore Ranges can be hit with a bit more snow than the Tenmile/Mosquito Range because they are located farther to the south and west and catch the prevailing fronts coming from the western United States, either from the Pacific California coast or the Pacific Northwest. The eastern side of the Sawatch Range is very dry, also due to the orographic effect. These general trends are important to keep in mind, especially with regard to understanding snowpack and avalanche potential with increasing elevation.

SNOW AND AVALANCHES IN THE COLORADO MOUNTAINS

Avalanches are the most unpredictable phenomenon related to weather forecasting and skiing in the major Colorado ranges. Most avalanches (up to 80 percent) are human triggered, and therefore nearly 100 percent preventable. However, the only way to prevent an avalanche is to not venture out to climb and ski in the backcountry in the first place. This is not realistic, of course, but there are many steps an educated and experienced backcountry skier and alpinist can take to decrease the chances of ever being caught in an avalanche.

Four Human Factors for Avalanche Avoidance

1. **Become Experienced and Educated.** Take avalanche courses, and if you have never been out climbing and skiing in the backcountry before, go with someone who knows what they are doing. You can always learn something from others. Get out and explore as often as possible. You can learn a great deal from just being out on the peaks all the time.

2. **Terrain Selection and Good Route-finding Habits.** Carrying the proper equipment is important, but if you steer clear of extremely steep slopes, avoid overhanging cornices, and stay away from glaciers that are heavily crevassed (this applies mainly to other parts of the world), you can minimize your risk. Proper backcountry travel is a skill that is learned over many years. Always consider what is above you when climbing, think often about your escape route, and never linger in an area that might be prone to avalanches. Travel through high-risk areas one at a time, and try to stay above and cross potential avalanche paths as high on the slope as possible.

3. **Never Go Out Alone.** I approach this one with discretion—about 60 percent of my adventures are done solo as I enjoy solitude. Going solo is a matter of preference, and can be very rewarding for the experienced alpinist. The rewards can also be great if you have an equal partner because you can learn a great deal from one another in the mountains.

4. **Start Early.** Many mistakes in the backcountry are created and compounded from other mistakes. The root of the problem is often not starting early enough and running out of time, which makes us rush and make rash decisions leading to mistakes and accidents. For example, in April, May, and June, the Colorado snowpack is generally more predictable and stable compared to winter months. Snow heats up and softens in the afternoons from warmer temperatures and direct sunlight. The snowpack settles, freezes,

and stabilizes overnight when it gets cold. It is generally a good rule to begin an ascent in safe, frozen, and stable snow well before dawn, to be on the summit at sunrise or at least before 9:00 a.m. on a very warm day, and to be skiing down a steep slope or narrow couloir when the snow becomes corn—when it is soft enough to ski but not soft enough to create a wet slab avalanche. Powder days are in a different category, but starting early is still a good rule so that you are down and out of harm's way before noon.

THE AVALANCHE TRIANGLE

The human factors mentioned above can be placed within the "Avalanche Triangle," first described by Fesler and Fredston in **_Snow Sense_**, first published in 1984. The triangle has three sides: terrain, weather, and snowpack. Each will be briefly described here.

Snowpack   Terrain

Weather

A fourth variable, human actions, creates the avalanche hazard.

Photo by Ivan Larson

Terrain. The magical slope angle for avalanches is 35 degrees. This is the most important factor to consider when evaluating whether a slide can occur. Slope aspect determines if sun exposure is hitting a slope indirectly. Slope aspect can also determine the impact of wind, which can load snow onto a slope. Overall, north-facing slopes tend to be more prone to avalanches because the snow is colder and slower to bond together. "Faceting," or crystallization of snow creating a weak layer, can also happen more on north-facing slopes. While slopes with northerly aspects (opposite in the southern hemisphere with southerly aspects) remain cold, slopes with south-facing aspects often develop a sun crust that can act as a sliding layer. Moderate warming on a slope can stabilize the snowpack, but rapid warming, especially within a day's time or on very warm spring days from direct sunlight, can have the opposite effect and can cause avalanches.

Weather. Snowpack is constantly changed by the weather. The best question to ask is, "How is the weather impacting the snow's strength?" Past, current, and future weather can dictate snowpack and the likelihood of avalanches. Digging a snow pit near a slope you want to ski is a good way to check snow layers for stability and to see what the weather was doing to the snowpack in the past months. Layers have different densities or hardness showing periods of drought, heavy snowfall, or mild days and cold nights when depth hoar was created.

Climbing high peaks in Colorado in the middle of winter to ski powder often includes having to deal with strong winds and ground blizzards! Photo by Chris Tomer

Understanding how current weather is impacting snow and conditions is critical. For example, is it snowing heavily or lightly, and how long has it been snowing? How much snow has fallen, and is the temperature rising or falling? Quickly rising temperatures combined with sunlight can lead to snow settling and creeping downhill due to gravity.

Heavy snowfall that accumulates at an inch per hour, or 12 inches in less than 24 hours, can have a significant impact on snowpack and snow stability. The weight of the snow is dictated by the moisture content and temperature. Colder snow is lighter and more powdery and can be less dangerous than warmer, wetter, and heavier snow. Wind plays a factor. If winds are stronger than 20 mph they can not only impact the visibility of route hazards, but can also transport snow to cornices and load it onto slopes, making them immediately more dangerous.

Knowing the future weather forecast is very helpful when planning a trip. I usually check the weather forecast to see what happened overnight and what is in store for the day. Red flags include more than six inches of new snow, high winds, more snow forecasted, and rapid warming during the day. Be aware that conditions may change while you travel into the backcountry or to a summit. Use general weather information to your advantage, but realize that "You never know until you go." I never cancel a trip because someone else told me to—I want to get into the field and see for myself. If conditions indicate too many hazards, I can always pull the plug 30 minutes into the trip, but will have learned more from firsthand experience.

The author stands atop a summit ridgeline in the San Juans. Note the wind loaded slabs to the left which are best avoided until late spring once the snowpack consolidates.
Photo by Eric Sangueza

Snowpack. To create a slab avalanche, the snowpack must have a slab, a weak layer, and a bed surface. What makes snow strong or weak, bonded or slippery, is mainly determined by how it changes when it hits the ground. These changes, called snow metamorphism, either create strong internal cohesion through rounding, or create weak cohesion through faceting and crystallization. The latter results in unstable snowpack and "sugar" snow, which is heavily avalanche prone.

THE COLORADO ROCKIES AS PART OF THE CONTINENTAL SNOWPACK

In Colorado, the central Rocky Mountains are considered continental in their location. They are relatively far from the ocean, and generally the winters are bitter cold, and include periods of extreme cold, but there can also be some warm days where the sun is intense at high elevations and the air temperature gets slightly above freezing. The following avalanche characteristics are true of the continental Colorado Rockies:

1. Moderate snowpack (more than a meter to upwards of 3 meters (3 to 9 feet).
2. Cold temperatures (–10 to 35 degrees Fahrenheit, –15 to 2 degrees Celsius).
3. Low-density snow (2 to 10 percent water by volume).
4. Storms with lots of snow, but dry periods of winter high pressure that help decrease the avalanche danger.
5. Weak layers are more pronounced and frequently persist.
6. Avalanches generally occurring during storms are triggered by precipitation or wind, as well as the human element. Wind slabs are common due to the increase in wind that occurs in winter and is caused by the jet stream.

7. Mid-winter rain is uncommon.
8. Slides are possible throughout the year, especially in the afternoon and on south facing slopes that are warmed by the sun.

These trends vary depending on elevation and orographic effects, as well as latitude and the actual location of specific mountain ranges.

A NOTE FOR OUT-OF-STATE VISITORS REGARDING WEATHER AND SNOWPACK

Conditions in Colorado can vary greatly from those in other parts of the country and differ within separate parts of the state. For example, conditions in the Wasatch Mountains of Utah are very different from those in Colorado's Rocky Mountains. And snow conditions in the San Juan Mountains can vary from those in the Elk Range or the Front Range. Learn about the snowpack history of a specific location to help you determine how safe conditions might be.

Before heading out into Colorado's backcountry, study the general conditions reports and forecasts from the Colorado Avalanche Information Center (CAIC), www.avalanche.state.co.us. Colorado is generally known for its weak-layered snowpack, which is a function of Colorado's climate. The snow-covered ground is almost always near the freezing point of water. Snow

To gain more knowledge about snowpack in Colorado, consider taking an avalanche certification course.

depth combined with air temperature can determine the temperature gradient across the snowpack. In fall and early winter, Colorado is notorious for snow that has crystalized facets formed by shallow snow and cold temperatures. The faceted snow can last all season long near the ground, under several feet of snow. This condition is a dangerous recipe for large slab avalanches.

From mid-May through June the snowpack usually stabilizes; this is the best ski season in Colorado. With long days and warm temperatures, afternoon thunderstorms or even "thundersnow" can develop, so start your climb pre-dawn and be off the summits by before noon. Starting early and finishing early will also help you avoid wet-slab avalanches.

The best way to stay safe, test out all of your ski gear, and prepare for a season in the backcountry is to ski uphill at your favorite local ski resort on an early morning in November or December.

TYPICAL SEASONAL CONDITIONS

The following conditions are typically encountered when skiing in Colorado's backcountry:

November—December: Backcountry ski season begins in Colorado, but the lack of snow can lead to exposed terrain hazards (rocks, bushes, tree stumps), and bare areas on peaks.

January—March: Snow is accumulating and snowpack is growing, but with large storms that dump a lot of snow and the lack of warmth and low sun angles, snow layers may not bond until well into March.

April—May: Spring ski season arrives with longer days, excellent snow coverage, warmer temperatures, and stable snowpack. With mid-day to afternoon warming, pre-dawn starts for big objectives should be routine. Steeper lines must be climbed and skied before 9 or 10 a.m. depending on slope aspect, solar heating, and overall snow coverage.

June—July: Summer snow conditions arrive; snow has settled, but may be sloppy, wet, and slippery by 8 a.m. Skiing can be good but sticky. Watch for unpleasant sun-cupped snowfields on some aspects.

August—October: Lack of snow coverage usually means the season is over. Consider taking a break from skiing and go for a trail run, mountain bike, or rock climb!

Good luck and have safe adventures!

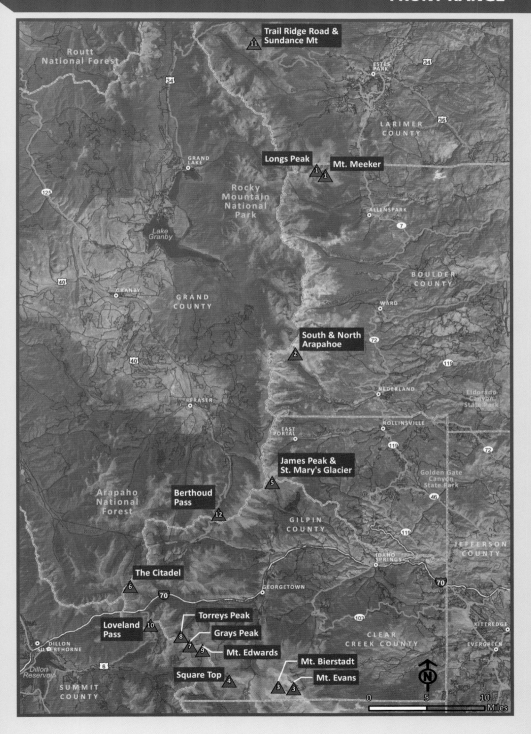

Routt
National Forest

Trail Ridge Road &
Sundance Mt
11

ESTES
PARK

34

34

LARIMER
COUNTY

36

GRAND
LAKE

Longs Peak

Mt. Meeker

1   1

Rocky
Mountain
National
Park

ALLENSPARK

125

7

Lake
Granby

BOULDER
COUNTY

40

GRANBY

WARD

GRAND
COUNTY

South & North
Arapahoe

72

40

2

119

FRASER

NEDERLAND

Eldorado
Canyon
State Park

ROLLINSVILLE

EAST
PORTAL

James Peak &
St. Mary's Glacier

119

72

5

Golden Gate
Canyon
State Park

Berthoud
Pass

Arapaho
National
Forest

46

12

GILPIN
COUNTY

119

IDAHO
SPRINGS

JEFFERSON
COUNTY

The Citadel

6

GEORGETOWN

70

70

Loveland
Pass

Torreys Peak

10

103

KITTREDGE

DILLON
SILVERTHORNE

8

Grays Peak

7

CLEAR
CREEK COUNTY

EVERGREEN

9

Mt. Edwards

6

Square Top

Mt. Bierstadt

4

Mt. Evans

Dillon
Reservoir

N

SUMMIT
COUNTY

3   3

0   5   10

Miles

1. Longs Peak

14,256 feet/4345 meters

SKIABLE VERTICAL:	Up to 5900 feet/1798 meters
ROUND-TRIP DISTANCE:	13–16 miles/21–26 kilometers
TRAILHEADS:	Longs Peak (9,400 feet), Copeland Lake (Sandbeach Lake/ Wild Basin) (8320 feet)
DIFFICULTY RATINGS:	◆ / ◆ ◆
SKI TERRAIN:	Ridgelines, couloirs, steep faces, and tree glades
OPTIMAL SEASON:	February to June. May and June are ideal.
MAPS:	Trails Illustrated Numbers 200 and 301, Longs Peak, Roosevelt National Forest

COMMENT: Longs Peak is the Front Range's monarch. It is seen easily from the Denver Metro area and cities along the Front Range corridor. Thousands climb Longs every year, but only a handful ski the peak because the most practical ski

Breaking trail on wind loaded slabs above Keplinger's Couloir near the Homestretch.
Photo by Chris Tomer

lines have technical descents and Longs lacks good snow cover for most of the year. Longs is probably the windiest 14er in Colorado and is undeniably one of the windiest peaks in all of North America, so most of the winter snow gets blown away in the consistently high winds. Therefore ski conditions are usually good only in the spring, when sticky upslope cakes the slopes with snow. If you are fortunate to get a calm day on Longs the day after a storm, take advantage of it and enjoy making turns!

GETTING THERE

Longs Peak Trailhead (9,400 feet). This trailhead is located at the Long's Peak Ranger Station just off Colorado Highway 7. If approaching from the north from Estes Park, travel 9 miles from the

Approaching the Loft in Chasm Meadows near Chasm Lake.

US Highway 36/Colorado Highway 7 junction in Estes Park. Turn right on the paved road marked for Longs Peak Trailhead and follow the road 1 mile to the parking area and ranger station. From the south, travel 10.5 miles north from the junction of Colorado Highway 7 and the Peak to Peak Highway (Colorado Highway 72). Turn left on the paved road marked for Longs Peak Trailhead and follow the road 1 mile to the parking area and ranger station.

Copeland Lake (Sandbeach Lake/Wild Basin) Trailhead. (8,320 feet). Copeland Lake Trail is also called the Sandbeach Lake Trailhead and is located at the entrance to Wild Basin just off Colorado Highway 7. If approaching from the north from Estes Park, travel 13 miles from the US Highway 36 and Colorado Highway 7 junction in Estes Park. Turn right on the paved road marked for Wild Basin and follow the road 0.4 mile to the parking area just north of the Wild Basin Park entrance. From the south, travel 6.5 miles north from the junction of Colorado Highway 7 and the Peak to Peak Highway (Colorado Highway 72). Turn left on the paved road marked for Wild Basin and follow the road for 0.4 mile to the parking area just north of the Wild Basin Park entrance.

THE CLIMBS

The Loft (Class 3). Start from the Longs Peak Trailhead and follow the East Longs Peak Trail for 4.5 miles to Chasm Meadows below Chasm Lake. On the way you

Skiing into Keplinger's from the Homestretch with the Palisades adding to the scene.
Photo by Scott Benge

will cross a stream near timberline at 2 miles. Turn left at Jims Grove Junction at 2.5 miles and reach Chasm Junction at 3.5 miles, where you will continue to the left toward Chasm Meadows. Instead of traveling to Chasm Lake and toward the east face of Longs, climb to the southwest toward a moderate face that rises to a saddle between Mt. Meeker and Longs Peak. The key to reaching the flat saddle known as the Loft is to take a left (south) and traverse a narrow but obvious ledge that heads south then southwest up class 3 slopes to reach the flat saddle. From the Loft, continue west for 0.25 mile, descending around the mountain for 150 feet. Then climb up and around into Keplinger's Couloir. Just before starting to gain elevation below the rock formations known as the Palisades (beautiful west facing rock slabs), you will pass an arrow painted on the rocks known as Clark's arrow.

From Clark's Arrow scramble north and descend slightly, then ascend a broken set of ledges up a couloir to 13,600 feet. From here the top of the couloir can be reached at a feature called the Notch but before you get to the notch, traverse left (northwest) on a snow-covered ledge and ramps for 200 yards to join the Homestretch at 13,900 feet. Follow the relatively easy slope to the summit of Longs.

Other popular routes to the top of Longs include the Keyhole, the North Face Cables, and Keiners.

Relaxing on the summit in early June waiting for the snow to soften. Photo by Scott Benge

Celebrating a fun ski of Keplinger's Couloir seen at center.

DESCENTS

1. ***Keplinger's Couloir*** ◆ / ◆◆ Leave the summit to the southwest. Ski the Homestretch for 300 feet down to the broad face and set of ledges that take a skiers left (east). Ski 200 yards to the east to enter the top of Keplinger's Couloir. Keplinger's Couloir is a spectacular line that when filled with snow skis for nearly 2000 feet to the valley below. If you ski the full line, a vehicle shuttle is necessary from Wild Basin below Sandbeach Lake. You can enjoy turns to 11,000 feet in the woods near Keplinger's Lake, and then find the hiking trail corridor near Sandbeach Lake to return via Wild Basin.

2. ***North Face Cables Route*** ◆ / ◆◆ The entire North Face of Longs rarely has enough snow to avoid a rappel off the route. If you are lucky enough in late May or early June to find the face in prime condition, you can make a clean descent at 50-degrees of steepness.

ALTERNATIVES

Exploring Longs extremes ◆◆ Any number of lines can be explored on Longs from the summit. Few skiers have tried descending the Notch or Keiners to Lambslide. It may also be practical to ski the Homestretch to Keplinger's Couloir, then climb up past Clark's Arrow to the Loft and descend the steep couloir/face from the Loft back to the northeast to Chasm Meadows, eventually hiking back to your vehicle at the Longs Peak Trailhead.

Another option includes climbing Mt. Meeker and descending its south face back to Sandbeach Lake on a ski line known as Dragon's Egg Couloir.

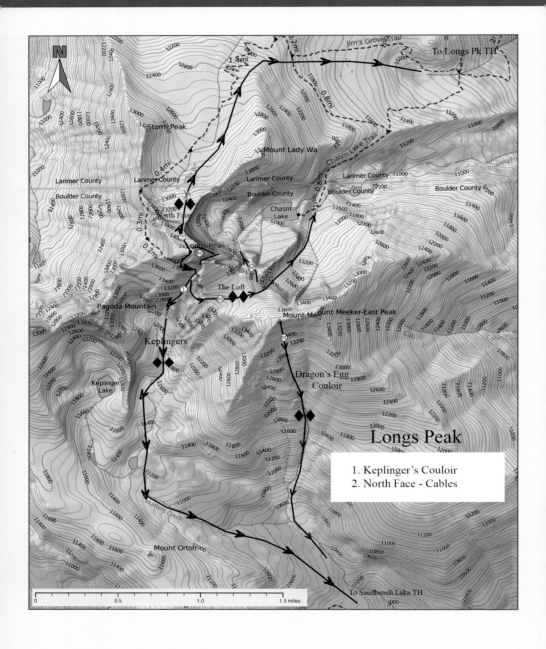

Longs Peak

1. Keplinger's Couloir
2. North Face - Cables

LONGS PEAK

2. South and North Arapahoe Peaks

13,502 feet and 13,397 feet/4115 meters

SKIABLE VERTICAL:	Up to 3400 feet/1037 meters
ROUND-TRIP DISTANCE:	7 miles/11.3 kilometers
TRAILHEAD:	Fourth of July (10,100 feet)
DIFFICULTY RATINGS:	■ / ◆ / ◆ ◆
SKI TERRAIN:	Ridgelines, couloirs, and moderate faces
OPTIMAL SEASON:	February through June. April and May are ideal.
MAPS:	Trails Illustrated Number 102, Arapaho National Forest

COMMENT: You can be to the trailhead in less than two hours from most Front Range locations, making Arapahoe Peaks an excellent ski choice. These peaks are the sentinels of the Indian Peaks Wilderness, offering stunning views and spectacular ski options.

Peering down the spectacular skiable Skywalker in late spring.

Approaching the Skywalker, the obvious line angles left towards 11-o'clock.

GETTING THERE

To get to the Fourth of July Trailhead (10,100 feet), follow Colorado Highway 119 south from Boulder to the small town of Nederland. From Nederland, head south on Colorado Highway 119 for 0.6 mile. Turn west (right) onto County Road 130, signed for Eldora. Follow the paved road through the town of Eldora, where the pavement ends. Continue on the road for 1.5 miles and turn right at the signed junction, and continue 4.5 miles to the trailhead, which is near the Buckingham and Fourth of July campgrounds. Typically the road at the end of the pavement gets plowed towards the trailhead by mid-April. By early May it is possible to drive all the way to the trailhead- and four-wheel-drive is not mandatory.

THE CLIMB

South Slopes/Southeast Ridge (Class 2). Start at the Fourth of July Trailhead. From the trailhead gate, skin or hike up the Arapahoe Pass Trail to the west. At 1.5 miles you will get close to timberline. At the Fourth of July Mine ruins (11,250 feet), double back to the northeast on the Arapaho Glacier Trail, which is signed and well-beaten. Travel northeast up relatively gentle slopes for 0.75 mile to reach the southeast ridge at 13,000 feet, where you will be able to see the Arapahoe Glacier to the north in the basin. Continue 0.3 mile to the summit of South Arapahoe Peak. From the basin at 11,500 below South Arapahoe's south face, it is possible to climb the steep Skywalker Couloir, which heads directly north toward the summit.

DESCENTS

1. *Skywalker Couloir* ◆ / ◆◆ Leave the summit to the south aspect on the steep ridge and look for the cornice at the top of the couloir. The top of Skywalker Couloir drops steeply to the south and is narrow, only about 30 feet across at first. The couloir is initially 50 degrees depending on the snow conditions but the angle lessens to 35 degrees once you are about 800 feet down. Most of the upper couloir is about 40 degrees. Once the couloir ends,

Skiing into the depths of Skywalker half way down.

enjoy easy snow slopes to the vicinity of the Fourth of July Mine ruins to the basin below.

2. ***Southeast Ridge and South Variations*** ■ / ◆ If you aren't feeling up to the steepness of the Skywalker Couloir, enjoy some fun turns down the southeast ridge. You can really open it up for some spring corn on the south couloir and southwest facing slopes of South Arapahoe Peak for over 2,000 feet. Once in the basin, follow the Arapahoe Pass Trail corridor east and ski back to the Fourth of July Trailhead.

ALTERNATIVES

North Arapahoe Peak Traverse ◆ ◆ From the summit of South Arapahoe Peak, traverse 0.50 mile to North Arapahoe Peak via the Class 3 and Class 4 ridgeline. Use maps and your own exploratory skills to locate options for skiing off the top of North Arapahoe to the north, or return to ski the routes off South Arapahoe Peak as described.

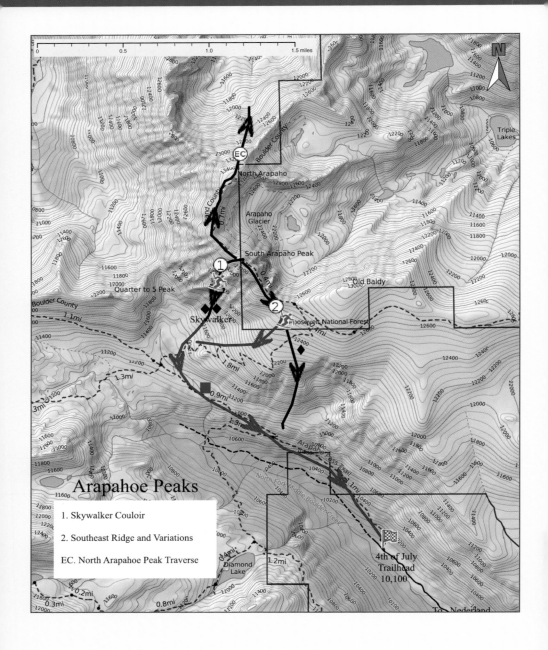

Arapahoe Peaks

1. Skywalker Couloir

2. Southeast Ridge and Variations

EC. North Arapahoe Peak Traverse

SOUTH AND NORTH ARAPAHOE PEAKS

3. Mt. Bierstadt
14,060 feet/4285 meters

SKIABLE VERTICAL:	3000 feet/914 meters
ROUND-TRIP DISTANCE:	7 miles/11.3 kilometers
TRAILHEAD:	Guanella Pass (11,669 feet)
DIFFICULTY RATINGS:	■ / ◆
SKI TERRAIN:	Ridgelines, moderate faces, and bowls
OPTIMAL SEASON:	February through June. April and May are ideal.
MAPS:	Trails Illustrated Number 104, Guanella Pass, Arapaho National Forest

COMMENT: The easiest 14er to get to from Denver and the Interstate-70 Corridor, Bierstadt is a fine ski tour in spring snow conditions.

GETTING THERE
Guanella Pass (11,669 feet). Travel west from Denver on I-70 for about 50 miles and take Exit 228 at Georgetown. Follow the signs into historic Georgetown. From downtown, continue following the signs out of town and head south above town on switchbacks on Guanella Pass Road. You will pass a power plant and a small lake in the deep valley on your left as you continue on a paved road for 10 miles from Georgetown to the top of Guanella Pass at 11,669 feet. In winter, the

In May you can experience a snow-loaded summit in solitude on Bierstadt before skiing down.

The west and northwest aspects provide great low angle turns.

road is generally plowed through to the power plant, which is in the vicinity of the reservoir, and by May 1 the road is sometimes plowed and open to the pass (but this is not considered a CDOT priority). Note that a slog up the road in winter or early spring might add up to 4 miles one way. In recent years the road has been consistently open to Guanella Pass Campground, which is 1.7 miles from the top of the pass and has ample parking. Consider using a snowmobile or starting early on this one in winter! If approaching from the south, follow the Guanella Pass Road north for 12.2 miles from US Highway 285 near the town of Grant.

THE CLIMB

West Slopes (Class 1). Start at the top of Guanella Pass and travel to the southeast from the parking lot on the east side of the road. You can easily see Mt. Bierstadt from the trailhead. You will gradually drop 300 feet for the first 0.50 mile and then cross Scott Gomer Creek. This is a popular winter climb, so if you are familiar with the summer route, it is generally easy to find snowshoe or ski tracks cutting through the willows on the actual summer trail. From above the creek crossing, zigzag skin to your east to gain an obvious shoulder and flatter area above timberline at 12,300 feet. The sharper northwest face of Mt. Bierstadt welcomes you at this point. It is now possible to skin up the west slopes angling to the southwest to a small saddle for a strong mile and connect to a gentle ridge that heads northeast and directly to the summit.

DESCENTS

1. *West/Northwest Slopes* ■ Leave the summit to the southwest on the narrow but relatively simple ridgeline and retrace your path to the flat saddle at 13,800 feet. From here, stay skiers right and ski straight back down 25 degree slopes to the west side of Mt. Bierstadt. These slopes are gentle and perfect for a first time 14er skier. Once back to the willows near Scott Gomer Creek, follow your tracks and the summer trail corridor back to the west to return to Guanella Pass. If the coverage on Mt. Bierstadt's west face is good enough, you can choose to ski the face direct between 13,900 feet and 13,600 feet instead of staying on the ridge.

Greeted by some early morning light while skinning up to Guanella Pass.

2. *Northwest Gully* ◆ This is a steeper and shorter way to ski down. From the summit, head northwest on the ridge for about 100 feet. You will drop down and be able to see a sharp ridgeline leading toward the Sawtooth and Mt. Evans (right) and Mt. Bierstadt's west face (left). The northwest gully is fairly broad and is steeper than the west face. If filled in well, it makes an excellent ski not exceeding 35–40 degrees. Ski the gully for 500 feet directly down to the northern flanks of the gentle west face and the easy slopes of the ridgeline. At times you can peer down into the deep basin below the Sawtooth and the upper reaches of Scott Gomer Creek. You may even be able to find a steep line directly north into this glacial basin, which makes a nice variation. Return to Guanella Pass through the willows once reaching 12,300 feet on the ridge.

ALTERNATIVES

Northeast Face ◆ Any number of lines can be explored to the northeast from the summit. Just remember that these routes will finish in the deep glacially carved basin at Abyss Lake. In winter or early spring, create an excellent ski tour by skiing from the northeast down to Abyss Lake and climbing north to Mt. Evans, eventually looping back to Guanella Pass.

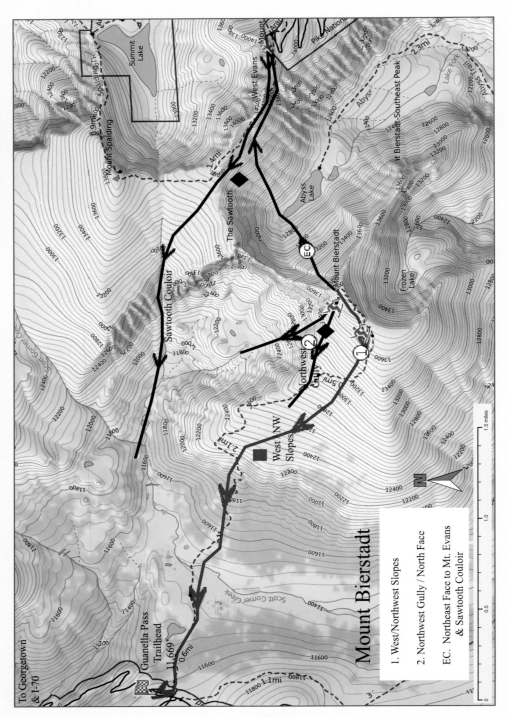

Mount Bierstadt

1. West/Northwest Slopes

2. Northwest Gully / North Face

EC. Northeast Face to Mt. Evans & Sawtooth Couloir

MT. BIERSTADT

4. **Square Top**
13,794 feet/4204 meters

SKIABLE VERTICAL:	3656 feet/1114 meters
ROUND-TRIP DISTANCE:	10 miles/16.1 kilometers
TRAILHEAD:	Guanella Pass (11,669 feet)
DIFFICULTY RATINGS:	■ / ◆
SKI TERRAIN:	Ridgelines, couloirs, moderate faces, and bowls
OPTIMAL SEASON:	February through June. April and May are ideal.
MAPS:	Trails Illustrated Number 104, Guanella Pass, Argentine, Arapaho National Forest

COMMENT: Easily accessible from Denver and the Interstate 70 corridor, Square Top is one of Colorado's bi-Centennial peaks, just shy of Centennial Peak status. When the spring hordes of early season 14er enthusiasts are bombarding Bier-

The east bowl of Square Top from a frozen Lower Square Top Lake.

Several north side options ski down to Silver Dollar lake, Argentine Peak (13,743') in the distance.

stadt to the southeast of Guanella Pass, choose this fresh alternative to the north for solitude and an enjoyable skiing experience.

GETTING THERE

**Guanella Pass** (11,669 feet). Travel west from Denver on I-70 for about 50 miles and take exit 228 at Georgetown. Follow the signs into historic Georgetown. From downtown, continue following the signs out of town and head south above town on switchbacks on Guanella Pass Road. You will pass a power plant and small lake in the deep valley on your left as you continue on a paved road for 10 miles from Georgetown to the top of Guanella Pass at 11,669 feet. In winter, the road is generally plowed through to the power plant, which is in the vicinity of the reservoir, and by May 1 the road is sometimes plowed and open to the pass (but this is not a CDOT priority). Note that a slog up the road in winter or early spring might add up to 4 miles one way. In recent years the road has been consistently open to Guanella Pass Campground, which is 1.7 miles from the top of the pass and has ample parking. Consider using a snowmobile or starting early on this one in winter! If approaching from the south, follow the Guanella Pass Road north for 12.2 miles from US Highway 285 near the town of Grant.

FRONT RANGE   47

THE CLIMB

East Slopes (Class 2). Start at the top of Guanella Pass. At the southwest corner of the Summit Overlook parking lot there is a detailed sign for the South Park Trail and Square Top Interpretive Trail. From the parking lot you can also look to the west and see Square Top in the distance. Follow the Square Top Interpretive Trail, or the approximate line of the trail across the basin, for nearly 2 miles to Lower Square Top Lake. You will lose a little elevation initially upon leaving the parking lot. Navigate between the lakes and aim to get to Upper Square Top Lake (12,220 feet) and travel to the right side of the lake. From here you can climb directly up the steeper runs of the east bowl, or trend right to the east slope and eventually to the summit. For an even easier climb, from the lower end of Upper Square Top Lake, travel south and then west and gain the southeast ridge of Square Top at 13,400 feet. From here it is possible to skin up the gentle ridge directly to the summit.

DESCENTS

1. *East Slopes/East Bowl* ■ / ◆ Leave the summit to the east on gentle ridgeline and retrace your path to the start of steeper terrain. You have two choices: stay skiers left and ski straight back down 30–35 degree slopes to the north side of Upper Square Top Lake. If you feel ambitious, take a skier's right as you ski down the southeast ridge and choose any number of small couloirs that get you into the spectacular east bowl of Square Top. Once back to the lake, follow contours to the east to return to Guanella Pass.

2. *Southeast Ridge* ■ This gentle ridge slopes skier's right from the summit. Follow the southeast ridge and stay in the sun, especially in the early morning hours, which can mean an excellent spring corn experience. Return to Lower Square Top Lake and Guanella Pass once reaching 13,300 feet on the ridge.

ALTERNATIVES

North Couloirs ◆◆ Any number of lines can be explored to the north from the summit. Just remember that these routes will finish in the vicinity of Silver Dollar Lake. In winter or early spring make an excellent loop by skiing back to the east down to the Guanella Pass Road and campground and to the Lower Silver Dollar Lake Trailhead (Silver Dollar Road junction). The Lower Silver Dollar Lake Trailhead (10,850 feet) and Silver Dollar Road junction is only about 0.50 mile south of the Guanella Pass Campground.

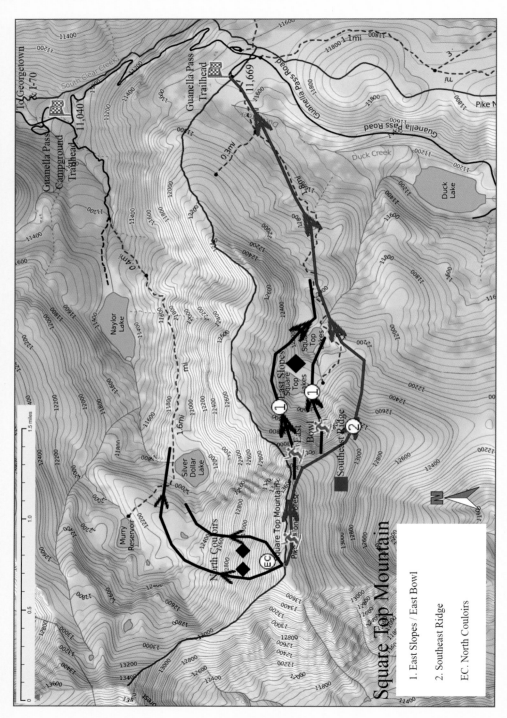

SQUARE TOP

5. James Peak and St. Mary's Glacier
13,294 feet/4052 meters

SKIABLE VERTICAL:	Up to 2894 feet/882 meters
ROUND-TRIP DISTANCE:	6.2 miles/10 kilometers
TRAILHEADS:	St. Mary's Glacier (10,400 feet)
DIFFICULTY RATINGS:	■ / ◆
SKI TERRAIN:	Ridgelines and moderate slopes
OPTIMAL SEASON:	February through July. May and June are ideal.
MAPS:	Trails Illustrated Number 103, St. Mary's Glacier, Indian Peaks Wilderness

COMMENT: The highest point in Gilpin County and the fifth highest summit in the Indian Peaks, James Peak provides the perfect winter or spring ski, and a great opportunity for a group outing on gentle ski terrain. You can get to the trailhead from Denver in less than an hour, making it easy to enjoy an outing close to home! St. Mary's Glacier is a permanent snowfield leading toward James Peak, so it may have glacial ice underneath.

GETTING THERE
St. Mary's Glacier Trailhead (9,400 feet). This trailhead is privately owned and maintained by a private subdivision in partnership with the US Forest Service. There is a $5 fee for self-issued parking permits. Traveling west from Denver on Interstate 70, take the Fall River Road Exit 238, 2 miles west of Idaho Springs. Travel 10 miles northwest on Fall River Road toward St. Mary's/Alice. The parking area is just past Lake Quivera.

Excellent Front Range views and ski terrain for all abilities can be found on James Peak. Photo by Colin Miller

Enjoyable turns can be found on St. Mary's Glacier nearly all year long. Photo by Tara Nichols

THE CLIMBS

St. Mary's Glacier and Southeast Slopes (Class 2). Start from the St. Mary's Glacier Trailhead and follow the St. Mary's Glacier Trail to the northwest and north for 0.5 mile to the base of St. Mary's Glacier at 10,800 feet. You will emerge past St. Mary's Lake, on the left. Climb the glacier for 600 to 800 feet, ascending through a narrowing gully at the top to your west and northwest, and reach gentle, flat slopes above timberline at 11,400 feet. From here look over gentle terrain to see James Peak to your northwest. Follow easy slopes for 1.5 miles to the summit.

DESCENTS

1. *Southeast Slopes to Saint Mary's Glacier* ■ Leave the summit of James to the southeast. Ski easy slopes that are at most 30 degrees, and much less steep for the majority of the descent. Ski the shallow gully onto St. Mary's Glacier and enjoy turns all the way back to the vicinity of St. Mary's Lake.

2. *Kingston Peak* (12,187 feet) ■ / ◆ The south slopes of Kingston Peak provide a shorter ski. From the top of Saint Mary's Glacier, climb 0.4 mile north to the top of Kingston Peak. Descend the south slopes back to the glacier. Peak 11,716 feet to the southwest is also an option here.

ALTERNATIVES

■ / ◆ / ◆◆ Any number of lines can be explored on James Peak from the summit. The steeper east face boasts ski lines such as Starlight, Shooting Star, Sky Pilot, and SuperStar, with access to James Peak Lake. You can also approach the peak from the west and from the north from Rogers Pass in Grand County.

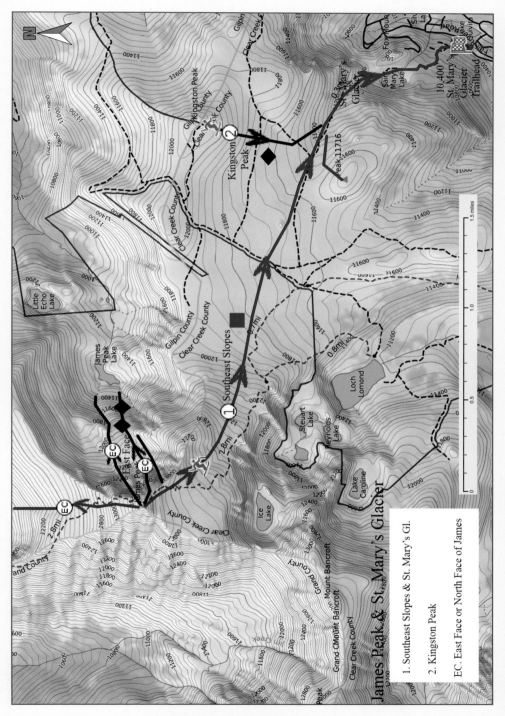

James Peak & St. Mary's Glacier

1. Southeast Slopes & St. Mary's Gl.

2. Kingston Peak

EC. East Face or North Face of James

JAMES PEAK AND ST. MARY'S GLACIER

6. The Citadel
13,294 feet/4052 meters

SKIABLE VERTICAL:	Up to 3000 feet/914 meters
ROUND-TRIP DISTANCE:	10 miles/16.1 kilometers
TRAILHEADS:	Herman Gulch (10,300 feet), Dry Gulch (10,630 feet)
DIFFICULTY RATINGS:	■ / ◆ / ◆ ◆
SKI TERRAIN:	Ridgelines, couloirs, moderate faces, and bowls
OPTIMAL SEASON:	February through June. April and May are ideal.
MAPS:	Trails Illustrated Number 104, Arapaho National Forest

COMMENT: Easily accessible from Denver and the Interstate 70 corridor, The Citadel is becoming a classic ski mountaineering destination. The peak is sometimes called "Snoopy" because the double summits of the summit ridge resemble Snoopy sleeping on his doghouse. On a weekend day in May, don't expect to be the only party on the mountain as the routes on this peak are well known. Nevertheless, The Citadel is worth multiple trips to take advantage of the three classic routes described here.

GETTING THERE
Herman Gulch (10,300 feet). Travel west from Denver on I-70. This trailhead is only a few miles east of the Eisenhower Tunnel. Use I-70 Exit 218 to access the

The Citadel from the southeast.

The steep and precarious summit perch.

The author about to drop into Snoopy's Collar from the notch. Photos by Chris Tomer

trailhead on the north side of the interstate in a large parking lot with some outhouses.

Dry Gulch Trailhead (10,630 feet). Use I-70 Exit 216 to access a small parking area immediately off of the westbound off ramp. This is the same exit for US Highway 6 and Loveland Pass. In winter the access road to the trailhead is closed, so park in a pull off to the right just before the off ramp goes under the interstate. In the spring you can continue northeast through the pull out on a dirt road to the gate at Dry Gulch, about 0.50 mile east along the westbound lanes of the interstate. There is no official Forest Service trailhead here. If you are coming from the west, exit the interstate, turn left on to US Highway 6, and then take an immediate left under the interstate.

THE CLIMB

South Face/Snoopy's Collar (Class 3). Start at the Dry Gulch Trailhead. From the gate skin or hike up the Dry Gulch Trail to the northeast, which turns north and away from the interstate. Follow the line of the creek west through the valley, staying on the right side of the creek to tree line. You will exit the forest and enter another forest on the way. Ascend northwest following the line of the creek drainage to 12,000 feet below Hagar Mountain and Golden Bear. This point is about 3 miles from the trailhead. Turn north from here and cross the high basin to the south face of Citadel. Climb the south face, which leads to the couloir on the upper reaches of the face. Once reaching the top of the couloir, you can scramble left (west) on some rocks for 200 feet to reach the true summit. In years when the April snowpack is big you can ski off the true summit. Otherwise, from the top of Snoopy's Collar Couloir on the south you can drop into the Northeast Chute/Snoopy's Backside Couloir.

Beautiful ski options abound in the Northeast Bowl while ascending the southeast ridge.

Stellar powder and easy cruising terrain on the Southeast Face.

DESCENTS

1. ***Snoopy's Collar/South Face*** ◆ / ◆◆ Leave the summit to the southeast aspect on the steep ridge and retrace your path to the top of the saddle between both summits. The top of Snoopy's Collar drops to the south and is narrow, only 15 to 20 feet across for about the first 300 feet. Once the couloir ends, there are wider turns on the 40 degree face for nearly 1000 feet to the basin below.

2. ***Northeast Chute/Snoopy's Backside Couloir*** ◆ When standing on the top of Snoopy's Collar, look down and to the north; you are at the top of the Northeast Chute, also called Snoopy's Backside Couloir. This chute is a classic because it is loaded with snow all winter, has a consistent pitch, is usually cornice free, and it starts in a great position between the two vertical summits of The Citadel. Snoopy's Backside Couloir starts off narrow and steep, then opens up for nearly 1,000 feet of bigger turns to just south of the small lake at about 12,000 feet. The Northeast Chute is not quite as steep and narrow as the south face described above, so it is slightly easier. Once in the basin, follow Herman Gulch east and ski back to the Herman Gulch Trailhead.

ALTERNATIVES

Northeast Bowl and Southeast Face ■ / ◆ Climb the southeast ridge of The Citadel to access the multi-faceted Northeast Bowl. Depending on cornice size and avalanche conditions, you can ski the bowl from closer to the east summit tower, or enter the bowl further to the southeast along the ridge. Moderate-angle northeast facing powder is a spring classic on this option. Return to the trailhead by way of Herman Gulch. If the Northeast Bowl doesn't feel right, you can also descend the moderate southeast face of The Citadel into Dry Creek Gulch.

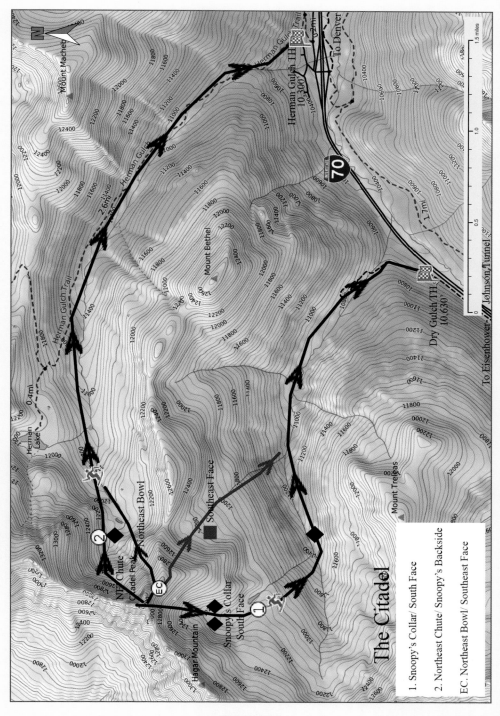

The Citadel

1. Snoopy's Collar/ South Face

2. Northeast Chute/ Snoopy's Backside

EC. Northeast Bowl/ Southeast Face

THE CITADEL

7. Grays Peak

14,270 feet/4349 meters

SKIABLE VERTICAL:	Up to 4440 feet/1359 meters
ROUND-TRIP DISTANCE:	13.0 miles/21 kilometers (distance from the bottom of Forest Service 189 (Stevens Gulch Road) at Bakerville)
TRAILHEAD:	Stevens Gulch (9,830 feet to 11,250 feet)
DIFFICULTY RATINGS:	■ / ◆
SKI TERRAIN:	Ridgelines, couloirs, and moderate faces
OPTIMAL SEASON:	February through June. April and May are ideal.
MAPS:	Trails Illustrated Number 104, Grays Peak, Arapahoe National Forest

COMMENT: Located right on the Continental Divide, Grays Peak is one of the most accessible 14ers in all of Colorado. Even in winter, an extra hour or two of effort from Interstate 70 will take you into the basin of upper Stevens Gulch below the magnificent east face of Torreys Peak, and the easy northeast slopes of Grays. Skiing this 14er giant is exhilarating and provides a nice long run with a variety of options.

Roger Carter tops out on Grays Peak on a bluebird spring morning.

Grays Peak provides skiers with moderate steepness and a long descent of the northeast face.

GETTING THERE

Stevens Gulch (9,930–11,250 feet). Travel west from Denver on I-70 to Exit 221 Bakerville. This exit is about 6 miles east of the Eisenhower-Johnson Tunnel. Stevens Gulch Road is directly to the south of the interstate. It is 3 miles from the exit to the Stevens Gulch (summer) Trailhead at 11,250 feet. By late April or early May the road melts out enough to allow four-wheel-drive vehicles to make it all the way up. In winter you can park in the lot just south of the interstate interchange, which has an old chimney frame on the side of the start of the road.

THE CLIMB

Northeast slopes (Class 1). Start at the Stevens Gulch (summer) Trailhead. Cross a creek on a good bridge, leave timberline, and after about 1 mile Mt. Edwards is visible above to your left (to the southwest). Within the first mile you will see both Grays (left) and Torreys Peaks (right) in the distance up the basin. In winter the trail through willows is often packed by snowshoers as you approach the peaks. You will switchback a few times and then head straight up to 12,000 feet and a nice view of Grays and Torreys at a large trail sign. Ascend the upper basin heading straight toward Torreys Peak. At about 12,400 feet, angle to the south (left) along the intermediate ridgeline and ascend directly toward the left side of the northeast face. Once on the face you can follow one of two routes: either stay left (east) and find your way onto Grays east ridge and follow the ridge to the summit, or zigzag up the face to the top. Depending on snow coverage, choose the line that works best for you.

It is possible to zig-zag skin all the way to the summit of Grays Peak.

DESCENTS

1. **_Northeast Face_** ■ Leave the summit by dropping directly onto the northeast face. The face is long and broad and if the coverage is good, you can choose a ski line of your choice. Enjoy the turns toward the valley for almost 2,000 feet. Once the face ends, take more turns in the easy to ski basin all the way back to the Stevens Gulch Trailhead.

2. **_Lost Rat Couloir_** ◆ Leave the summit and travel east on Grays east ridge for about 300 yards. After dropping about 400 feet, stay left (north side of the ridge) to find the entrance to the Lost Rat Couloir. There is a fully direct and unobstructed line that faces slightly northeast, but mainly to the east. Drop in and enjoy steep turns for 800 feet. Arrive at the bottom of the basin and ski east then northeast back down gentle slopes to Stevens Gulch Trailhead.

ALTERNATIVES

Two-for-one with Torreys ◆◆ Climb and ski the broad slopes of Grays Peak's northeast face with an early morning start as a warm up. Once down in the basin, ascend the Dead Dog Couloir as described for Torreys Peak. Both peaks together provide two amazing ski lines and up to 6,000 feet of vertical climbing and skiing.

◆ There is a wealth of terrain to explore on Grays Peak's south aspects. For example, take a look at the Mt. Edwards entry. You can approach Grays and its outstanding southeast bowl from Horseshoe Basin on Mt. Edwards and Grays Peak's south sides. Ski descents from here take you down to Peru Creek.

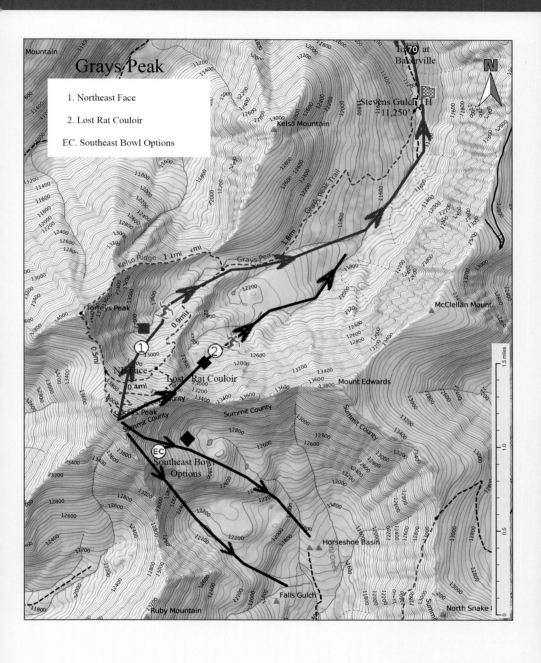

GRAYS PEAK

8. Torreys Peak
14,267 feet/4348 meters

SKIABLE VERTICAL:	Up to 4437 feet/1358 meters
ROUND-TRIP DISTANCE:	13.0 miles/21 kilometers (distance from the bottom of Forest Service 189 (Stevens Gulch Road) at Bakerville)
TRAILHEAD:	Stevens Gulch (9,830 feet to 11,250 feet)
DIFFICULTY RATINGS:	◆ / ◆ ◆
SKI TERRAIN:	Ridgelines, couloirs, and moderate faces
OPTIMAL SEASON:	February through June. April and May are ideal.
MAPS:	Trails Illustrated Number 104, Grays Peak, Arapahoe National Forest

COMMENT: Like it's neighbor Grays Peak, Torreys Peak is located right on the Continental Divide and is one of the most accessible 14ers in Colorado. In winter, the extra hour or two of effort from Interstate-70 will take you into the basin of upper Stevens Gulch below the magnificent east face of the peak, which takes on a dramatic appearance in snowy months. Skiing this 14er giant from any of its many ski lines that leave the summit in all directions rewards the effort of getting there.

The east face of Torreys almost looks Himalayan.

GETTING THERE
Stevens Gulch (9,930 to 11,250 feet). Follow the directions for Grays Peak.

THE CLIMB
Dead Dog Couloir (Class 2+, Moderate Snow). Start at the Stevens Gulch (summer) Trailhead at 11,250 feet. Cross a sturdy bridge and head southwest, quickly climbing above timberline. Within the first mile you will see both Grays Peak (left) and Torreys Peak (right) in the distance up the basin. In winter the trail

Roger Carter descending the ridgeline and skirting the east face of Torreys to access the top of the Dead Dog Couloir.

through willows is often packed by snowshoers. As you approach the peaks, switchback a few times and then head straight up to 12,000 feet and a nice view of Grays and Torreys. Ascend the upper basin heading straight toward Torreys Peak. At about 12,400 feet, leave the trail and drop into a small basin as you head towards Torrey's east face. Dead Dog Couloir is the primary couloir that splits the face and angles right (northwest). Climb this spectacular couloir for 1,500 feet. The early morning sun in early spring will reach you as you climb. At about 14,100 feet the couloir ends on Kelso Ridge. From the top of Dead Dog Couloir, follow the summit ridge west for about 150 yards to the top of Torreys Peak.

DESCENTS

1. ***Dead Dog Couloir*** ◆ Leave the summit to the west along Kelso Ridge for 150 yards down to a prominent notch. The notch is just before the jagged white granite shark-fin feature on the ridge. The Dead Dog Couloir is a classic, not too wide nor too narrow. Enjoy turns toward the valley that widen as the couloir open to the easy to basin all the way back to Stevens Gulch Trailhead.

2. ***Tuning Fork*** ◆ Leave the summit and travel west on Torreys' west ridge for about 150 yards. There is a relatively unobstructed line that faces slightly northwest at first, and then cuts directly north and into a slightly wider

Skiing Dead Dog Couloir. Photo by Drew Warkentin

snow face below. This is one of Colorado's longest sustained ski faces! Ski this line for about 2,500 feet into Grizzly Gulch below and follow it back to the trailhead toward Bakerville and I-70. A variation of the Tuning Fork is a line I call the "Tuning Knife," a fun separate couloir that can be started about 200 yards further west on Torreys' ridge.

ALTERNATIVES

East Face Direct and South Paw Couloir ◆ / ◆◆

There are two additional lines that offer excellent skiing when the snow is prime in May on Torreys Peak's east face. When covered with deep snow, the east face, which is accessed directly from the summit, can be skied top to bottom. The South Paw Couloir can be accessed 250 yards south of the summit on a corniced notch at 13,900 feet, below Torreys Peak's summit on the connecting ridge toward Grays. Use caution entering this couloir, which can have a dangerous cornice most of the season. With either of these fine lines, return to the trailhead by way of Stevens Gulch.

Snow nearly buries the trail signs at 12,000' below Torreys.

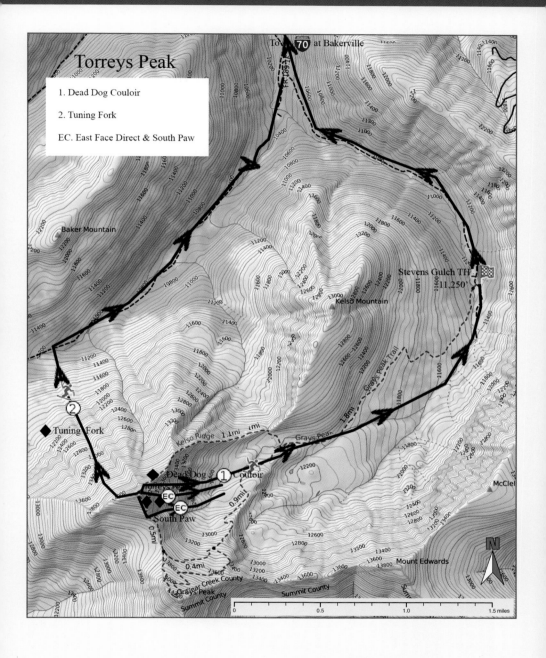

TORREYS PEAK

9. Mt. Edwards
13,850 feet/4221 meters

SKIABLE VERTICAL:	Up to 2750 feet/838 meters
ROUND-TRIP DISTANCE:	6.2 miles/10 kilometers
TRAILHEADS:	Horseshoe Basin (11,100 feet), Stevens Gulch (9,930 feet to 11,250 feet)
DIFFICULTY RATINGS:	◆ / ◆◆
SKI TERRAIN:	Ridgelines, couloirs, moderate faces, and bowls
OPTIMAL SEASON:	February through June. April and May are ideal.
MAPS:	Trails Illustrated Number 104, Grays Peak, Argentine, Arapahoe National Forest

COMMENT: Situated east along the Continental Divide, and in the shadow of its higher twin neighbors Grays and Torreys, Mt. Edwards offers a rewarding and isolated experience, especially on its southern routes. Mt. Edwards is among the 100 highest peaks in the state, and offers challenging lines that until recently were rarely skied.

Magnificient view of Mount Edwards approaching from Stevens Gulch.

The north face of Edwards with the Goat Finger Couloir (skier's left of summit) and the North Couloir (skier's right of summit). There are literally half a dozen variations on this face.

GETTING THERE

Horseshoe Basin (11,100 feet). This trailhead is east of the Keystone Ski Resort on the west side of the Continental Divide, and allows access to the south side of Mt. Edwards. From the town of Keystone, travel east toward the settlement of Montezuma. Montezuma is the last exit off of US Highway 6 when traveling toward Loveland Pass and the Arapahoe Basin Ski Resort. From its start at US Highway 6 (Loveland Pass Road), drive on Montezuma Road for about 4.5 miles to the intersection with Peru Creek Road. Turn left on Peru Creek Road. The start of this dirt road has Forest Service signs and is well marked. Drive up Peru Creek Road another 4.5 miles to the Horseshoe Basin Trailhead, where the road is closed in the summer. (If you reach the town of Montezuma, you've gone too far.) This road isn't very rough, and there are several campsites along the trail. Before May 1 the road won't be melted out, so an early spring ascent might be much longer than anticipated.

Stevens Gulch (9,930 feet to 11,250 feet). Follow the directions for Grays Peak.

THE CLIMB

South Face/Edwardian Couloir (Class 2+, Moderate Snow). Start at the Horseshoe Basin Trailhead. From the gate and old inactive mine, skin or hike up the mining road trail to the north. At the start you are nearly at timberline and the south face of Mt. Edwards can be seen to the north almost immediately. Follow gentle slopes for almost 1 mile north to get to the base of the most obvious opening at the bottom of the face. The introduction is over, and it's time to climb! Follow the Edwardian Couloir up for a few hundred feet to a narrower and slight right

The Eduardian Couloir (center) holds snow well into June most years.

turn. For about 250 feet the couloir becomes relatively narrow, then at about 13,100 feet the face opens to your west. You can remain in the center of the broad gully and head to a small saddle on the ridge at 13,580 feet. From the saddle turn right (east) and follow the easy ridge for 0.25 mile to the summit.

DESCENTS

1. *Edwardian Couloir/South Face* ◆ Leave the summit to the west along the ridge for 0.25 mile and find the first small saddle at 13,580 feet, between the top of Mt. Edwards and its subsidiary summits along the ridge to the west. Ski south down the center of the funneling face for several hundred feet until the gully narrows into the Edwardian Couloir. Enjoy the narrow but easily skiable "S" turns, and then face southwest down to about 12,600 feet. Once the couloir opens, there are wider turns in the basin all the way back to the Horseshoe Basin Trailhead.

2. *North Couloir* ◆ Leave the summit and travel west on Mt. Edwards' west ridge for about 150 yards. There is a relatively unobstructed line that faces slightly northeast at first, then cuts directly north and into a wider snowfield below. Ski this steep line for about 1,500 feet into Stevens Gulch below and follow Stevens Gulch back to the trailhead toward Bakerville and I-70.

ALTERNATIVES

North Face Variations ◆ / ◆◆ There are two additional lines that have excellent skiing when the snow is peaking in May on Mt. Edwards' north face. One is the narrow Goat Finger Couloir, which is skiers left of the summit. The other line is nearly directly off the summit. It starts near the top of Goat Finger Couloir but turns skiers right just below the summit ridge cliffs and enters a tight couloir leading directly down the center of the face from north of the true summit. (The author skied this line in 2011, and Chris Davenport skied a slight variation of this line in late May 2013). From either one of these fine lines, return to the trailhead by way of Stevens Gulch.

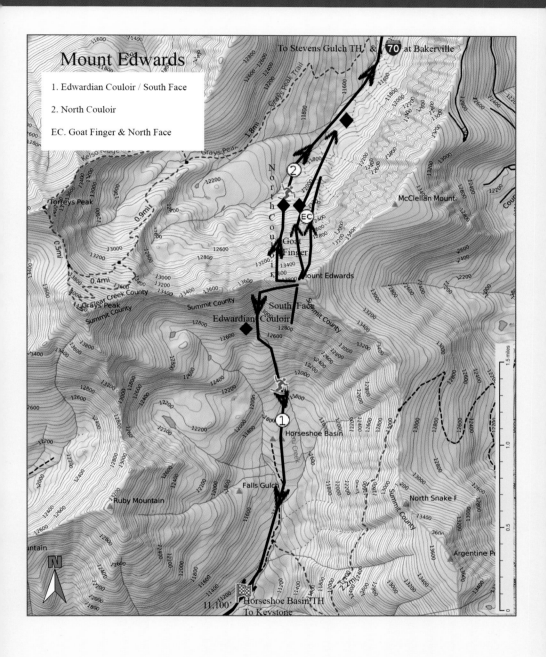

MT. EDWARDS

10. Loveland Pass
11,990 feet/3654 meters

SKIABLE VERTICAL:	Up to 1600 feet/305 meters
ROUND-TRIP DISTANCE:	Varies
TRAILHEAD:	Loveland Pass (11,990 feet)
DIFFICULTY RATINGS:	■ / ◆
SKI TERRAIN:	Ridgelines, couloirs, and moderate faces
OPTIMAL SEASON:	January through June. April through June are ideal. Some 4th of July weekends can even be fun on the pass!
MAPS:	Trails Illustrated Number 104, Arapahoe National Forest

COMMENT: Located right on the Continental Divide, Loveland Pass is one of the most accessible places for a fun ski outing with great views. Grab three or four of your friends and have a blast switching drivers and shuttling each other up the road. You can ski off the Pass in either direction.

GETTING THERE
Loveland Pass (11,990 feet). Travel west from Denver on Interstate 70 to Exit 216. Follow the signs for US Highway 6 West over Loveland Pass and after 4 miles

Skiing a moderate face directly north from the Continental Divide.

There is limited parking at Loveland Pass, so get there early on weekends.

A calm morning on the divide as the author drops into a powder stash near Loveland Pass.
Photo by Chris Tomer

reach the top of the Pass. If you are coming from the west, drive east on US Highway 6 for 16 miles from Exit 205 in Dillon/Silverthorne to reach Loveland Pass.

DESCENTS

1. *Northern Faces* ■ Leave the pass directly to the north (which is the east side of the Pass facing I-70). There are several lines down the face and into relatively gentle trees, which you will have to navigate for about 100 yards to get down to Highway 6. Switch drivers to shuttle back up to the Pass and ski some more!

2. *Southern Faces* ■ / ◆ Leave the Pass and walk east along the ridgeline in the direction of Sniktau, East Loveland Pass Peak, and Cupid Peaks. Hike as far as you want, then ski down into the bowl to the south in the direction of the Arapahoe Basin Ski Area. Once descending into the basin, You will reach the road (U.S. 6), which is above timberline.

ALTERNATIVES

Point 12,594 feet ◆ Climb and ski the steeper slopes above Loveland Pass to the west and southwest of the pass. If you reach Point 12,594 feet you can either drop back down to the northern faces (described above), or ski the steep southern face known as the Professor toward Arapahoe Basin Ski Area.

13er Potpourri Sniktau, Cupid, or Grizzly ■ / ◆ From the top of the Pass, climb east along the Continental Divide toward any of these three peaks. Choose your own ski line!

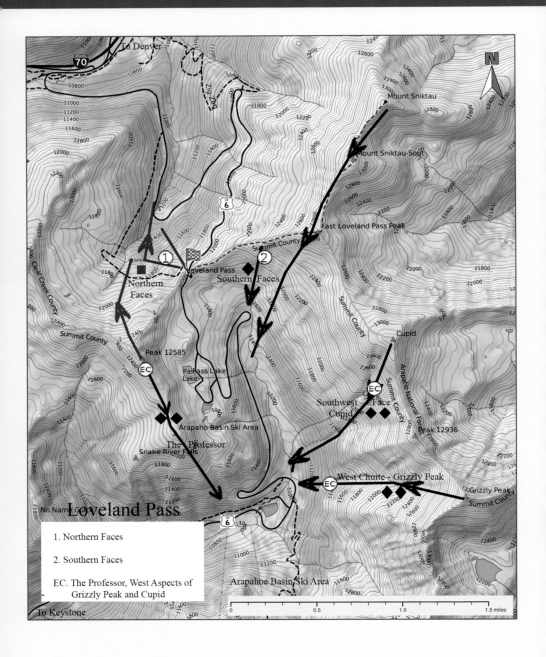

1. Northern Faces

2. Southern Faces

EC. The Professor, West Aspects of
    Grizzly Peak and Cupid

LOVELAND PASS

11. Trail Ridge Road—Sundance Mountain
12,486 feet/3806 meters

SKIABLE VERTICAL:	Up to 2,200 feet/670 meters
ROUND-TRIP DISTANCE:	Varies
TRAILHEAD:	Toll Memorial Saddle (12,000 feet)
DIFFICULTY RATINGS:	■ / ◆
SKI TERRAIN:	Ridgelines, couloirs, and moderate faces
OPTIMAL SEASON:	May through July. In big snow years you can make August turns!
MAPS:	Trails Illustrated Number 200 and 301, Rocky Mountain National Park

COMMENT: Located directly on Trail Ridge Road, North America's highest continuous paved road, Sundance Mountain is an excellent way to enjoy spring or summer skiing in Rocky Mountain National Park. Grab three or four friends and have a blast shuttling each other from Fall River Road below, or hike the ski line back up for an hour or so back to your car.

Stairway to heaven as skiers boot up the north side of Sundance Mountain. Fall River road is visible below.
Photo by Alessandro Sacerdotal.

Low angle powder is excellent and safe from avalanches on this north facing terrain.

GETTING THERE

Trail Ridge Road—Toll Memorial Saddle (12,000 feet). Travel west of Estes Park on US Highway 34/Trail Ridge Road for 14 miles. Along the road park at the low saddle in a small parking lot to the southeast of the Toll Memorial (12,310 feet) and to the west of 12,486 foot Sundance Mountain. If you chose to shuttle skiers from Fall River Road, note that the road is one way uphill to the Alpine Visitor Center, so descend Trail Ridge Road to Fall River Road and loop back up to pick up skiers. In most years, Fall River Road might not be cleared until mid-June.

DESCENTS

1. *Toll Memorial* ■ / ◆ Leave the parking area and ascend the easy hillside to the northwest for 0.25 mile and 300 feet to the Toll Memorial at 12,310 feet. From the top you can ski to the north and then angle to the northwest for 2,000 feet down into the wide trough of the valley toward Fall River Road.
2. *Sundance Mountain* ■ / ◆ Leave the parking area and travel east on easy slopes for 0.25 mile to the top of Sundance Mountain (12,486 feet). Keep in mind that some years by the time Trail Ridge Road opens, the top and western/northwest aspects of Sundance Mountain might be devoid of snow. If this is the case, simply depart the parking lot to your north and head straight down the north broad gully of the mountain to Fall River Road.

ALTERNATIVES

Climb on! ■ / ◆ Instead of using a car shuttle from Fall River Road, which might not yet be open in late May or early June, hike up the route you skied back to your car and get a nice workout!

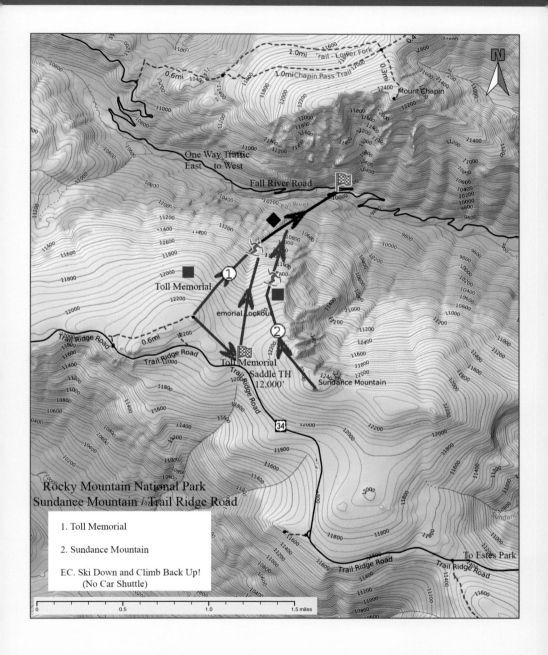

Rocky Mountain National Park
Sundance Mountain / Trail Ridge Road

1. Toll Memorial

2. Sundance Mountain

EC. Ski Down and Climb Back Up!
    (No Car Shuttle)

TRAIL RIDGE ROAD—SUNDANCE MOUNTAIN

12. Berthoud Pass

11,306 feet/3446 meters

SKIABLE VERTICAL:	up to 2,500 feet/762 meters
ROUND-TRIP DISTANCE:	Varies
SKIABLE ACRES:	1,200, with a summit elevation of 12,493 feet
TRAILHEAD:	Berthoud Pass (11,306 feet)
DIFFICULTY RATINGS:	■ / ◆
SKI TERRAIN:	Ridgelines, couloirs, tree glades, and moderate faces
OPTIMAL SEASON:	January through June.
MAPS:	Trails Illustrated Number 103, Arapaho National Forest

For an excellent online resource and trail maps of the terrain, visit www.BerthoudPass.com.

COMMENT: Located on US Highway 40, Berthoud Pass is a backcountry skier's paradise. Named for Edward L. Berthoud, the chief surveyor of the Colorado Central Railroad during the 1870s, the Pass was not deemed suitable for a railroad crossing, but decades later in 1937 a ski area opened there. Unfortunately, by 2002 the ski area closed, but with the removal of the lifts, the backcountry terrain still remains, along with a warming hut and restroom facilities, making the pass very popular for backcountry outings, and crowded on weekends. Some popular ski runs are discussed here, but the terrain on Berthoud Pass is expansive, so use online resources to maximize your ability to explore.

Fresh tracks in Floral Park.

GETTING THERE

Berthoud Pass. Travel west from Denver for 65 miles on Interstate 70 to Exit 232. Follow US Highway 40 west for 14 miles to the top of Berthoud Pass, where a parking area is located on the right (east) side of the highway.

Scott Benge takes advantage of the nice cold conditions. Photo by Anne Marie Migl

DESCENTS

1. *East Side* ■ / ◆ / ◆◆ Expansive terrain to the east of the Pass includes Hell's Half Acre, which is northeast of the Pass, and Floral Park, which skis to the southeast of the Pass. All lines are accessed by ascending east toward Colorado Mines Peak.

2. *West Side* ■ / ◆ Leave the parking area and cross US Highway 40 to the west of the Pass. Expansive terrain includes Current Creek to the northwest and Pumphouse Basin to the southwest. West side terrain can also include a climb of Russell Peak (12,240 feet), which also allows access to both Current Creek and Pumphouse Basin.

*Note that nearly all terrain allows for climbing short distances and descending to US Highway 40. This maximizes opportunities for skiing and for vehicle shuttles on either side of the Pass.

ALTERNATIVES

Mines Peak, East Side ◆ / ◆◆ Leave the parking lot and travel east for a mile, ascending above timberline to the summit of 12,493-foot Mines Peak. From the top of Mines Peak you can ski to your west and northwest and take advantage of steep terrain on runs such as Mines 1 and 2 (to the northwest), The Fingers, The Knuckle, The Choke, North Chute, Sentinel Chute, and Hanging Meadow to the west. Skiing from the summit of Mt. Flora is also a great descent. The various chutes lead down to US 40 on the north side of the Pass at a USFS access point that is near a hairpin turn on the highway. At this point you can shuttle back up to the Pass.

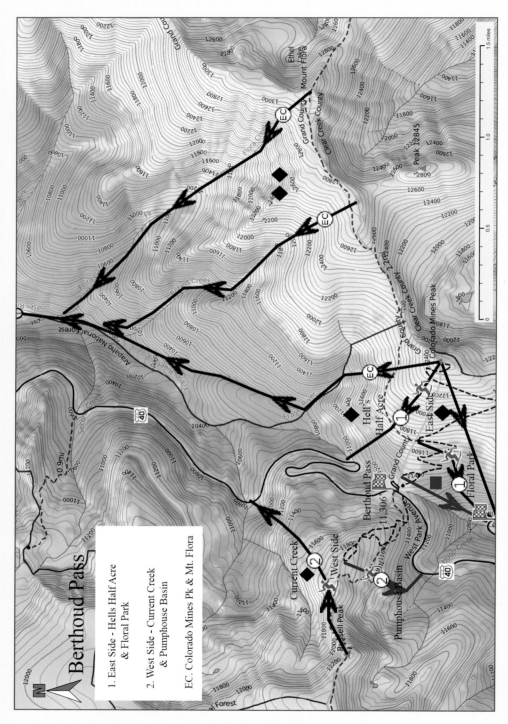

BERTHOUD PASS

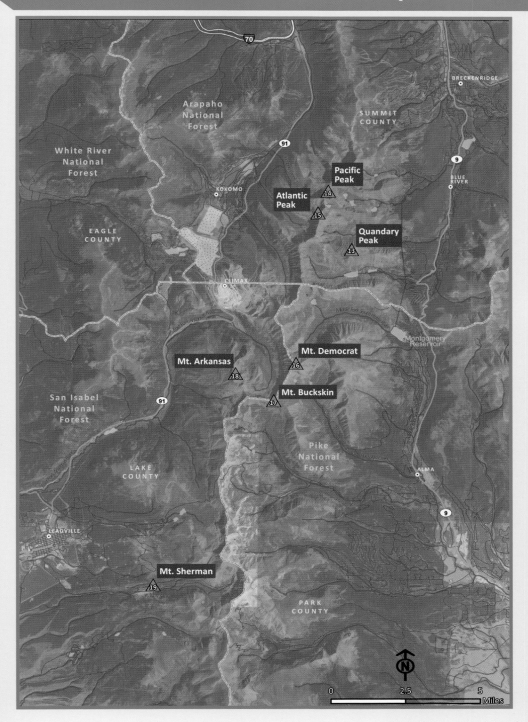

13. Quandary Peak
14,265 feet/4348 meters

SKIABLE VERTICAL:	3365 feet/1025 meters
ROUND-TRIP DISTANCE:	5.5 miles/8.9 kilometers
TRAILHEAD:	Monte Cristo (10,900 feet)
DIFFICULTY RATINGS:	■ / ◆
SKI TERRAIN:	four-wheel-drive road ■, tree glades, ridgelines, steep faces, and couloir options
OPTIMAL SEASON:	Dec through May. April and May are ideal.
MAPS:	Trails Illustrated Number 109, Breckenridge, Arapaho National Forest

COMMENT: Quandary Peak should be on the list of every ski mountaineer. For experienced skiers who want to take someone into the backcountry for the first time, Quandary offers easy access, even in winter. If your goal is to climb and ski a 14er, the high trailhead and relative ease of the east slopes route make this peak a fun and safe outing, relatively free of avalanche danger, particularly when you stay on the ridge. Enjoy the gentle terrain this high peak offers, and the summit views, clear across most of Colorado!

Skinning up Quandary's long east ridge.

Skiing Quandary's east ridge in January. Snow is generally best in April or May but its possible to get a true winter descent if desired. Photo by Chris Tomer

GETTING THERE
Monte Cristo. At 10,900 feet, this trailhead is very close to Colorado Highway 9 and is open year-round. From the center of Breckenridge, travel 8 miles south on Colorado Highway 9. After a pair of sharp switchbacks, turn right on Summit County Road 850. The large parking lot is immediately on the right. In late spring, it is possible to take the first right from Summit County Road 850 onto Summit County Road 851 (McCullough Gulch Road) and travel about 200 yards to the start of the summer Quandary Peak Trail and park on the east side of County Road 851.

THE CLIMB
East Slopes (Class 1). The well marked start of the Quandary Peak Trail is easy to find and follow, even in the winter. Follow a northwest and then west trajectory through spruce and pine forest for 0.5 mile to gain a flat shoulder and a few small meadows. From here on a clear day Quandary Peak's upper slopes will be seen clearly to the west. Stay left (south just below timberline) to gain the east slopes and eastern ridge and follow the ridge for 2 miles to the summit. Unless it's a powder day in the middle of the winter, there will likely be a skin track or snowshoe path through the woods for most of February, March, April, and May, which will help you find the start of the east ridge.

DESCENTS
1. _East Ridge/East Slopes_ ■ / ◆ Leave the summit and basically retrace the route you climbed to summit by way of the East Ridge. Just below the sum-

mit ridge there is a nice broad face that provides excellent skiing from 14,000 feet down to 13,200 feet. Just remember to stay to skier's right (south) side of the ridge when you drop below 13,200 feet. Do the same when nearing treeline to mitigate any avalanche danger to the northeast of the East Ridge.

2. *Monte Cristo Couloir* ◆ / ◆◆ This south facing ski line is an excellent April to mid-May choice. The couloir narrows near the bottom and is about 45 degrees. From the summit, the couloir is slightly broad, and be aware that snow on skier's right (west) can get windblown and avalanche prone, especially any time before April. Nearly a 0.75 mile of solid turns and 2,500 vertical feet carry you to the base of the chute. In another 0.25 mile, complete the route near the dam for Upper Blue Lake. In summer or late spring you can park below the dam; this is the Blue Lake Trailhead. Before May, ski the road east back to the Monte Cristo Trailhead for almost 2.5 miles.

Quandary's North Face as seen from Pacific Peak.

ALTERNATIVES
North Face and Quandary Couloir

◆ / ◆◆ Two spectacular options await more experienced skiers on Quandary's north side. In good snow years, it's possible to ski directly north/northwest off the summit into a broad gully. Skiing the north face into upper McCullough Basin for 2,500 feet is a spectacular line! For the second option, traverse the summit ridge east for 150 yards. When you get to the crest of the ridge above Quandary's east face, turn skier's left (northeast) and follow the crest of the ridge on the north side of the east face. The crest of the ridge gets steeper and steeper for another 200 yards and at about 14,000 feet you will be standing at the top of a very fine and direct inset couloir looking northwest for almost 3,000 feet into McCullough Gulch below. The Quandary Couloir is best skied in May, when you know the windblown cornice near the top won't avalanche. Drop in and enjoy steep turns that get narrow in a few places, but for the most part, the skiing is direct and straightforward. Once at timberline, ski down the basin and find the McCullough Gulch Road (Summit County 851), which will take you back to the Monte Cristo Trailhead in 2 miles.

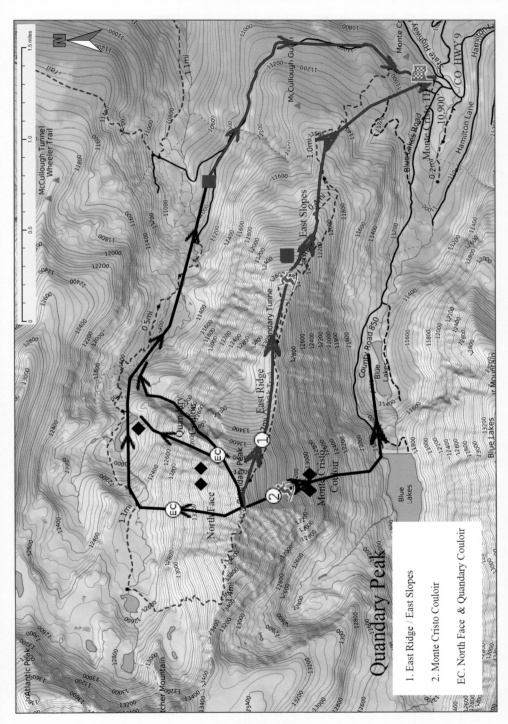

QUANDARY PEAK

14. Pacific Peak
13,951 feet/4250 meters

SKIABLE VERTICAL:	3551 feet/1236 meters
ROUND-TRIP DISTANCE:	10.6 miles/17.1 kilometers
TRAILHEAD:	Mohawk Lakes/Spruce Creek Road (10,400 feet).
DIFFICULTY RATINGS:	◆ / ◆ ◆
SKI TERRAIN:	Couloirs, steep slopes, tree glades, and forest service roads
OPTIMAL SEASON:	March through June. May and June are ideal.
MAPS:	Trails Illustrated Number 109, Breckenridge, Copper Mountain, While River National Forest

COMMENT: This is a Colorado ultra classic ski experience! The North Couloir on Pacific Peak is known for its steep and narrow character, and thrilling ski-ability. Pacific Peak is a Centennial Colorado 13er with plenty to offer the expert ski mountaineer.

Pacific Peak and the North Couloir viewed from the north above Mohawk Lakes basin.

Ryan Belanger scouts the North Couloir.

GETTING THERE

Mohawk Lakes/Spruce Creek Trailhead (10,400 feet). From the Boreas Pass Road junction at the south end of Breckenridge (the final traffic light on the south end of town), travel south on Colorado Highway 9 for 1.7 miles to Spruce Creek Road. Turn right (west) onto Spruce Creek Road. Pass through a housing development and you will reach the winter trailhead parking after 1.2 miles. The trailhead is marked for the Mohawk Lakes Trail. After the snow melts out in the spring, four-wheel-drive vehicles can travel another 1.8 miles along the road, reaching the water diversion dam at 11,100 feet.

THE CLIMB

North Couloir (Class 4). The Mohawk Lakes Trail travels from the winter parking area up the Spruce Creek Road and passes the water diversion dam at the end of the road. From here stay left at a trail junction near the end of the water diversion dam. Just before reaching Continental Falls, about 2.5 miles above the water diversion dam, pass some log buildings and continue up the basin to the left of the falls. There are plenty of mine buildings en route to the upper basin. In gentler terrain, the upper basin greets you with Mohawk Lake at 12,100 feet. Continue skinning up the flat basin for 1 mile and reach Pacific Peak's north couloir. The challenge is obvious. Ascend the couloir toward the large and obvious cornice on the north ridge. On the ascent, pass a prominent rock tower on your left, after which turn left into the upper portion of the couloir. The steepest and narrowest sections are in this area at about 13,400 feet. Climb the couloir to the summit, which is just to the east of the top of the chute.

A stunning bluebird spring day ascending the Hawaii Chute near the top of Pacific Peak.

DESCENTS

1. *North Couloir* ◆◆ Leave Pacific's tiny summit by skiing first to the west for 25 feet and down 75 feet into the jaws of the upper North Couloir. The couloir is steep, narrow, and nearly 50 degrees up top. Jump turn your way down the top of the couloir for the first 300 feet as the it turns from northwest to north and eventually funnels all the way onto a northeast aspect for another 800 feet down into Upper Mohawk Lakes Basin. Ski the basin back to the trailhead.

The author at nearing the top of Pacific's Southwest Face.

ALTERNATIVES

Southwest Face ◆ Ski south from the summit on Pacific's south ridge. Descend about 300 feet to a prominent notch along the ridge. The notch drops directly down onto the southwest face. Ski the face into the basin between Pacific Peak and Atlantic Peak to the south, eventually skiing toward the Mayflower Gulch Trailhead and Colorado Highway 91. See Atlantic Peak for directions to the Mayflower Gulch Trailhead.

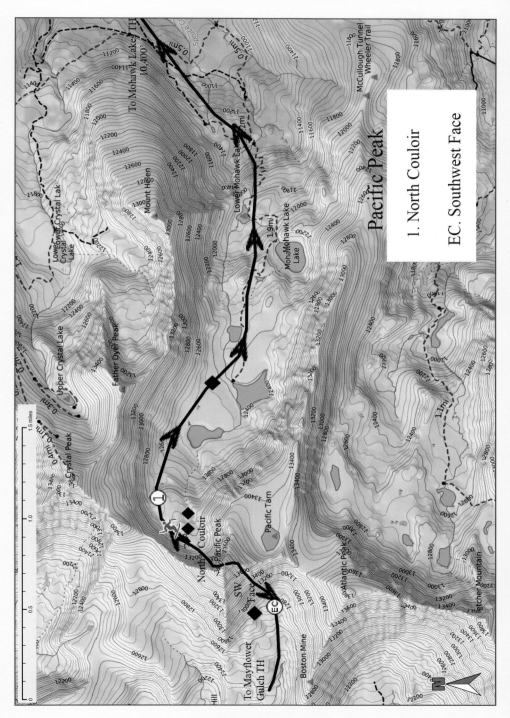

Pacific Peak

1. North Couloir

EC. Southwest Face

PACIFIC PEAK

15. **Atlantic Peak**
13,841 feet/4218 meters

SKIABLE VERTICAL:	2841 feet/866 meters
ROUND-TRIP DISTANCE:	7 miles/11.3 kilometers
TRAILHEAD:	Mayflower Gulch (11,000 feet)
DIFFICULTY RATINGS:	■ / ◆
SKI TERRAIN:	Four-wheel-drive road ■, tree glades, ridgelines, steep faces, and couloir options
OPTIMAL SEASON:	January through May. April and May are ideal.
MAPS:	Trails Illustrated Number 109, Breckenridge, Copper Mountain, White River National Forest

COMMENT: Atlantic Peak is perhaps one of the most easily accessible areas for backcountry skiing in the Colorado Rockies outside the Front Range. Atlantic Peak by way of Mayflower Gulch boasts plenty of excellent ski touring options, some of which won't even take you to the top of the peak, as the basins have lots of low angle terrain for beginner ski mountaineers.

Descending the north ridge of Pacific with Atlantic's Northwest Face as the backdrop.

GETTING THERE

Mayflower Gulch (11,000 feet). This trailhead is right off of Colorado Highway 91 and is open year-round. From 75 miles west of Denver, take Exit 195 at Copper Mountain and travel 6 miles south on Colorado Highway 91. The trailhead is on the east side of the highway in a large paved parking area that is plowed. If approaching from Leadville to the south, the trailhead is 4 miles north of the top of Freemont Pass. In late spring, it is possible to take the forest road for a mile and a half up to abandoned cabins near the old Boston Mine at 11,600 feet.

THE CLIMB

<u>*Northwest Face (Class 2).*</u> This climb ascends the pyramidal broad northwest face of Atlantic Peak. Start at the Mayflower Gulch Trailhead and go up the often packed-down road for about 1 mile toward the southeast. (Sometimes it's possible to leave the road before travelling a mile and turn northeast to head up Pacific Creek Basin.) Before heading into the trees and up the basin you will have to cross Mayflower Creek. Then zigzag among trees and leave timberline behind through a narrow valley (which is easiest on the west and northwest side of Pacific Creek) leading to a broad valley at the base of Pacific Peak to the northeast, and Atlantic Peak to the southeast. From 12,400 feet the basin is quite flat for several hundred yards. This is where you will see the broad slopes of Atlantic's northwest face. It is possible to skin up the face zigzagging the entire way. This is a good way to check the slope's stability. Climb the face for about 1,200 feet to reach Atlantic's broad, flat summit.

Jump Turns into the Atlantis.

▼ The Hawaii Chutes near Pacific and Atlantic peak are excellent choices as well.

Myreh Luallen carves powder turns on the Atlantic's Northwest Face.

DESCENTS

1. *Northwest Face* ■ / ◆ Leave the summit and basically retrace the route you climbed by way of the northwest face. Just below the summit there are sometimes windblown slabs that can be a problem in winter. Otherwise, Atlantic's broad face provides excellent skiing for at least 1,200 feet. I've seen many dogs chasing their owners down this face on a warm weekend in May! Just remember to stay to skier's left (west) side of the face when you drop below 12,600 feet. This will help you funnel back down the Pacific Creek valley and eventually back into Mayflower Gulch.

2. *A-Pac Couloir* ◆ / ◆◆ This west facing ski line is an excellent April to mid-May choice. The couloir broadens near the bottom and is about 40 degrees near the top portion. From the summit, the couloir is easy to get to: ski north on the gentle slopes of Atlantic's northeast ridge to the 13,400-foot connecting saddle between Pacific and Atlantic Peaks, to a point just to the north of the flattest and longest saddle area. Before heading up the slopes toward Pacific Peak, look west and down into the obvious couloir. Cornices are usually minimal on this route, and dropping into the couloir is a blast! Ski down into the basin for about 800 feet and then proceed back down Pacific Creek Basin to the Mayflower Gulch and trailhead.

ALTERNATIVES

The Atlantis Couloir ◆ / ◆◆ This southeast facing hidden couloir is narrow and steep and takes you down the east side of Atlantic. You will eventually ski out toward McCollough Gulch in the McCollough Basin near Quandary Peak.

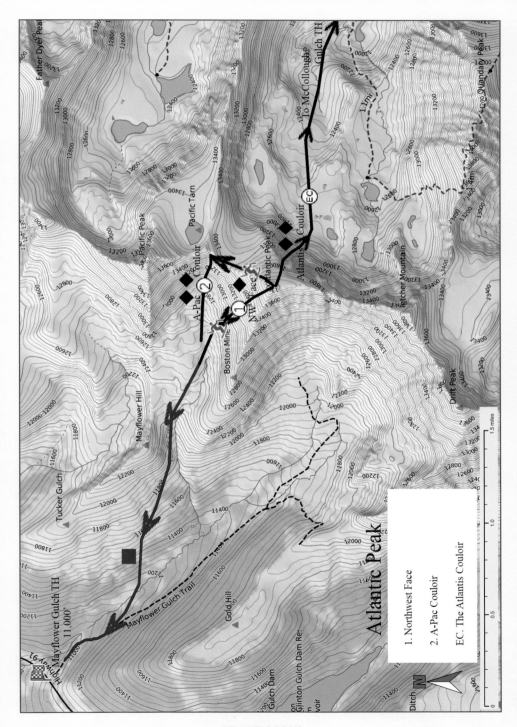

ATLANTIC PEAK

Atlantic Peak

1. Northwest Face

2. A-Pac Couloir

EC. The Atlantis Couloir

16. Mt. Democrat
14,148 feet/4312 meters

SKIABLE VERTICAL:	Up to 3148 feet/960 meters; 2148 feet/654 meters back to Kite Lake.
ROUND-TRIP DISTANCE:	4 to 6 miles / 7 to 10 kilometers
TRAILHEADS:	Kite Lake or below depending on seasonal road snow coverage (12,000 down to 11,000 feet).
DIFFICULTY RATINGS:	■ / ◆ / ◆ ◆
SKI TERRAIN:	Ridgelines, couloirs, and moderate slopes
OPTIMAL SEASON:	February through June. April through June are ideal.
MAPS:	Trails Illustrated Number 109, Alma, Climax, Pike National Forest

COMMENT: Democrat is a high peak in the Tenmile/Mosquito Range with easy access and a handful of excellent faces to climb and ski. Most of the year the peak is quite windy, but in April, May, and June when the coverage is good and the wind settles down, there are excellent descents here.

Democrat's Southeast Face.

The South Face Couloir.

Democrat's North Face.

GETTING THERE

Kite Lake Trailhead (12,000 feet). This trailhead is privately owned and maintained by a partnership with the US Forest Service. A $2 to $10 fee is charged through self-issued parking permits. In past years the fees have fluctuated. From the center of Alma, travel west and then north on Park County 8, which is a dirt road. Follow the signs to Kite Lake for 6.0 miles. You can reach the center of Alma from Colorado Highway 9 either from the north, 6 miles south from Hoosier Pass. From the south, travel north on Colorado Highway 9 for 6.0 miles north from US Highway 285 in Fairplay.

THE CLIMB

East Ridge (Class 1–2). Start from the Kite Lake Trailhead and aim for the 13,380-foot connecting saddle between Democrat and Cameron, which is to your north/northwest. Turn left (west) and follow the ridgeline for 0.5 mile to the summit of Democrat.

Democrat's West Face.

A perfect day on the summit of Democrat with Mount Arkansas in the next valley over and the Sawatch Range on the horizon.

DESCENTS

1. *South Face Couloir.* ■ / ◆ Leave the summit to the south. Ski easy slopes that are only 30 degrees at first and angle to the southeast (skier's left) to find a nice couloir that drops toward Lake Emma. Ski this couloir, which is the steepest through the cliff bands, but never exceeds 40 degrees. Once in the basin, take a left at 13,000 feet and ski back toward Kite Lake and the basin below the lake on easy slopes.

2. *Southeast Face.* ◆ This face is only slightly more challenging than the south face couloir, but similar in steepness. You can also scout this face from Kite Lake to find the correct line through some of the cliff bands. Leave the summit of Democrat on gentle slopes for 200 yards to the east. At the top of a 13,900-foot flat spot on top of the southeast face, choose your line carefully and enjoy almost 2000 feet of skiing back to Kite Lake.

ALTERNATIVES

1. ■ / ◆ / ◆◆ From Kite Lake, access the famous DeCaLiBron Loop. The 14ers Lincoln, Cameron, and Bross can also be skied in the right conditions. Enjoy your explorations of this area and make some turns!

2. ◆◆ Democrat's west and north faces are steep and classic when covered by enough snow in May and early June.

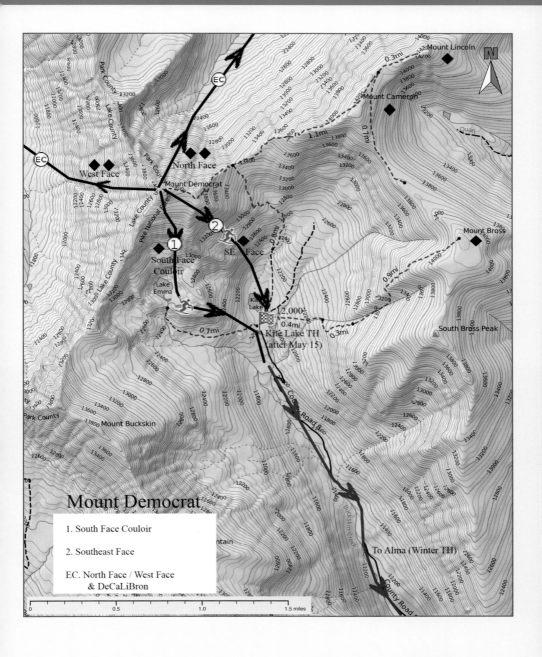

Mount Democrat

1. South Face Couloir

2. Southeast Face

EC. North Face / West Face
& DeCaLiBron

MT. DEMOCRAT

17. **Mt. Buckskin** 13,865 feet/4226 meters
18. **Mt. Arkansas** 13,795 feet/4205 meters

SKIABLE VERTICAL:	2,865 feet/873 meters
ROUND-TRIP DISTANCE:	Buckskin summit, 9.0 miles/11.3 kilometers; Arkansas summit, 8.0 miles/10.6 kilometers
TRAILHEAD:	Fremont Pass (11,000 feet)
DIFFICULTY RATINGS:	■ / ◆ / ◆ ◆
SKI TERRAIN:	Four-wheel-drive road ■, tree glades, ridgelines, steep faces, and couloir options
OPTIMAL SEASON:	January through May. April and May are ideal.
MAPS:	Trails Illustrated Number 109, Alma, Climax, Pike National Forest

Two skiers begin their exploration of the Buckskin Couloir.

Skinning in the upper Arkansas basin towards Mount Buckskin.

Skiing the northwest face of Buckskin.

COMMENT: The headwaters of the Arkansas River form a long and gradual basin, formerly covered by glaciers. These gentle slopes are ideal for touring, while the surrounding peaks, Buckskin, Arkansas, and Democrat, offer unlimited ski options from their summits and connecting ridges. Just a few favorites are described here that allow beginners and experts alike to take advantage of this special place.

GETTING THERE

Fremont Pass (11,000 feet). This trailhead is right off of Colorado Highway 91 and is open year-round. From 75 miles west of Denver, take Exit 195 at Copper Mountain and travel 10 miles south on Colorado Highway 91 to the top of Fremont Pass near the Climax Mine. The trailhead is 0.75 mile from here on the south side of the Pass, on the downhill and east side of the sharp curve on the highway. The east side of the road is plowed enough for a handful of cars to park in winter, and I've never seen more than 3 cars parked here at any time. If approaching from Leadville to the south, the trailhead is 12 miles north of Leadville on Colorado Highway 91. In summer, it is possible to take the forest road that heads east from the highway 1.5 miles up to a road closure and trail junction.

THE CLIMB

Mt. Buckskin West Ridge (Class 2). This climb ascends the basin and follows a moderately steep slope to the west ridge, finishing on the spectacular summit.

Follow the four-wheel-drive road up the right side of the broad basin as it heads southward to the obvious triangle known as Mt. Buckskin. After 2 miles you will be above timberline. You will bypass Mt. Democrat, which is high and to the west, and then you will see Mt. Buckskin to your south. Skin up into a flat area below a broad chute at 12,500 feet and the steep northwest face of buckskin. It is possible to climb a moderately steep but wide couloir to the ridge on the western end of the steep northwest face. Gain the ridge at 13,400 feet. From here stay to the right side (south) on the west ridge and follow it east for 450 feet to the summit. Some sections you might be able to skin up, others you will have to boot pack.

DESCENTS

1. *Northwest Face* ◆ / ◆ ◆ Leave the summit and travel slightly down and northwest for less than 50 yards. There is a small flat spot or notch that leads directly onto the steep northwest face. The face begins as a couloir, then opens up onto a series of rocky bands with openings in between the rocks. The face is best skied in a big snow year in May. About 600 feet down

Mount Arkansas and the North Couloir visible in the left center of the photo.

Climbing the North Couloir on Arkansas.   **Skiing the North Couloir.**

the face you will meet the Buckskin Couloir, which is more of a northerly facing wide slope, at 13,000 feet. Ski this enjoyable face north down and into the basin. Follow the broad valley north and then northeast back to the trailhead.

2. **_Buckskin Couloir_** ■ / ◆ This north facing ski line is easily accessible and is an excellent April to mid-June option. The couloir broadens greatly on the bottom half and is only about 35 degrees near the top portion. Ski between cool towers on the way down. You can make some fast turns when snow conditions are right. From the summit, ski west on the south slopes of Buckskin's west ridge to the 13,400-foot notch just to the west of some large buttresses on the ridge. Before heading any further down west to the true saddle between Arkansas and Buckskin, look north and down into the obvious face. Cornices are sometimes large on the ridge on this route, but dropping into the broad couloir is exhilarating. Ski down into the basin for about 1000 feet and then proceed back down gentle slopes to the northwest to the trailhead.

Ryan Belanger pondering his next turn in the North Couloir.

ALTERNATIVES

Mt. Arkansas North Couloir ◆ / ◆◆ This north facing couloir is narrow and steep (sustained at 50 degrees) and takes you down the north side of Mt. Arkansas. Follow the four-wheel-drive road up the right side of the broad basin as it heads southward. After the first 1.5 miles stay to the right (west) of some trees to get above timberline. Once above the timber, Buckskin's triangular face remains to the southeast. Look south to the closer Mt. Arkansas and in another 0.3 mile, arrive at a frozen lake at 12,100 feet. From here the challenge is obvious. Up in the basin to your south is the steep and narrow North Couloir. Skin up the gentle basin to the base of the couloir for another 0.5 mile. May and June are probably the safest months to climb and ski this aesthetic couloir. The top may be up to a 70-degree cornice, so use caution. The couloir provides more than 1000 feet of narrow jump turns and is actually oriented slightly to the northeast. Enjoy one of Colorado's Classics!

Headwaters Basin Ski Tour ● / ■ For a fun beginner ski mountaineer tour, follow this route to the lake in the basin below the north side of Mt. Arkansas, and ascend any of the moderate slopes for several hundred feet above the lake before enjoying turns on the way back to your vehicle at the trailhead. This route is 5 to 6 miles round-trip and has 1,500 feet elevation gain.

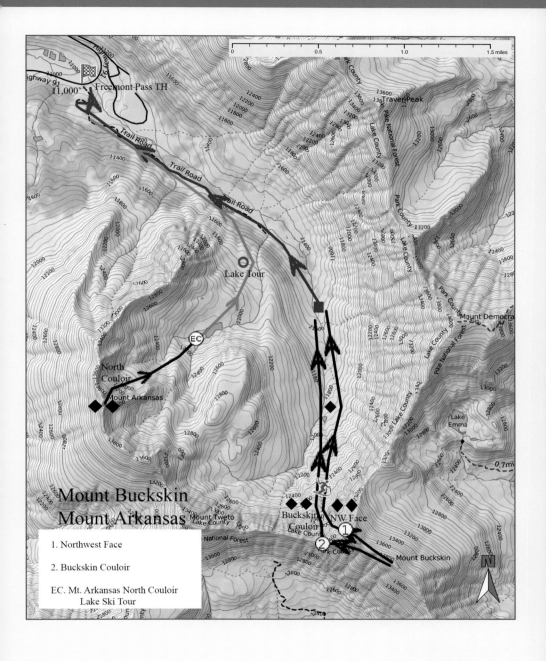

Mount Buckskin
Mount Arkansas

1. Northwest Face

2. Buckskin Couloir

EC. Mt. Arkansas North Couloir
    Lake Ski Tour

19. Mt. Sherman
14,036 feet/4278 meters

SKIABLE VERTICAL:	2836 feet/980 meters
ROUND-TRIP DISTANCE:	7.5 miles/12 kilometers
TRAILHEAD:	Iowa Gulch near ASARCO Mine (11,200 feet).
DIFFICULTY RATINGS:	■ / ◆ / ◆ ◆
SKI TERRAIN:	Ridgelines, steep and moderate faces, and bowls
OPTIMAL SEASON:	March through June. April and May are ideal.
MAPS:	Trails Illustrated Numbers 149 and 110, Mt. Sherman, Pike National Forest

COMMENT: Mt. Sherman is an easy winter ascent for a 14er, but unfortunately the snow coverage on the peak is rarely adequate for skiing. Strong winds are the norm here, and usually it takes the spring snowstorms of April and May to put certain lines on Sherman into prime ski condition. If you are looking for a true winter ski descent, be sure to go immediately after a storm hits, before the powder is blown away.

Following the power lines up Iowa Gulch to the West Face of Sherman.

Climbing the south ridge on Sherman to access east-facing ski terrain.

GETTING THERE

Iowa Gulch at ASARCO (11,200 feet). This trailhead is accessed from the west side and the town of Leadville. From the central part of Leadville follow US Highway 24 for 0.3 mile. Before US Highway 24 takes a sharp right turn, turn left onto Monroe Street and follow it up the hill for 0.3 mile. Next turn right (south and then southeast) onto Lake County Road 2. Follow Lake County Road 2 for 3.4 miles as it climbs to an obvious turnout. This road is plowed all winter long. At the turnout, the winter parking is on Lake County 2, while the narrower dirt road continues to the left on a road shelf. Lake County 2 drops to the right and down to the ASARCO mine. Take the left fork, which you can skin up in the winter. The road will melt out by late May.

THE CLIMB

West Slopes (Class 2). From the trailhead/road intersection, travel east following the four-wheel-drive road. After ascending about 0.75 mile you can easily see Mt. Sherman to the east above you. At about 1.0 mile near power lines to the left you will gradually drop down 300 feet for the next 0.5 mile to cross the shallow basin and reach the base of the gully between Mt. Sherman and Mt. Sheridan. Zigzag up the gully from 12,000 to 13,000 feet to reach the 13,140-foot saddle between Mt. Sherman and Mt. Sheridan. Travel north and then northeast for 1 mile to reach the summit of Mt. Sherman.

Powder turns on the southeast face.

DESCENTS

1. *West Face* ◆ / ◆◆ Leave the summit directly and choose any number of lines on the steep west face. The face needs lots of snow to cover up the small cliff bands and ledges, and not every season will bear fruit. Generally, May finally delivers enough snow to ski any number of variations on the face.

2. *Southeast Face* ■ / ◆ The eastern reaches of the southeast face are excellent and easy skiing; that's the good news. The bad news is that skiing this route means descending into Fourmile Basin, and if you parked in Iowa Gulch, you will have to climb back over to the 13,140-foot saddle between Mt. Sheridan and Mt. Sherman. Descent of the west gully is easy and leads you into the fantastic powder of Iowa Gulch. Do some research and consider accessing this southeast face line by coming from Fairplay and the Fourmile Basin Trailhead. You can also ski a variation off the much steeper southeast face of Mt. Sherman, farther to the south, which begins at the top of Sherman's broad summit ridge and the start of Sherman's south ridge.

ALTERNATIVES

Centennial 13ers. ◆ Any number of lines can be explored to the north from the summit of 13,951-foot Gemini Peak, or 13,855-foot Dyer Mountain, which in recent years has hosted a new ski mountaineering race. Mt. Sheridan's north face is interesting as well.

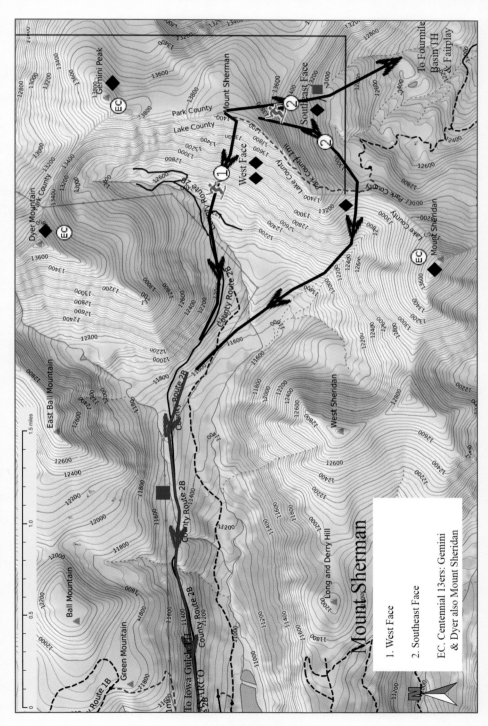

MT. SHERMAN

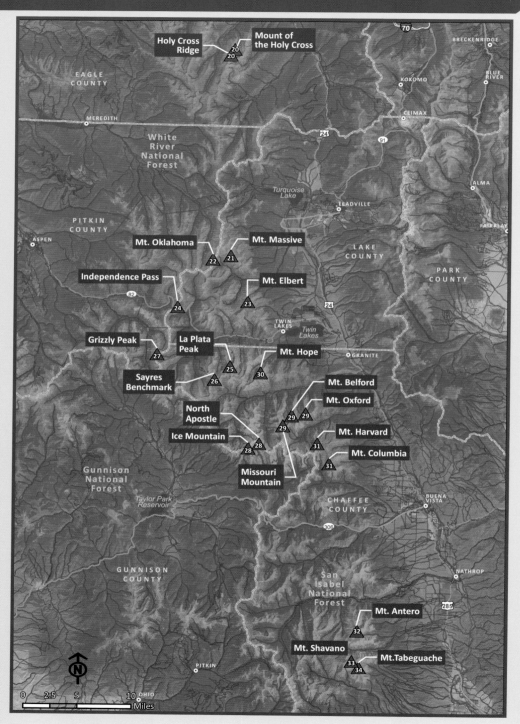

20. Mt. of the Holy Cross
14,005 feet/4269 meters

SKIABLE VERTICAL:	Up to 5625 feet/1715 meters
ROUND-TRIP DISTANCE:	12 miles/19.4 kilometers
TRAILHEADS:	Halfmoon Trailhead (10,320 feet)
DIFFICULTY RATINGS:	■ / ◆ / ◆ ◆
SKI TERRAIN:	Ridgelines, couloirs, tree glades, and steep slopes
OPTIMAL SEASON:	February through June. April through June are ideal.
MAPS:	Trails Illustrated Number 126, Mt. of the Holy Cross, White River National Forest

COMMENT: Mt. of the Holy Cross is a Colorado Classic. The legendary cross is visible from the top of the Vail Mountain Ski Area and from the west portals of the Interstate 70 Eisenhower-Johnson Tunnel. Many have seen the cross but few have skied this uniquely challenging objective. Travel here in a big snow year and you will have a rewarding adventure!

Alpenglow on Holy Cross from East Cross Creek basin. The Couloir is visible to the left side of the mountain. Photo by Andrew Warkentin

The Notch Mountain Shelter.
Photo by Andrew Warkentin.

Brad Burgtorf climbs the Cross Couloir.

GETTING THERE

Halfmoon (10,320 feet). From Vail, travel west on I-70 for 5 miles to Exit 171. Take US Highway 24 east for 5 miles, passing through the town of Minturn to Tigiwon Road Number 107. Turn right onto Tigiwon Road and follow the road as it switches back several times for 8.5 miles to the Halfmoon Trailhead, where there is ample parking as well as a campground. The road usually opens by mid-June. For winter and spring access, consider using snowmobiles to get to the summer trailhead.

THE CLIMB

Cross Couloir (Class 3). Start from the Halfmoon Trailhead and hike or skin 1.7 miles to reach Halfmoon Pass at 11,640 feet. From the pass there are a couple of options. Some hearty souls have managed to traverse basically to the west and southwest along the slopes of Notch Mountain to find their way into the basin near Lake Patricia and eventually to the Bowl of Tears at 12,000 feet. Also, it is possible to follow the summer trail corridor and descend nearly 1,000 feet into the East Cross Creek Basin. Once down to East Cross Creek, ascend a boulder-strewn basin to Lake Patricia and then reach the Bowl of Tears. Once you arrive at the Bowl of Tears, you will realize the effort was worth it! Climb 800 feet of snow slopes angling to the north to get into the lower third of the Cross Couloir. Aim for a notch at 12,800 feet above the cliffs that guard the bottom of the couloir. (When skiing the Holy Cross, make sure to exit the couloir at this notch.) Once in the couloir, climb for 1,200 feet to the summit. The couloir barely exceeds 40 degrees at the steepest parts, but be aware of any cornices at the top of the couloir. Exit the couloir and walk north for less than 100 feet to reach the true summit.

DESCENTS

1. *Holy Cross Couloir* ◆ Leave the summit to the south to ski the classic Cross Couloir. In April and May it is wise to ski this couloir before 9 a.m. as the sun can warm it rapidly, contributing to avalanche danger. By June, the snow will be nice and soft by 8 a.m. Descend for 1,200 feet in the cross and make sure to exit the couloir to the right at the 12,800-foot notch before skiing easy slopes down to the Bowl of Tears 12,000 feet.

2. *Angelica Couloir* ◆ This couloir is only slighty more challenging at the top than the Holy Cross Couloir, but becomes broader and easier after the first 400 feet. You can scout this face from Halfmoon Pass to find the correct (southern) branch through some of the cliff bands. Leave the sum-

Skiing the long and narrow Cross Couloir in June requires precision to avoid the center runnel.

mit of Holy Cross on gentle slopes for 200 yards to the northwest, angling toward Holy Cross' north ridge. At 13,700 feet there is a flat spot on the ridge; ski from here to the northeast into the narrow upper portion of the Angelica Couloir. At 13,000 feet you will meet the northern branch of the couloir, and from here you can enjoy 1,000 feet of great skiing on a 35-degree slope to the vicinity of Lake Patricia.

ALTERNATIVES

1. *Notch Mountain to the Holy Cross Couloir*: ■ / ◆ / ◆◆ From the Halfmoon Trailhead parking lot, use the Fall Creek Trail and head toward Lake Constantine instead. After 2.5 miles, follow a trail junction and climb another 2.5 miles to the south of the summit of Notch Mountain, 13,237 feet. You will arrive at the famous Notch Mountain shelter at 13,100 feet, which is in clear view of Mt. of the Holy Cross and the Cross Couloir. Ski down to the west into the basin toward the Bowl of Tears and the base of Holy Cross.

Making turns down the Cross Couloir near the exit notch.

There are a couple of couloirs that provide excellent skiing down into the basin. From the basin at the Bowl of Tears ascend the Cross Couloir to ski it as well!

2. ***Holy Cross(Halo) Ridge***: ◆ / ◆◆ Holy Cross Ridge, also known as Halo Ridge (13,831 feet), is one of Colorado's hundred highest peaks and is located 0.5 mile west of Mt. of the Holy Cross. The east face of Holy Cross Ridge boasts a broad and distinguishable couloir that skis into the basin toward the Bowl of Tears. This line is seldom skied, but terrific if you have lots of extra energy!

3. ■ / ◆ Skiing Mt. of the Holy Cross by its north ridge is a spectacular tour in itself when the conditions of the Cross Couloir are not ideal.

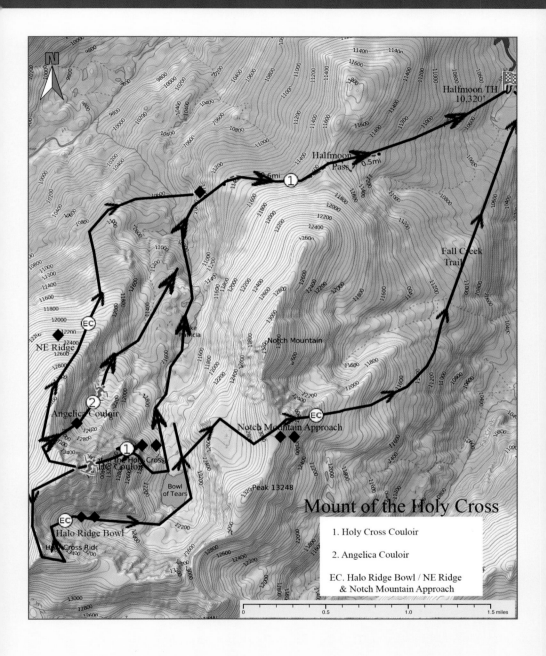

Mount of the Holy Cross

1. Holy Cross Couloir

2. Angelica Couloir

EC. Halo Ridge Bowl / NE Ridge
& Notch Mountain Approach

MT. OF THE HOLY CROSS

21. Mt. Massive
14,421 feet/4395 meters

SKIABLE VERTICAL:	4181 feet/1275 meters
ROUND-TRIP DISTANCE:	7 miles/11.3 kilometers (from North Halfmoon Creek Trailhead); 8 miles/12 kilometers (from Halfmoon Creek Trailhead, FS 110/FS 1103A junction)
TRAILHEAD:	Halfmoon Creek (10,240 feet) or North Halfmoon Creek (10,500 feet)
DIFFICULTY RATINGS:	■ / ◆
SKI TERRAIN:	Four-wheel-drive road ■, tree glades, ridgelines, faces, and couloir options
OPTIMAL SEASON:	January through June. April, May, and June are ideal. Maps: Trails Illustrated Numbers 149 and 127, Mt. Champion, Mt. Massive, San Isabel National Forest

COMMENT: As one of Colorado's 14ers, Mt. Massive in the northern part of the Sawatch Range is truly a skier's paradise. There is unlimited potential to explore here. The North Halfmoon four-wheel drive road allows access to multiple ski options on the peak. Returning to ski Mt. Massive again and again can be a lifetime learning experience. The five total summits above 14,000 feet along the 3-mile ridge all have at least half a dozen options each to explore. You could spend days and days skiing different lines on the peak. My favorites are described here.

A look at the west slopes and face of Massive from Mount Oklahoma across the valley. Several ski lines are possible.

Skiing June corn on Massive. Make sure avalanche conditions are stable before bringing dogs on ski outings.

GETTING THERE

Halfmoon Creek Trailhead (10,240 feet). Access to the trailhead varies depending on whether the four-wheel-drive road is driveable to its end, which usually happens in May. In winter you may have to skin up the road for several miles. From the center of Leadville on Main Street (Highway 24), travel 3.5 miles southwest from town and turn right (west) on Colorado 300. Travel 0.7 mile west on Colorado 300 and take a left on Lake County 11. After 1 mile on Lake County 11, take a right and follow signs for Halfmoon Creek. After leaving Lake County 11, the road turns to dirt. After 2 miles on this road you will enter the San Isabel National Forest. Halfmoon Campground is at 3.5 miles, Mt. Elbert Trailhead and Elbert Creek Campground are at 4.7 miles, and the Colorado Trail and Mt. Massive Trailhead are at mile 5. Continue to the FS 110/FS 1103A junction at mile 7. Lower-clearance vehicles can park near this junction while four-wheel-drive higher clearance vehicles can proceed another 0.5 mile up a steeper road and reach the start of the North Halfmoon Creek Trail at 10,500 feet.

APPROACH

Standard route: Southwest slopes. Travel 1.0 mile along the North Halfmoon Creek Trail starting at the Mt. Massive Helicopter Memorial at 10,500 feet. You will reach the first major meadow after crossing through the forest and some willows at 11,100 feet. At the end of the meadow turn northwest to head up the peak.

THE CLIMB

Southwest slopes (Class 2). From the meadow at 11,100 feet, begin your climb by following the evergreen trees to the northeast. In several hundred feet you will make it to timberline and be directly in the shallow gullies and bowls of the southwest slopes. In good snow conditions, it is easy to zigzag your way up the face and slopes for nearly 2,000 feet. You will see 14,132-foot South Massive Peak to your right (southeast), and nearing the 13,500-foot mark, aim for the shallow saddle that is just north of South Massive. From the saddle, you will see the summit ridge to your north. Climb west and then northwest and finally north to reach the true summit of Mt. Massive. Staying on the ridge or slightly to the right side of the ridge will allow you to skin the entire way.

DESCENTS

1. *South Ridge to Southwest slopes* ■ / ◆ Leave the summit and retrace your ascent route. Enjoy 3,000 feet of wide-open turns on excellent slopes that have several different minor gullies that are easy to ski. Just remember that near the bottom of the run at about 11,400 feet you must ski to the right (north) into the trees to avoid the cliffs that guard the meadow at the base of the valley, and use the trees to ski back into the valley and finish in the meadow below.

2. *"Massive" Couloir to West Slopes* ■ / ◆ This ski line is usually in safe condition by mid-May. This broad couloir is more like a gulley that opens up to the expanse of Massive's west face. It is an excellent way to ski down to North Halfmoon Lake in the basin below Mt. Oklahoma. You can scout the entire line from the summit of Massive. Look north and down to the northwest and the line is easily seen starting from a saddle just south of a small sub-summit at 14,300' known as "Massive Green." You can ski the ridge over to the top of the line, which sometimes slightly cornices, and drop down to your left. The steepest portions are at the top. The line drops into excellent turns several hundred feet down and then turns into wide open slopes all the way down to North Halfmoon Lake. Ski southwest and south for 1.0 mile to reach the base of the southwest slopes route.

ALTERNATIVES

East and Southeast Slopes ◆ The five total summits above 14,000 feet along the 3 mile ridge all have at least half a dozen options each to explore. Any line you take to the eastern sides of Mt. Massive will eventually take you down to timberline and the Colorado Trail. If you ski the east face of Massive from the southern end of the summit ridge, it will take you into a broad bowl and back to the Colorado Trail. Once you are down to the Colorado Trail corridor, you can follow it back to the south for 4 miles to return to the Mt. Massive Trailhead along Halfmoon Creek Road.

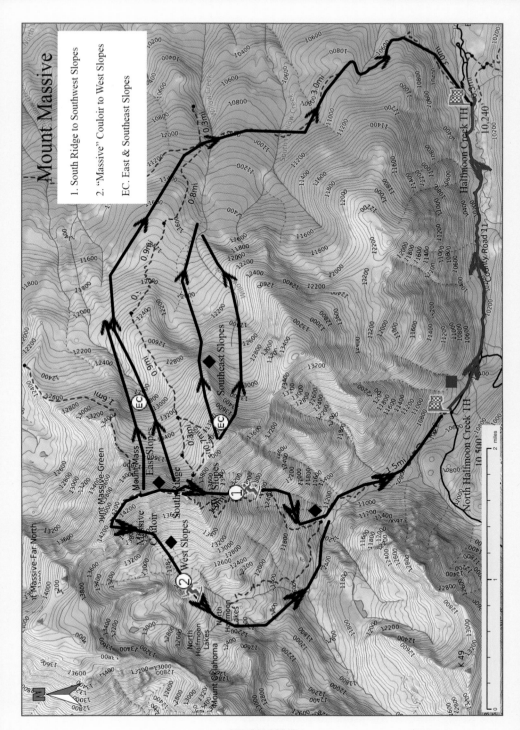

Mount Massive

1. South Ridge to Southwest Slopes
2. "Massive" Couloir to West Slopes
EC. East & Southeast Slopes

MT. MASSIVE

22. Mt. Oklahoma
13,845 feet/4220 meters

SKIABLE VERTICAL:	3605 feet/1098 meters
ROUND-TRIP DISTANCE:	14 miles/22.6 kilometers (from North Halfmoon Creek Trailhead); 16 miles/26 kilometers (from Halfmoon Creek Trailhead, FS 110/FS1103A junction)
TRAILHEAD:	Halfmoon Creek (10,240 feet) or North Halfmoon Creek (10,500 feet)
DIFFICULTY RATINGS:	■ / ◆ / ◆ ◆
SKI TERRAIN:	Four-wheel-drive road ■, tree glades, ridgelines, steep faces, and couloir options
OPTIMAL SEASON:	March through June. May and June are ideal.
MAPS:	Trails Illustrated Numbers 148, 149, and 127, Mt. Champion, Mt. Massive, San Isabel National Forest

COMMENT: Centennial peak Mt. Oklahoma in the northern part of the Sawatch Range is tucked away to the southwest in the shadow of its larger neighbor, Mt. Massive. The North Halfmoon four-wheel drive road allows access to multiple ski options on the peak. Skiing Oklahoma is a true wilderness experience, as the summit straddles two wilderness areas: Mt. Massive to the east, and the Hunter Fryingpan to the west. The climb also offers an excellent opportunity above treeline to scout the west slopes and faces of Mt. Massive.

GETTING THERE
North Halfmoon Trailhead (10,240 feet). Access to the trailhead varies. It is driveable to the end of the four-wheel-drive road by sometime in May. During winter you may have to skin up the road for several miles. From the center of Leadville on Mainstreet (Highway 24), travel 3.5 miles southwest from town and turn right (west) on Colorado 300. Travel 0.7 mile west on Colorado 300 and turn left on Lake County 11. After 1 mile on Lake County 11, turn right and follow signs for Halfmoon Creek. After leaving Lake County 11, the road turns to dirt. On this road you will enter the San Isabel National Forest in 2 miles, then pass Halfmoon Campground at 3.5 miles, Mt. Elbert Trailhead and Elbert Creek Campground at 4.7 miles, and the Colorado Trail and Mt. Massive Trailhead at

The east face of Oklahoma, the narrow "Sooner" Couloir at the right center of the pyramidal face.

mile 5.0. Continue to the FS 110/FS 1103A junction at mile 7.0. Lower clearance vehicles can park near this junction while four-wheel-drive higher clearance vehicles can proceed another 0.5 mile up a steeper road and reach the start of the North Halfmoon Creek Trail at 10,500 feet.

APPROACH
North Halfmoon Lakes. Travel 2 miles along the North Halfmoon Creek Trail starting at the Mt. Massive Helicopter Memorial at 10,500 feet. You will reach the lower North Halfmoon Lake first at mile 2.0 at 12,000 feet. Skin up northwest for 0.25 mile to reach the largest of the North Halfmoon Lakes at 12,300 feet in a large basin. From here the east face and northeast bowl of Oklahoma are impressive.

THE CLIMB
Northeast Bowl (Class 2). Coming from Upper North Halfmoon Lake at about 12,300 feet, skin south and southwest up steeper slopes to reach Mt. Oklahoma's east/southeast ridge at around 13,000 feet. To gain the ridge you may have to boot pack, but with careful zigzag skinning it is possible to skin onto the ridge. From the ridge you will see Oklahoma's broad summit to your northwest. Follow the gentle ridge for 0.3 mile to the summit. By climbing the bowl you have a great opportunity to see the conditions not only in the bowl but also in the east and northeast facing Sooner Couloir.

Easy turns are found on the upper southeast ridge.

Ascending the southeast ridge with Mount Elbert in the distance.

DESCENTS

1. ***Southeast Ridge to Northeast Bowl*** ■ / ◆ Leave the summit and enjoy 1,000 feet of excellent wide open turns on a broad slope that narrows the farther east you ski. The views coming down the ridge to above the start of the northeast bowl to your left are among the finest in Colorado. At 13,000 feet, choose a line directly into the northeast bowl, which is generally steeper to skier's left than skier's right. Manage any cornices or terrain features according to the conditions. At the bottom of the bowl you can ski down to North Halfmoon Lakes.

2. ***Sooner Couloir*** ◆ / ◆◆ This advanced ski line is usually safe by mid-May. You must evaluate a series of small chutes on the upper east face of Mt. Oklahoma. The clearest route into the central part of the Sooner Couloir is about 400 feet below the summit. The couloir narrows near the bottom and is about 45 degrees. Scout the face and your line carefully on your approach from near the North Halfmoon Lakes.

ALTERNATIVES

South Bowl and Southeast Slopes ◆ From the upper reaches of the southeast ridge, ski farther right (south). Choose one of the steep and narrow chutes around 13,000 feet to reach a flat platform on the south face at 12,700 feet. Turn skier's left, heading back southeast and down into the North Halfmoon Basin at the confluence of creeks from the south and the north. Once you reach the timber, ski down the basin and find the North Halfmoon Creek Trail, which will take you back to the trailhead.

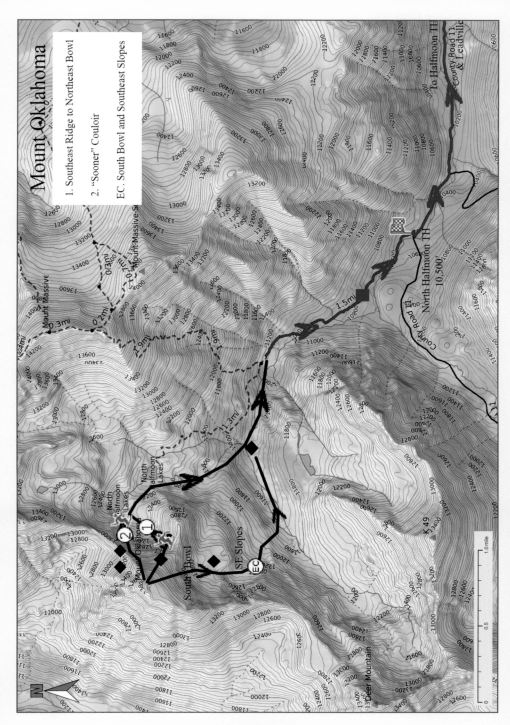

Mount Oklahoma

1. Southeast Ridge to Northeast Bowl
2. "Sooner" Couloir
EC. South Bowl and Southeast Slopes

MT. OKLAHOMA

23. Mt. Elbert
14,440 feet/4400 meters

SKIABLE VERTICAL:	4880 feet/1487 meters
ROUND-TRIP DISTANCE:	11.2 miles/18.5 kilometers (from South Elbert Trailhead); 9 miles/12.6kilometerskilometers(from North Elbert Trailhead)
TRAILHEADS:	South Mt. Elbert (9,560 feet) or North Mt. Elbert (10,050 feet)
DIFFICULTY RATINGS:	■ / ◆
SKI TERRAIN:	Four-wheel-drive road ■, tree glades, ridgelines, faces, and couloir options
OPTIMAL SEASON:	January through June. April and May are ideal.
MAPS:	Trails Illustrated Numbers 127 and 148, Mt. Elbert, San Isabel National Forest

COMMENT: The granddaddy of them all, Mt. Elbert is the highest of Colorado's 14ers in the northern part of the Sawatch Range and is a relatively easy ski objective. There are numerous ski lines off many aspects for all ability levels. Climb high and enjoy the views from the rooftop of Colorado before clicking in and skiing down at least 4,000 vertical feet on nearly every route.

Full view of multiple ski lines in the Box Creek Chutes from the northeast ridge.

GETTING THERE

South Elbert Trailhead (9,650 feet). Travel south on US Highway 24 from Leadville, or north on US Highway 24 from Buena Vista. From the US Highway 24/Colorado Highway 82 junction, travel west on Colorado Highway 82 for 4 miles, or 2.3 miles east on Colorado Highway 82 from the town of Twin Lakes. Turn onto paved Lake County Road 24, which ascends north/northwest away from and above Twin Lakes Reservoir. After 1 mile on this road, you will arrive at the paved South Mt. Elbert Trailhead, marked clearly by a good sign. Four-wheel-drive vehicles can ascend the separate dirt road leading west and northwest, but in winter and early spring, parking in the plowed and paved lot is the best option.

North Elbert Trailhead (10,050 feet). Access to the trailhead varies; you can drive all the way to the trailhead by sometime in May, or in winter you may have to skin up the road for several miles. From the center of Leadville on Mainstreet (Highway 24), travel 3.5 miles southwest from town and turn right (west) on Colorado 300. Travel 0.7 mile west on Colorado 300 and take a left on Lake County 11. After 1 mile on Lake County 11, take a right and follow signs for Halfmoon Creek. After leaving Lake County 11, the road turns to dirt. You will enter the San Isabel National Forest in 2 miles, Halfmoon Campground at 3.5 miles, and Mt. Elbert Trailhead and Elbert Creek Campground at 4.7 miles. The Mt. Elbert Trailhead is marked and on the left, and can accommodate over a dozen vehicles.

THE CLIMBS

East slopes (Class 2). Starting from the South Elbert Trailhead, follow the four-wheel-drive road for 2 miles. This road is easy to skin or hike. Near the end of the road you will meet the Colorado Trail, and a large set of signs marking the Mt. Elbert climb. Cross a footbridge and follow the Colorado Trail north for 0.3 mile through aspens. There will be a clear trail junction and sign marking the Mt. Elbert Trail. Turn left (west) and ascend through the aspens and pine for a mile to a broad ridge that eventually reaches timberline and Mt. Elbert's long east ridge. Follow the ridge to the summit.

Northeast Ridge (Class 2). Follow the Colorado Trail south as it climbs through the evergreen forest for nearly 1.5 miles. In winter the trail corridor is easy to follow. Before crossing Box Creek, take the well-marked right trail fork, which leads toward Mt. Elbert to the southwest. Reach timberline and follow the northeast ridge to the summit.

DESCENTS

1. *Southeast slopes to southeast couloirs* ■ / ◆ You can ski right off the top of Mt. Elbert and toward the east ridge by taking the upper southeast slopes for

Skinning up the southeast ridge with the southeast couloirs in full view to the upper left.

Skiing gentle slopes near the summit of Elbert.

the first 800 feet or so. Before getting on the east ridge, angle to the steepening southeast portions of the ridge and aim for a pair of couloirs that empty into the basin to the south/southeast of Mt. Elbert. The chutes ski down from 13,200 to 12,400 feet and are lots of fun. Once reaching the basin, either follow the basin back toward the Colorado Trail, or ascend slightly to the east ridge near timberline to follow the trail corridor back to the South Elbert Trailhead.

2. **_Box Creek Chutes_** ◆ The top of the Box Creek chutes are about 0.5 mile from the summit of Mt. Elbert. Ski gentle slopes for 600 feet down to the northeast. Choose any of the small couloirs that empty into the Box Creek Basin between the northeast ridge (left) and the east ridge (right and south of you). Ski from 13,800 feet down to 12,400 feet, and then it's time to make a decision. Where did you park? Ski north for the North Elbert Trailhead, and ski south and east to get back to the South Elbert Trailhead.

ALTERNATIVES

West Face ◆ Depending on your exact line off the summit, up to a 3,000-foot ski line on the west and northwest aspects awaits your adventurous spirit. If you ski any of the west aspects, you will arrive at the South Halfmoon Creek drainage and can find your way back to the North Elbert Trailhead.

East Bowl ◆ For east bowl options, ski south off the summit of Mt. Elbert and down to the saddle between Mt. Elbert and South Elbert (14,134 feet). The east bowl skis beautifully into the basin that funnels all the way back toward the South Elbert Trailhead. Join the east ridge descent route once you reach timberline.

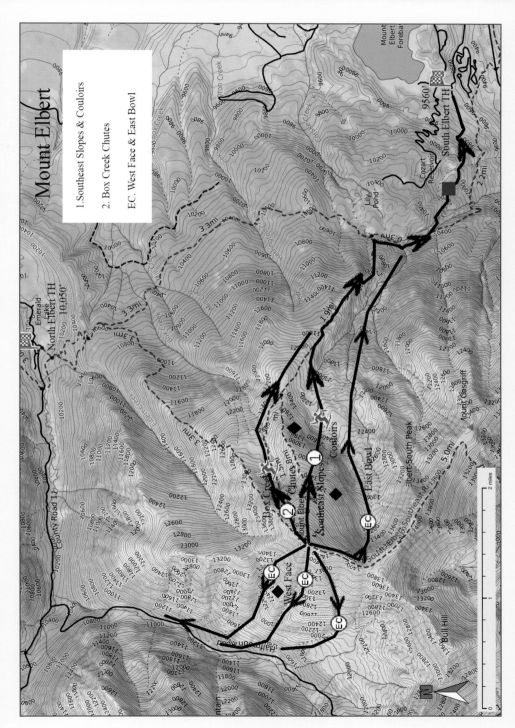

Mount Elbert

1. Southeast Slopes & Couloirs

2. Box Creek Chutes

EC. West Face & East Bowl

MT. ELBERT

24. Independence Pass

12,095 feet/3687 meters

SKIABLE VERTICAL:	Up to 2,500 feet/762 meters
ROUND-TRIP DISTANCE:	Varies depending on your ski objective
TRAILHEAD:	Independence Pass (12,095 feet)
DIFFICULTY RATINGS:	■ / ◆ / ◆ ◆
SKI TERRAIN:	Ridgelines, couloirs, tree glades, and moderate faces
OPTIMAL SEASON:	May through June. Early July in some years still delivers. Usually the pass opens by Memorial Day weekend, or the weekend prior depending on CDOT and snow remaining.
MAPS:	Trails Illustrated Numbers 127 and 148, Independence Pass, Mt. Champion, White River National Forest

COMMENT: Independence Pass is one of Colorado's truly scenic mountain passes. Backcountry skiing in this stunning setting is simply spectacular. Once the road is opened for the spring, there is a two to three week window where the ski potential to the north and south ridgelines of the Pass and multiple directions is unlimited. Several 12,000- and 13,000- foot peaks can be accessed from the Pass and provide stellar ski outings.

Climbing the final steps to the summit of Mountain Boy Peak (13,198'). Photo by Chris Tomer

GETTING THERE

Independence Pass. The Pass is located west of Denver and east of Aspen on Colorado Highway 82. If travelling from Denver, Leadville, or Buena Vista, follow Colorado Highway 82 west for 18 miles from Twin Lakes to the top of Independence Pass. There is a parking area on the left (east) side of the highway. If travelling from Aspen, drive on Colorado Highway 82 for 20 miles to the top of Independence Pass.

Atop Mountain Boy Peak, the options are unlimited in the sea of mountains.

DESCENTS

1. *Indy North of the Pass* ■ / ◆ / ◆◆
   This is expansive terrain to the north of the Pass that you can climb to the north and then ski toward the west to the Aspen side of the Pass. Destinations and objectives include Blarney Peak and Blue Peak, both over 12,500 feet.

2. *Indy South of the Pass* ■ / ◆ Leave the parking area to the south and follow the ridgeline to access multiple objectives. Snowfence Ridge and Mountain Boy Gulch as well as Mountain Boy Peak (13,198 feet) along the east side ski down to Highway 82.

*Note that nearly all terrain allows climbing and then descending to Colorado Highway 82. This maximizes skiable vertical terrain and facilitates vehicle shuttles on either side of the Pass.

Mountain Boy Peak's east bowl.

ALTERNATIVES

Peaks Accessed by Highway 82 on the west side of Independence Pass ◆ / ◆◆
Several peaks require a bit more work and effort from below the top of the Pass by parking on Highway 82. Independence Peak (12,703 feet) and Green Mountain are further south and above the old mining town of Independence, while Linkins Peak and Geissler Mountain are further north and can be accessed from the first hairpin turn below the west side of Independence Pass.

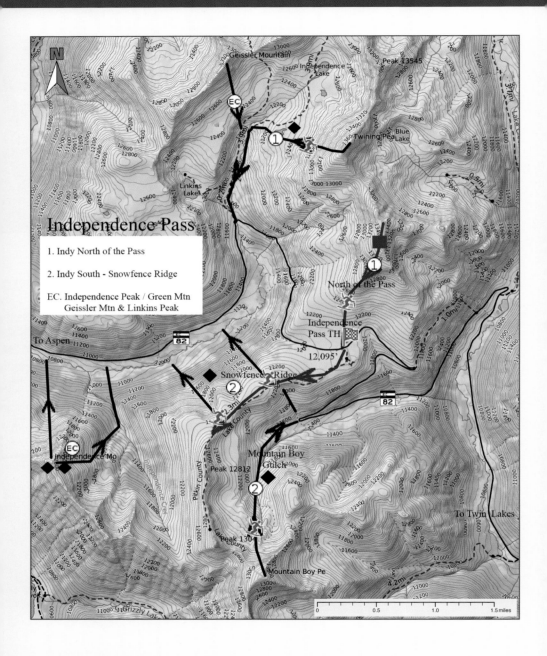

25. La Plata Peak
14,336 feet/4370 meters

SKIABLE VERTICAL:	Up to 4,300 feet/1310 meters
ROUND-TRIP DISTANCE:	From Lake Creek Trailhead: 9.0 to 11 miles/13.8 to15 kilometers
TRAILHEAD:	Lake Creek (10,100 feet)
DIFFICULTY RATINGS:	■ / ◆ / ◆ ◆
SKI TERRAIN:	Four-wheel-drive access road, narrow trail, tree glades, ridgelines, steep faces, and couloirs
OPTIMAL SEASON:	January through June. April through June are ideal.
MAPS:	Trails Illustrated Numbers 127 and 148, Mt. Elbert, Winfield, Independence Pass, San Isabel National Forest

COMMENT: La Plata is the perfect setting for a winter or spring outing with moderate to steep skiing on a challenging 14er. Because the trailhead is right on Highway 82, you can give this peak a try in all seasons.

The Northwest ridge generally skis right off the summit. Also consider a couple of lines off the North Ridge direct (left) once the avalanche conditions are favorable.

Skiers marching out of the basin after skiing the North Face of La Plata.

Scott Benge on the Northwest Ridge.

GETTING THERE

Lake Creek Trailhead (10,100 feet). This trailhead is located on Colorado Highway 82 and is open in winter. Travel 14.5 miles west of the US 24/Colorado Highway 82 junction south of Leadville. Pass west through the small town of Twin Lakes and park on Colorado Highway 82 where it meets South Fork Lake Creek Road (FS 391). This trailhead is clearly marked "La Plata 14er Trailhead."

THE CLIMB

Northwest Ridge (Class 2). Start at the Lake Creek Trailhead and go south on South Fork Lake Creek Road for 0.3 mile. You will pass many "No Trespassing" signs. Leave the road before it takes a turn to the southwest and travel south through the trees on a trail. In 250 yards, cross a creek on a good footbridge. Once across the bridge, travel east for 0.5 mile through the forest on easy flat terrain. After crossing La Plata Gulch Creek, the summer trail travels south and steepens into the woods. Stay just east of the creek, climbing 1.5 miles and find your way up to a flat meadow at 11,000 feet. From here you will be able to see La Plata's west face and northwest ridge. If conditions permit, follow the creek in the valley for several hundred yards and then choose the best chute to ascend to your east. You will gain the northwest ridge between 12,600 and 12,800 feet. Follow the ridge to the summit.

DESCENTS

1. *North Face Bowl* ◆ / ◆◆ Leave the summit heading north and evaluate several options. The entrance to the North Couloir is almost directly off the summit. The further you travel down the northwest ridge, the easier the lines dropping into La Plata Basin become. If you drop down to 13,800 feet on the

ridge, there are several relatively easy east facing lines into the basin. Once down to the La Plata Basin at 12,000 feet, ski north into the woods and carefully navigate the forest until you arrive at Lake Creek at around 10,000 feet.

2. *Northwest ridge to West Chutes* ◆ Leave the summit and travel down slopes for about the first 500 feet on the northwest ridge. Between 13,600 and 13,200 feet the west face (skier's left) has several long gullies that are excellent when snow-filled. If you prefer, ski down the ridge to a small saddle at about 12,700 feet. From here, an easier slope funnels into a minor and steeper gully, which will take you to the valley floor at 11,000 feet. Travel/ski north down La Plata Gulch to reach the trailhead.

ALTERNATIVES

Southwest Ridge Ski Tour ■ / ◆ This long ski loop can be delightfully easy on a warm spring day. Start out by leaving La Plata's summit down its long and gentle southwest ridge. At 13,600 feet an obvious ridge crest drops to a slightly steeper slope. From here you will see Sayres Peak to your southwest. Ski toward the peak on excellent 30-degree slopes. To get into the basin directly below Sayre's north face, ski east until reaching 12,200 feet in the basin. From this point ski down the valley to your north, eventually following La Plata Gulch back to the trailhead. As you ski, notice La Plata's imposing west face looming above you.

A beautiful day on a snowy summit looking south.

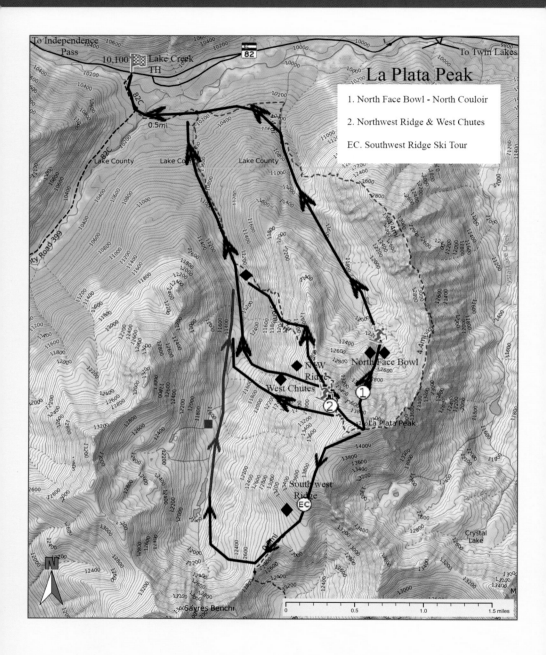

LA PLATA PEAK

26. Sayres Benchmark
13,738 feet/4187 meters

SKIABLE VERTICAL:	Up to 3,700 feet/1128 meters
ROUND-TRIP DISTANCE:	From Lake Creek Trailhead: 10.5 miles/17 kilometers
TRAILHEAD:	Lake Creek (10,100 feet)
DIFFICULTY RATINGS:	■ / ◆ / ◆ ◆
SKI TERRAIN:	Four-wheel-drive access road, narrow trail, tree glades, steep faces, and couloirs
OPTIMAL SEASON:	January through June. April through June is ideal.
MAPS:	Trails Illustrated Numbers 127 and 148, Winfield, Independence Pass, San Isabel National Forest

COMMENT: Sayres Benchmark is a steep and inviting peak deep in the Sawatch Range. Its north face boasts a couple of classic lines that are well worth the effort.

GETTING THERE
Lake Creek Trailhead (10,100 feet). See La Plata Peak.

THE CLIMB
La Plata Gulch to North Face (Class 3). Start at the Lake Creek Trailhead and go south on South Fork Lake Creek Road for 0.3 miles. You will pass many "No Trespassing signs." Leave the road before it takes a turn to the southwest and travel south through the trees on a trail. In 250 yards, cross a creek on a good footbridge. Once across the bridge, travel east for 0.5 mile through the forest on easy flat terrain. After crossing La Plata Gulch Creek, the summer trail travels south and steepens into the woods. Stay just east of the creek, climbing 1.5 miles and find your way up to a flat meadow at 11,000 feet. From here you will be able to see La Plata's west face and northwest ridge. Continue south and slightly southwest toward the obvious peak in the distance (Sayres). Travel for 1.5 miles to the base of the north face. From here you have two options. Climb the north slopes into the narrowing north couloir (right), or ascend the slightly more difficult X-rated Couloir (left). Climb either route for nearly 2000 feet from the basin to the summit.

Powder conditions in the X-rated.
Photo by Dennis Humphrey

Approaching Sayers Benchmark.

Calen Orlowski skiing a narrow portion of the X-rated Couloir. Photo by Dennis Humphrey

DESCENTS

1. **_X-Rated Couloir_** ◆ / ◆◆ X-rated Couloir gets its name from the "X" shape of two gullies that appear to cross each other when viewing the face from the north. You can ski this line directly from the summit, and then follow the deepest inset portion of the couloir near the bottom to reach the valley floor. The couloir doesn't exceed 45 degrees at its steepest. Or vary the line by skiing the skier's left portion of the "X" lower down.

2. **_North Couloir_** ◆ Leave the summit and travel skier's left toward the west and northwest ridge. In about 50 yards you will see the obvious gully leading north into the inset North Couloir. Ski the line down for 1,000 feet before it opens up into a broader apron leading to the valley floor. Travel/ski north down the relatively flat La Plata Gulch ■ to reach the trailhead.

ALTERNATIVES

Sayres South Faces ◆ / ◆◆ Take some time to explore Sayres' steep and complicated south and southeast face lines. You can also travel east on the east ridge a bit toward La Plata Peak before dropping in and skiing down toward the old Winfield town site.

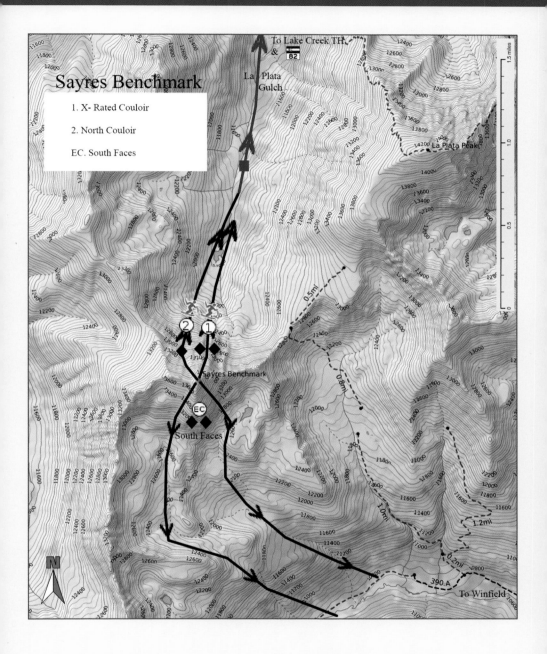

Sayres Benchmark

1. X- Rated Couloir

2. North Couloir

EC. South Faces

SAYRES BENCHMARK

27. Grizzly Peak
13,988 feet/4263 meters
North and East Approaches

SKIABLE VERTICAL:	Up to 4,000 feet/1220 meters
ROUND-TRIP DISTANCE:	From Lake Creek Trailhead: 14.8 miles/24 kilometers; from McNasser Gulch Trailhead: 8.2 miles/13.2 kilometers
TRAILHEADS:	Lake Creek (10,100 feet); McNasser Gulch (10,740 feet); Grizzly Reservoir Trailhead (10,560 feet)
DIFFICULTY RATINGS:	■ / ◆ / ◆ ◆
SKI TERRAIN:	Four-wheel-drive access road, narrow trail, tree glades, steep faces, and couloirs
OPTIMAL SEASON:	January through June. April and May are ideal.
MAPS:	Trails Illustrated Numbers 127 & 148, Independence Pass, San Isabel National Forest

COMMENT: Colorado's highest 13er, Grizzly Peak is situated on the geographical border between the Elk Range and the Sawatch Range. The peak is truly isolated, so you will likely not encounter another soul while on a ski mission to

Standing atop the North "Grizzly" Couloir before dropping in.

this peak. Climb to the top and enjoy mountains in all directions. Enjoy amazing skiing with endless peaks as your backdrop. There are truly classic lines on Grizzly, and because it's the highest 13er, there is plenty of vertical as well!

GETTING THERE

Lake Creek Trailhead (10,100 feet). See La Plata Peak.

McNasser Gulch (10,740 feet). In some years, by mid-May you can drive up South Fork Lake Creek Road (FS 391). Travel south then southwest for 3.3 miles and reach a small parking area near FS 394. Depending on the year, the snow may be melted in late May or early June and you can continue on FS 394 on a rougher four-wheel-drive road for up to 1.2 miles to the northwest to reach a locked gate in McNasser Gulch at 11,350 feet.

Kuma the ski dog climbing the North "Grizzly" Couloir in prime conditions.

Grizzly Reservoir Trailhead (10,560 feet). Use this trailhead to ski the classic North "Grizzly" Couloir. This trailhead is typically inaccessible until after Memorial Day because Independence pass (Colorado Highway 82) may not be open until then. You can use a snowmobile before the road opens to access this trailhead. If coming from the east, follow Colorado Highway 82 for 9.7 miles west from the top of Independence Pass. If approaching from the west, travel about 10 miles east from Aspen on Colorado Highway 82. Turn south on Lincoln Creek Road (FS 106). Travel 6.5 miles up Lincoln Creek Road to the marked trailhead on the left. You will pass the Lincoln Gulch Campground before the first mile on Lincoln Creek Road. You will also pass Grizzly Reservoir and Dam.

Ascending the east ridge above McNasser Gulch.

THE CLIMB

**East Ridge (Class 2+)**. Follow FR 391 from Lake Creek Trailhead in winter, and arrive at McNasser Gulch Trailhead after 3.3 miles. Next, follow FR 391 to the northwest for 1.2 miles to a locked gate. If you were able to drive up the road, which is generally possible in late May or early June, you can climb and ski from the locked gate. Prior to Mid-May, it is possible to skin up the road all the way from CO Hwy 82. Continue another 1.4 miles to the west, taking a sharp right for 0.2 mile to where the road ends at 12,000 feet at an inactive mine. From here you can skin to the west about 0.5 mile to 12,500 feet, above timberline and into a basin. The east face of Grizzly has greeted you by now, and the introduction is over. From some flat rocks in the basin at 12,500 feet, take a sharp right and zigzag for 0.25 mile up a small southeast-facing bowl. Your goal is a small saddle on the east ridge at 13,300 feet. From the saddle the jagged portions of the often-corniced ridge can be avoided by traversing on the south side of the ridge for 0.5 mile to reach the shoulder of Grizzly's minor 13,940-foot northern summit. Crampons are useful for gaining this small sub-summit, from which you can peer down to check the condition of the north-side Grizzly Couloir. From the northern ridge summit, follow the western edge of the north ridge to the summit for 0.25 mile, making sure to stay on the western windward side of the cornices that can form, especially on the summit block.

DESCENTS

1. _**East Ridge/Southeast Bowl**_ ■ / ◆ Leave the summit, retracing your route via the north ridge, returning to the 13,940-foot north ridge sub-summit. From this point, where you can again look into the Grizzly Couloir, ski east

down the often-windblown east ridge. For the first 300 feet veer skier's left toward the ridge crest, where it's possible to choose a careful line skier's right into the southeast-facing bowl. About 1,000 feet of excellent skiing will take you into McNasser Basin and the valley to the east of Grizzly's east face. Continue into McNasser Gulch and eventually back to the forest access roads in the direction of the Lake Creek Trailhead.

2. *North "Grizzly" Couloir* ◆ This ultra-classic north facing ski line is an excellent April to mid-May choice, and even skis well into late June most years. The couloir opens right into Grizzly Lake at 12,500 feet near the bottom, stays pretty wide throughout and is about 35 to 40 degrees. From the summit, the couloir is slightly broad, and be aware that snow on skier's left (west) be wind-blown and avalanche prone, especially any time before April. Nearly 0.5 mile of solid turns and 1,500 feet of vertical will take you to the base of the chute to finish near the glacial Grizzly Lake. Continue down the basin to the north and west ski back to the Grizzly Reservoir Trailhead for almost 3 miles.

ALTERNATIVES

East Couloirs ◆ / ◆ ◆ Two spectacular couloirs await more experienced skiers off of Grizzly's east side. In good snow years, it's possible to ski directly off of the summit to access both. Standing on the summit and facing east, one of the couloirs is skier's right (to the south) and the other is skier's left (to the north). The couloir to the south is slightly narrower than the other. Both start out very steep, up to 55-degrees. Use caution when entering either couloir as westerly winds create large cor-

The steep and narrow east couloirs on Grizzly.

niced wind slabs that might become safe enough to navigate only after mid- to late May. Choose your couloir wisely and enjoy nearly 2,000 feet of skiing into the McNasser Basin to the east of the peak.

West Gullies ◆ Leave the summit to the west to explore nearly 3,000 feet of skiing via either of the west gullies on the west face of Grizzly. These chutes take you down to Lincoln Creek and the Lincoln Creek Road and back to the Grizzly Reservoir Trailhead.

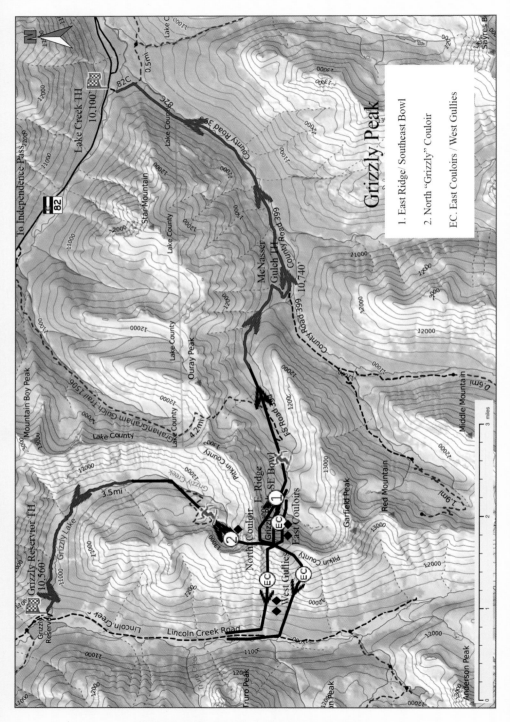

Grizzly Peak

1. East Ridge / Southeast Bowl

2. North "Grizzly" Couloir

EC. East Couloirs / West Gullies

GRIZZLY PEAK: NORTH AND EAST APPROACHES

28. Ice Mountain
13,951 feet/4252 meters
(The Three Apostles)

SKIABLE VERTICAL:	Up to 3,691 feet/1125 meters
ROUND-TRIP DISTANCE:	From South Winfield Trailhead, 10.2 miles/16.5 kilometers; from Huron Gate Trailhead, 6.2 miles/10 kilometers
TRAILHEADS:	South Winfield (10,260 feet); Huron Gate (10,600 feet)
DIFFICULTY RATINGS:	■ / ◆ / ◆ ◆
SKI TERRAIN:	Four-wheel-drive access road, narrow trail, tree glades, steep faces, and couloirs
OPTIMAL SEASON:	March through June. April and May are ideal.
MAPS:	Trails Illustrated Numbers 129 and 148, Winfield, San Isabel National Forest

COMMENT: The Three Apostles (Ice Mountain, North Apostle, and West Apostle) are arguably the Sawatch Range's most jagged peaks. Most people view them from the summit of Huron, which is only a few miles to the north. If these

The Three Apostles from the north in January. Snow coverage generally fills in better by March or April most years.

Skinning towards the 'Western Bowl' including North Apostle and Ice Mountain. Photo by Andrew Warkentin

Ascending the Refrigerator. Photo by Andrew Warkentin

gorgeous peaks arouse your curiosity, seek out the famous Refrigerator Couloir. Climbing the couloir is an adventure in itself, and skiing the couloir is the kind of epic descent that backcountry skiers dream of. Combine Ice Mountain with a climb and ski of North Apostle, and you will be on your way to one of the finest ski missions in Colorado!

GETTING THERE

South Winfield Trailhead (10,260 feet). This trailhead is open by about May 1 most seasons. Take US Highway 24 south from Leadville for 19.5 miles, or north from Buena Vista for 14.5 miles to access the area via Chaffee County 390. Turn west onto Chaffee County 390, which is a dirt road, and measure from this point. Travel 11.8 miles to Winfield, which is a clearly marked abandoned town site. The road is closed until late April, but in winter is usually driveable for 4 to 5 miles. From there, a snowmobile or an ambitious slog on skis can take you the rest of the way. Pass west through Winfield and turn left (south), crossing to Clear Creek's south side. Take an immediate right (west) onto South Fork Clear Creek Road (FS 390.2B). Travel 0.25 mile west on FS 390.2B to the trailhead. There are plenty of parking and camping spaces here.

Huron Gate Trailhead (10,600 feet). Follow the directions for South Winfield Trailhead to South Fork Clear Creek Road (FS 390.2B). Sometimes by mid-May you can continue to drive past the South Winfield Trailhead traveling west then southwest for 2.0 miles to reach a small parking area near a Collegiate Peaks Wilderness gate. This gate is the start of two trails: the trail to Huron Peak (left), and Lake Ann (right). The Lake Ann Trail leads to the Three Apostles, including Ice Mountain.

Plenty of Powder in the Refrigerator.
Photo by Andrew Warkentin

The sun sets over the Refrigerator.

THE CLIMB

The Refrigerator (Class 3). Follow the Lake Ann Trail (right and straight ahead from the gate) south for 0.5 mile to the Collegiate Peaks Wilderness boundary. From the boundary follow the trail another 0.75 mile through a mix of open meadows and timber to the old Hamilton town site at 10,820 feet. Here you will find a trail junction; stay left (straight) at the junction and follow the Lake Ann Trail, which at this point is also the Continental Divide Trail and the Colorado Trail. The Lake Ann Trail leaves Hamilton and quickly crosses the South Fork of Clear Creek, offering amazing views of the Three Apostles. After the creek crossing, take a sharp left (south-southeast) on the Three Apostles Trail. Once on this new trail, cross a side creek that flows from the Lake Ann Basin, and travel for 1 mile through woods toward a spectacular flat basin at the base of the Three Apostles at 11,400 feet. Some trail signs may be visible even in deep snow in the spring.

From 11,400 feet the trail soon disappears near some large boulders. The basin you need to climb into between North Apostle and Ice Mountain is obvious. Climb or skin just over 0.5 mile up to a tiny lake or frozen tarn at 12,100 feet in the basin between North Apostle's west face and Ice Mountain's north face. From here use your best judgment to navigate the slope toward the 13,460-foot saddle between North Apostle and Ice Mountain. Half way up this basin, at about 13,000 feet, you will come to a relatively flat area before the basin's angle increases. Look slightly to the right (almost southwest) and the entrance to the Refrigerator Couloir is apparent, beckoning to the big climb ahead. The beginning of the couloir is steep, but for less than 1,000 feet. Climb south up the couloir to 13,500 feet. Here the couloir becomes steeper and narrower, and it splits into two branches. By this point you will understand the snow conditions.

The Three Apostles along the Lake Ann Trail.

Be sure to take the right (west) branch of the couloir, not the left (east) branch. The correct branch becomes very narrow, is steep (up to almost 55 degrees), but then gets wider and easier near the crest of the couloir and the ridge at 13,900 feet. Due to lack of sun on this aspect, a cold morning climb might make you feel like you are in more of a freezer than a refrigerator! Follow the ridge east for 100 feet or so to the small summit.

DESCENTS

1. *The Refrigerator* ◆ / ◆◆ Leave the summit and ski across the ridge for 100 feet to the west, retracing your path back to the top of the Refrigerator Couloir, one of the finest lines in Colorado. Drop in and enjoy nearly 1000 feet of steep turns. Remember, the steepest and narrowest portions are about 400 feet below the top; use caution, as this section can be thinner than the rest of the couloir. Toward the bottom you can open it up and ski to the left (north) into the basin between North Apostle and Ice Mountain, finishing near the small tarn that you climbed past hours earlier. Continue into the basin toward the Lake Ann Trail and eventually back to the forest access roads in the direction of the South Winfield Trailhead.

ALTERNATIVES

North Apostle, Southwest Ridge, and Western Bowl ■ / ◆ If you don't have ice in your veins, from 13,000 feet in the basin take a slight left turn (east, then northeast) and climb to the 13,460-foot saddle between North Apostle and Ice Mountain. From the saddle, turn left and follow the southwest ridge of North Apostle to the 13,860-foot summit. The ridge and moderately steep face of the southwest ridge and the spectacular western bowl that you climbed to get to the top of the peak are excellent options for skiing nearly 2,000 feet into the basin to the tarn at 12,100 feet.

In addition to the above-described routes, there are perhaps half a dozen options here that have never been skied on North Apostle and Ice Mountain, as well as West Apostle (13,568 feet). Explore, enjoy and be safe out there!

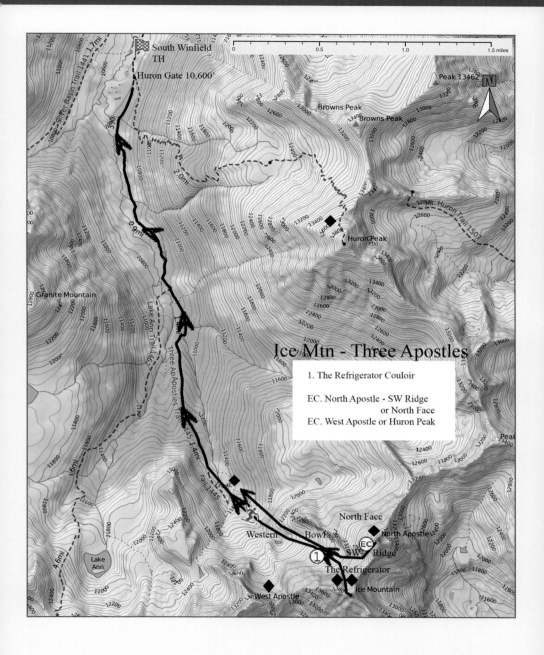

Ice Mtn - Three Apostles

1. The Refrigerator Couloir

EC. North Apostle - SW Ridge
           or North Face
EC. West Apostle or Huron Peak

ICE MOUNTAIN (THE THREE APOSTLES)

29. Missouri Mountain
14,067 feet/4288 meters

SKIABLE VERTICAL:	Up to 4500 feet/1372 meters
ROUND-TRIP DISTANCE:	10 miles/16.1 kilometers
TRAILHEAD:	Missouri Gulch (9640 feet)
DIFFICULTY RATINGS:	■ / ◆
SKI TERRAIN:	Narrow trail, tree glades, steep faces, and couloirs
OPTIMAL SEASON:	March through June. April and May are ideal.
MAPS:	Trails Illustrated Numbers 129 and 148, Winfield, Mt. Harvard, San Isabel National Forest

COMMENT: Missouri Mountain boasts some of the best moderately steep skiing in all of the Sawatch Range. Usually by late March the Missouri Gulch Trailhead melts out, making spring skiing access easy.

GETTING THERE
Missouri Gulch Trailhead (9,640 feet). This trailhead is open by about April 1 most years. Take US Highway 24 south from Leadville for 19.5 miles or north

The snow is loaded along the northwest ridge of Missouri. There are several ski lines to the left and into the upper Missouri Gulch.

from Buena Vista for 14.5 miles to access the area via Chaffee County 390. Turn west onto Chaffee County 390, which is a dirt road, and from this point travel 7.7 miles to Vicksburg. The trailhead is well marked on the left (south) side of the road.

THE CLIMB

The North Couloir (Class 3).

This is actually more of a northeast facing couloir. Follow the Missouri Gulch Trail for 2 miles to timberline at 11,400 feet. You will pass the ruins of a small cabin that might be buried in snow just before breaking out of the trees into the basin. From here follow the basin south for another 1.5 miles to the base of Mt. Missouri at 12,400 feet. The introduction is over. You will see the obvious North Couloir leading up the basin to your west.

Skiing the west face of Belford with just enough coverage. Missouri Mountain's North Couloir at center.

Ascend moderate slopes that get steeper as you enter the couloir. Halfway up, at about 13,300 feet, follow the main branch as it broadens (right and to the west), or a narrower and thinner eastern (left branch). The west branch is more likely climbable and skiable. This couloir emerges just 100 feet to the north of the true summit. If the couloir doesn't look optimal, you can always follow the standard summer route, which heads north from the valley to gain the north ridge and then travels south along the ridge to eventually reach Mt. Missouri's summit.

DESCENTS

1. *The North Couloir* ◆ / ◆◆ Leave the summit and retrace your steps on skis along the ridge for 100 feet to the north. This will allow you to get back to the top of the most prominent North Couloir. Drop in and enjoy nearly

A nice view of the North Couloir from the saddle at the northwest ridge.

Turns in prime conditions part way down the North Couloir on Missouri.

1000 feet of steep turns. Halfway down the couloir narrows, but never exceeds 40 degrees in steepness. The North Couloir usually holds excellent snow until mid-June in good snow years. Toward the bottom you can open it up and ski to the right (east) down into the basin between Mt. Missouri and Mt. Belford. Continue into the basin toward timberline on easy slopes and eventually back in the direction of the Missouri Gulch Trailhead.

2. *West Bowl* ■ / ◆ This line directly off the summit skis very well in May when the snow is deep and stable. Once down from the top, steeper portions and into the bowl, ski a couple thousand feet to Clohesy Lake at 10,850 feet.

3. *Southeast Face* ■ / ◆ This is an alternative line directly off the summit that tackles the face leading into Pine Creek Basin to the south of Elkhead Pass. The steepness of the line when covered in snow is in the excellent 40-degree range. The downside to this line is that you have to climb back over 13,200-foot Elkhead Pass to ski back to Missouri Gulch Trailhead. But this makes for an excellent ski tour.

ALTERNATIVES

Mt. Belford ■ To the east of Mt. Missouri is the 14er Mt. Belford. You can climb the gentle slopes of Mt. Belford to its summit and either continue to Mt. Oxford to ski another 14er, or choose relatively gentle ski lines off the west face of Mt. Belford. Steeper lines exist off the north aspect of Mt. Belford back toward Missouri Gulch Trailhead.

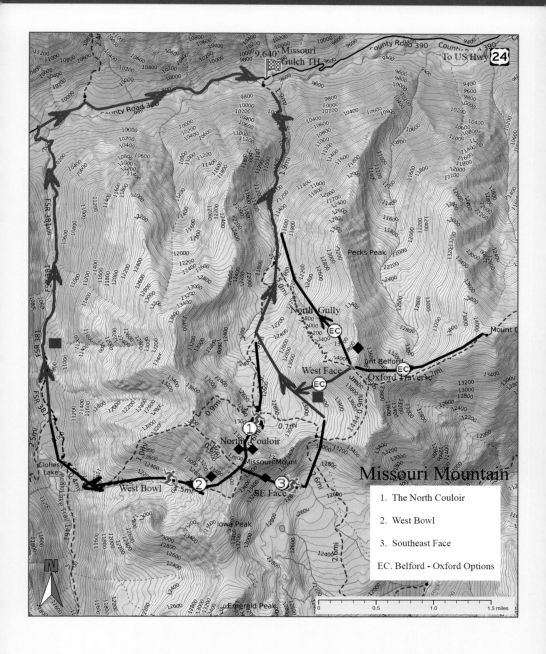

MISSOURI MOUNTAIN

30. Mt. Hope
13,933 feet/4247 meters

SKIABLE VERTICAL:	Up to 4653 feet/1418 meters
ROUND-TRIP DISTANCE:	12 miles/19.35 kilometers
TRAILHEADS:	Willis Gulch (9280 feet)
DIFFICULTY RATINGS:	■ / ◆
SKI TERRAIN:	Narrow trail, tree glades, moderate faces, and couloirs
OPTIMAL SEASON:	March through June. April and May are ideal.
MAPS:	Trails Illustrated Numbers 127 and 148, Mt. Elbert, Winfield, San Isabel National Forest

COMMENT: Mt. Hope is a high Centennial 13er situated between giants Mt. Elbert and La Plata Peak in the Sawatch Range. It's just north of the Belford group. The peak is commonly mistaken for a 14er when seen from surrounding valleys, which makes this peak a great ski tour option because you likely will not see another soul. The Willis Gulch Trailhead is located right off Colorado Highway 82, making spring skiing access easy.

Upper Little Willis Gulch is a special place with the Hopeful Couloir.

GETTING THERE

Willis Gulch Trailhead (9,280 feet). This trailhead is accessible year-round. From the east (Leadville or Buena Vista), travel 8.5 miles west on Colorado Highway 82 from its junction with US Highway 24. You will pass through the small town of Twin Lakes. If coming from the west and the top of Independence Pass (which opens in mid-May) travel 15.3 miles east from the pass to a dirt road. Turn south on the dirt road and travel a little more than 100 yards southwest to reach parking at the trailhead. There is a footbridge here that leads across Lake Creek. Park along Colorado Highway 82 if the road access is not plowed in the winter.

THE CLIMB

The Hopeful Couloir (Class 2, Moderate Snow). This is actually more of a northeast facing couloir. Start by crossing the Lake Creek on a good bridge. Travel 1.2 miles east along the south side of Lake Creek. Turn right (south) and follow the Hope Pass Trail (Also the Colorado Trail and the Continental Divide Trail) for 1.3 miles to a trail junction at 10,300 feet. Continue south to the left (straight fork) for 2 more miles into Little Willis Basin to reach a frozen lake at 11,780 feet. In winter this route will be snow covered and you can skin into the basin. From the vicinity of the lake looking to your south the Hopeful Couloir is obvious. Ascend the basin to 12,600 feet, to the west of Hope Pass. If spring conditions are stable, climb the couloir for 1200 feet to reach the summit ridge just a couple hundred yards east of the true summit. Near the top of the couloir at 13,700 feet, stay to the left (south) to avoid any cornices. Enjoy this snow climb; it never exceeds about 35 degrees near the top.

Ryan Belanger ascends the Hopeful Couloir, Twin Lakes in the Distance.

Ashley Belanger carving nice snow in the lower Hopeful.

Ryan Belanger skiing one of Colorado's more underrated couloirs.

The fun always feels like it comes to an end way too soon when the snow is good!

DESCENTS

1. ***The Hopeful Couloir*** ◆ Leave the summit and retrace your steps on skis along the ridge for 150 yards to the east to get back to the top of the Hopeful Couloir. Drop in and enjoy nearly 1200 feet of excellent turns. Half way down the couloir opens up and never exceeds 35 degrees in steepness. The Hopeful Couloir usually holds excellent snow until mid-June or even July in good snow years, and might make for a great way to ring in Independence Day due to its north aspect. Toward the bottom you can open it up and ski to the left (north) down into the basin of Little Willis Gulch. Follow the trail corridor on easy slopes back across Lake Creek to the Willis Gulch Trailhead.

2. ***Northeast Bowl*** ◆ A line directly off the summit skis very well in May when the snow is deep and stable. Ski north and then east into the bowl from the summit. Once below the top 400 feet, use caution to avoid cliff bands on the eastern portion of the face by staying skiers left along the banks of the northeast ridge.

3. ***East Face*** ■ This is an alternative line directly off the summit that skis the much gentler face leading to Hope Pass. When avalanche conditions are not as stable, you can enjoy the broad ridge. To ski back to Willis Gulch Trailhead, ski north from Hope Pass into Little Willis Basin, which makes an excellent ski tour.

ALTERNATIVES

West/Northwest/North ◆◆ The west and north aspects of Hope are guarded by very steep terrain. There are two or three hidden lines in some narrow couloirs that ski toward Willis Lake and also to the north into Willis Gulch. These are rarely skied, but worth exploring.

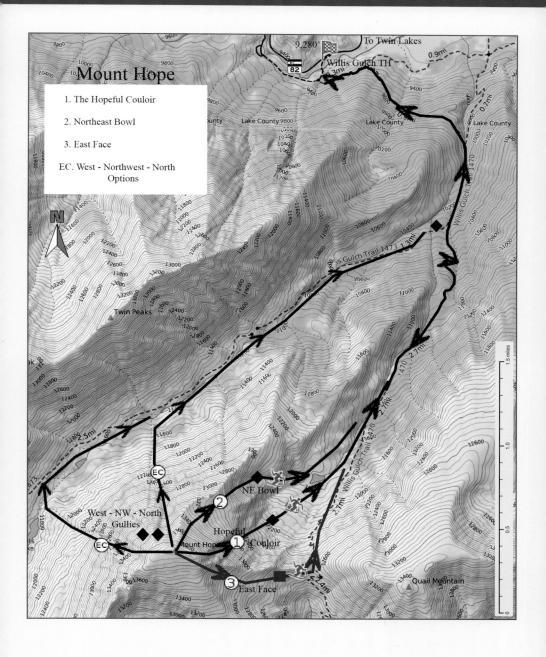

Mount Hope

1. The Hopeful Couloir

2. Northeast Bowl

3. East Face

EC. West - Northwest - North
    Options

MT. HOPE

31. Mt. Harvard
14,420 feet/4395 meters

SKIABLE VERTICAL:	Up to 4550 feet/1385 meters
ROUND-TRIP DISTANCE:	From North Cottonwood Trailhead: 12.5 miles/20.2 kilometers
TRAILHEADS:	North Cottonwood (9,880 feet)
DIFFICULTY RATINGS:	■ / ◆ / ◆ ◆
SKI TERRAIN:	Narrow trail, tree glades, moderate faces, and couloirs
OPTIMAL SEASON:	March through June. April and May are ideal.
MAPS:	Trails Illustrated Numbers 129 and 148, Mt. Harvard, Mt. Yale, San Isabel National Forest

COMMENT: Colorado's third highest peak, Mt. Harvard boasts long ski runs down its south aspect. The approach to this peak is a good distance, but excellent powder, rolling terrain, and winter solitude reward the effort.

GETTING THERE
North Cottonwood (9,880 feet). From the Chaffee County 306/US Highway 24 junction in the center of Buena Vista (at the stoplight), travel 0.4 mile on US

Ascending the south slopes of Harvard near Bear lake gives you a nice view of 14,073' Mount Columbia which isn't in ski condition just yet (December photo).

Pointing at the "South K" Couloir after skiing the narrow chute off the summit of Harvard.

Photo by Torrey Udall

Several options off the South Face including the direct line (left) and the "South K" Couloir (center) is the narrow slot seen at middle of the face.

Highway 24. Turn west on Chaffee County 350 (Crossman Avenue) and measure your distance. Travel west on Chaffee County 350 for 2.1 miles and upon reaching a T-junction, turn north (right) onto Chaffee County 361. Chaffee County 361 turns to dirt at mile 2.5 and angles to the northwest. At mile 3.0, turn left (south) onto Chaffee County 365, which quickly turns to the west, entering the San Isabel National Forest at 5.5 miles. Through the forest you will pass the Harvard Lakes Trailhead (mile 6.6) and the Colorado Trail. Continue on the road as it narrows and climbs to the North Cottonwood Trail and a circular turn-around area with parking at mile 8.2.

THE CLIMB

The South Slopes (Class 2). The first several miles of this climb is a long slog through the trees. The trek begins by skinning or hiking up the North Cottonwood Trail and crossing to the south side of North Cottonwood Creek on a bridge. Follow the trail corridor for 1.5 miles and then cross the creek again to the north side and reach a trail junction. Take the right (north fork), which leads to Horn Fork Basin and Bear Lake in the direction of Mt. Harvard. After another 2 miles enter the basin and break out of the trees and into the meadows above timberline. From here you can look north and see Harvard's south face. Skinning up this basin is quite easy. Once in the upper basin, continue past Bear Lake (which will be to your west) and climb to a relatively flat basin below Harvard's south face. Choose your line wisely; climb the south face directly to the summit, or do a variation of the south ridge, which is slightly to climbers left. See you on the summit!

The southwest aspect of Columbia can provide a nice little side trip if you've got extra energy on the way to Harvard.

DESCENTS

1. *The "South K" Couloir* ◆ / ◆◆ Leave the summit and ski east along the ridge for about 200 yards. As you ski the ridge, look to your right (south) and choose the best line. Near some prominent rock piles or angular blocks on the ridge you can begin your descent off the ridge into the top of the broad couloir known as the South K Couloir. Drop in and enjoy nearly 1500 feet of moderately steep turns. A third of the way down the couloir narrows, but never exceeds 35 to 40 degrees in steepness. The bottom third of the couloir broadens and offers many outstanding lines. This couloir usually holds excellent snow until mid-June in good snow years. Toward the bottom you can open it up and ski to the left (east) down into the basin. Continue into the basin toward timberline on easy slopes and eventually back in the direction of the North Cottonwood Trailhead.

2. *South face* ■ / ◆ A line directly off the summit block skis very well in May when the snow is deep and stable. From the summit, retrace your climbing line up the final 100 foot summit block. Once off the block, ski the relatively easy slopes of the south face and chose a fun line into the bowl below Harvard's south face.

ALTERNATIVES

Harvard and Columbia Ski Tour ■ / ◆ On a warm spring day or stable winter day with an early start, ski Harvard's east ridge, descend into upper Frenchman Creek Basin, and climb Columbia's north face. From Columbia's summit, choose your own adventure from possible lines on the peak's west and southwest aspects (depending on coverage and conditions) to get back into North Cottonwood Basin and the trailhead.

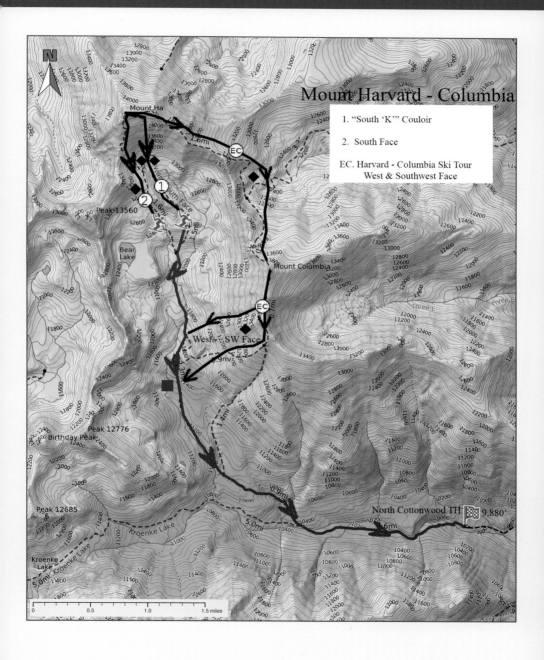

Mount Harvard - Columbia

1. "South 'K'" Couloir

2. South Face

EC. Harvard - Columbia Ski Tour
West & Southwest Face

MT. HARVARD

32. Mt. Antero: North and West Approach
14,269 feet /4350 meters

SKIABLE VERTICAL:	4,849 feet/1478 meters
ROUND-TRIP DISTANCE:	16 miles/26 kilometers
TRAILHEAD:	Baldwin Gulch, 9,420 feet/2871 meters
DIFFICULTY RATINGS:	● / ■ / ◆ / ◆◆
SKI TERRAIN:	Four-wheel-drive road ●, tree glades, ridgelines, steep faces, and couloirs
OPTIMAL SEASON:	March through May
MAPS:	Trails Illustrated Number 130, St. Elmo, Mt. Antero, San Isabel National Forest

COMMENT: Mt. Antero, one of Colorado's famed 14ers, is a spectacular peak to climb and ski in the southern part of the Sawatch Range. A long, gradually climbing four-wheel drive road allows you to skin up to almost 14,000 feet and access to multiple ski options. The road serves as an excellent high altitude catwalk and offers manageable terrain for beginner backcountry skiers. Wind often scours the peak's ridges and some of the upper slopes bare, so it may be best to climb Antero after a storm cycle in March or April when the snow actually sticks. South slopes of the peak get strong sunlight in May, making the road sometimes the only reasonable higher up option for skiing. Note that the lower parts of the west-face chutes can be prone to avalanches in mid-winter, but stabilize during the warmer transition to late spring. One thing is certain on Antero; you can ski nearly a vertical mile from the summit down to the Baldwin Gulch Trailhead, covering up to 8 miles or more in the right conditions, so enjoy the journey!

A warm spring day climbing Antero with Centennial 13er Cronin behind.

Standing on the summit pondering the options. Photo by Tara Nichols

GETTING THERE
Baldwin Gulch. The trailhead is at 9,420 feet and allows easy access to Baldwin Creek and the west and south sides of Antero, including Antero's standard route. When travelling from Denver or Buena Vista from the north, drive 5.5 miles south from the US Highway 24/US Highway 285 junction just west of Johnson's Village near Buena Vista to Chaffee County Hwy 162. This junction is 15.5 miles north of the Poncha Springs junction of US Highway 285 and US 50. Follow Chaffee County 162 west for 11.6 miles past Princeton Hot Springs and Cascade Campground to Baldwin Creek Road, located on the south side of Chaffee 162. You must park on the north side of the road just east of where you can start skinning up the Baldwin Creek Road. This road is also popular with snowmobilers.

APPROACH
Baldwin Gulch. Skinning 3 miles southeast then south up the Baldwin Creek Road will bring you to a very well marked trail junction and creek crossing at 10,840 feet. Take a left and continue south after crossing the creek to access the upper Baldwin Gulch and climbing routes to Antero.

THE CLIMB
West Slopes/Baldwin Gulch (Class 2). The best and safest way to summit Antero in winter conditions is to follow the four-wheel-drive road up the west slopes of the peak. At about 13,000 feet the switch-backing road flattens out on a vast high tundra shoulder to the southwest of Antero's summit. Continue east and wrap around to the south side of the peak, climb a few more switchbacks while heading north, and reach the end of the road at about 13,750 feet. Here is an excellent view of Antero's south ridge and south/southeast face leading to the summit. Follow the rocky and jagged lower portions of the ridge for less than 1 mile to

Skiing one of the West Gullies.
Photo by Anne Marie Migl

A view up the deepest gully looking east to the summit in excellent snow coverage.

the top. The final 0.25 mile is relatively steep but can be an excellent snow climb up the summit pyramid.

DESCENTS

1. *South Ridge to the Service Road* ■ / ◆ Approximately 400 vertical feet will take you south directly from the summit to the rocky portions of the south ridge. If you prefer to backtrack and take the four-wheel-drive road back down the mountain, you may be able to ski near the ridge crest to the east of the small rock towers on the ridge and not have to remove your skis to navigate back to the end of the road. Follow the road down as it crosses and traverses the south and west sides of Antero. At timberline, a glade takes you to the creek crossing at 10,840 feet and then down the gentle Baldwin Creek Road to your vehicle.

2. *West Face and West Gullies* ◆ Three deep gullies begin as broad couloirs and lead west from different sections of the south ridge, beginning from the summit of Antero. These faces/gullies may be up to 45 degrees, depending on how close you are to the ridgeline.

ALTERNATIVES

Northeast Bowl ◆◆ From the summit, the steep northeast bowl of Antero provides a lot of potential. You can ski directly into the bowl from the highest point, or traverse a bit to the north down Antero's north ridge to less steep east-facing terrain. Alternatively, traverse Antero's east ridge and drop into the bowl to the north utilizing a few small couloirs. The bowl empties to the north into complex terrain, so use caution, or skin/climb out of the bowl back toward the north ridge on moderate slopes and then ski Antero's west face to get back to Baldwin Gulch.

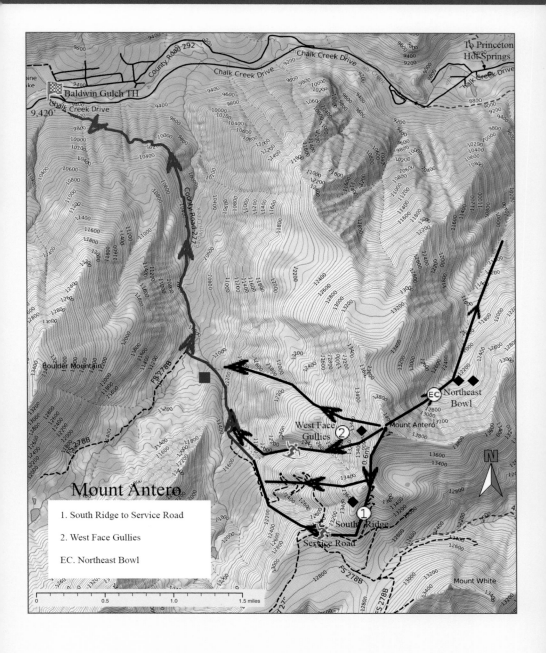

Mount Antero

1. South Ridge to Service Road

2. West Face Gullies

EC. Northeast Bowl

MT. ANTERO: NORTH AND WEST APPROACHES

33. Mt. Antero: South and East Approach
14,269 feet /4350 meters

SKIABLE VERTICAL:	5,300 feet/1615 meters
ROUND-TRIP DISTANCE:	18 miles/29 kilometers
TRAILHEAD:	Browns Creek, 8970 feet/2735 meters
DIFFICULTY RATINGS:	■ / ◆ / ◆ ◆
SKI TERRAIN:	Tree glades, ridgelines, steep faces, and couloirs
OPTIMAL SEASON:	March through May
MAPS:	Trails Illustrated Number 130, St. Elmo, Mt. Antero, San Isabel National Forest

COMMENT: Antero's more rugged and isolated route! Mt. Antero's south and east approach is an off-the-beaten-path way to test your skills on this famous 14er. Wind often scours the peak's ridges and some of the upper slopes bare, so it is best to climb Antero after good snow deposits from a March or April storm cycle. Mid-winter descents in January or February can be difficult, but are not unheard of. The south slopes get strong sunlight in May, and the routes from Browns Creek can be rewarding with a little extra effort. One thing is certain on Antero; you can ski over a vertical mile from the summit down to the Baldwin Gulch Trailhead, covering 9 miles or more in the right winter or spring conditions.

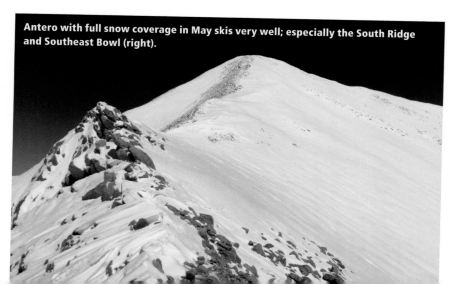

Antero with full snow coverage in May skis very well; especially the South Ridge and Southeast Bowl (right).

Moderate and low angle bowls are usually safe to ski in April and May.

GETTING THERE

Browns Creek. The trailhead is at 8970 feet, has a toilet building, and is a nice alternative to the much more frequented Baldwin Gulch. From US Highway 285, midway between Poncha Springs and Buena Vista, take County Road 270 west for approximately 1.5 miles to a four-way intersection. From the yield sign, continue traveling west. The road continues as Forest Road 272. Stay on FR 272 for about 2 miles. A sign at the cattle guard indicates the entrance to national forest lands. Continue traveling west on FR 272 from the boundary sign for 2 miles. At the intersection, turn left and travel south for 1.5 miles to the trailhead, which is right along the banks of Little Browns Creek.

APPROACH

Browns Creek. This uncrowded and scenic alternative is a true gem. Skin up west for 4.5 to 5 miles into the valley that divides the double 13er to the south of Antero, Mt. White, from the 14er Shavano/Tabeguache massif further south. After passing Browns Lake at mile 4, will wrap around to the southwest side of Mt. White until you reach timberline, then turn to the north and skin up gentle slopes into a broad and relatively gentle landscape. You will eventually reach the four-wheel-drive road to the south of Antero, meeting the Baldwin Gulch Route above 13,000 feet.

THE CLIMB

Browns Creek (Class 2). Coming from upper Browns Creek at about 11,400 feet near timberline, skin north up moderately steep slopes to gain flatter terrain and reach the Baldwin Gulch four-wheel-drive road around 13,000 feet. From here you will see Antero and can travel east then north along the four-wheel-drive road to climb to the summit via the south ridge, as described for the North and West Antero approach.

The South Ridge and Southeast bowl can lack coverage near the summit during dry and windy periods.

DESCENTS

1. ***South Ridge to Southeast Bowl*** ■ / ◆ Once on the summit pyramid, find a small flat saddle along the south ridge before the rocky portions of the ridge begin. From this saddle the sweeping southeast bowl lies in front of you to the south. Drop into the bowl to your left and enjoy several hundred feet of additional turns before skiing across a small lake in the bottom, which is usually hidden by snow cover. This line never exceeds about 35 degrees. To return to the four-wheel-drive road traverse around to the right (south then southwest) of the prominent summit that protrudes from the south ridge of Antero. Join the four-wheel-drive road and continue west then north around Antero and back into Baldwin Gulch.

2. ***South Slopes to Browns Creek*** ■ / ◆ Follow option 1, but instead of rejoining the four-wheel-drive road to head toward Baldwin Gulch, continue south and ski a delightful broad valley to the west of Mt. White, eventually dropping into the Browns Creek Basin, and then ski east back through the forest, past Browns Lake and back to the Browns Creek Trailhead. You can also ski east staying to the north of Mt. White, descend into Little Browns Creek, and eventually make your way back to the Browns Creek Trailhead.

ALTERNATIVES

Southeast Face from the end of the east ridge ◆ / ◆◆ Carefully follow the east ridge of Antero to a prominent point at 13,900 feet and take a look at the relatively narrow southeast facing slope that drops directly into Little Browns Creek. Ski the slope with the best looking snow and exit into the basin below. Ski east into the Little Browns Creek drainage, eventually finding your way back to the Browns Creek Trailhead.

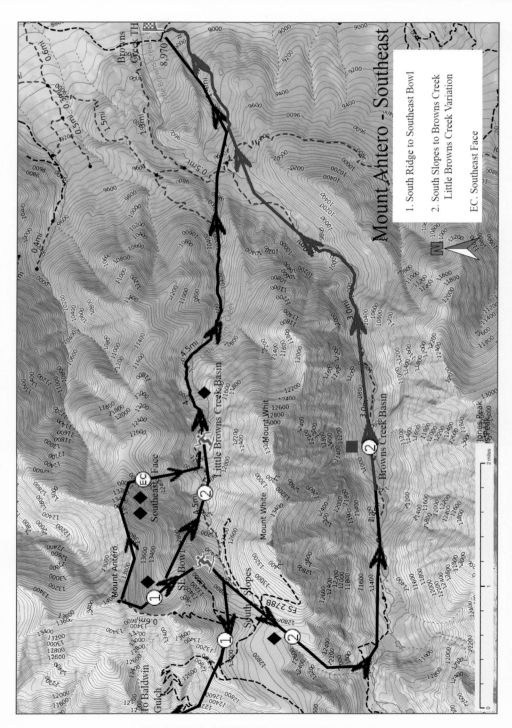

Mount Antero – Southeast

1. South Ridge to Southeast Bowl

2. South Slopes to Browns Creek
   Little Browns Creek Variation

EC. Southeast Face

MT. ANTERO: SOUTH AND EAST APPROACHES

34. Mt. Shavano
14,229 feet/4337 meters

SKIABLE VERTICAL:	Up to 4430 feet/1350 meters
ROUND-TRIP DISTANCE:	8 mi/13 kilometers
TRAILHEADS:	Blank Gulch Trailhead (9,800 feet)
DIFFICULTY RATINGS:	■ / ◆
SKI TERRAIN:	Ridgelines, couloirs, tree glades, and moderate slopes
OPTIMAL SEASON:	February through June. April and May are ideal.
MAPS:	Trails Illustrated Number 130, Maysville, St. Elmo, Mt. Antero, San Isabel National Forest

COMMENT: The legendary Angel of Shavano is visible from the lower Arkansas Valley near Salida. This southernmost Sawatch 14er bears a religious significance that dates back over a century. Climbing and skiing the Angel is fun, relatively straightforward, and not terribly steep. This is a great peak to take a group to enjoy spring skiing in Colorado for awesome views and excellent spring corn.

GETTING THERE
Blank Gulch Trailhead (9,800 feet). From Buena Vista, travel south on US Highway 285 from the US Highway 24 junction near Johnson's Village for 20 miles. Do not go all the way to Poncha Springs. One mile north of the US Highway 285/US Highway 50 junction in Poncha Springs, turn west onto Chaffee County 140. From the start of Chaffee County 140, travel west for 1.7 miles. Turn right (north) onto Chaffee County 250 (initially paved) and follow the road as it turns to dirt. Turn left at 5.7 miles onto Chaffee County 252. Cross Placer Creek at 6.5 miles, head through meadows and forests, and arrive at the Blank Gulch Trailhead at 9.0 miles.

THE CLIMB
Angel of Shavano (Class 2). Start from the Blank Gulch Trailhead and hike or skin for 0.25 mile to the north on the Colorado Trail. You will leave aspen forests and gorgeous meadows to take a left (west) and head up the clearly marked Mt. Shavano Trail. After 1.5 miles, the trail will switchback sharply at 11,100 feet and turn away from the drainage; before this switchback, leave the trail and continue

Ascending the basin and approaching the Angel, visible near treeline.

west toward timberline in the basin. Once you break out of the trees, you will see the Angel of Shavano above and to the west in the basin. Climb the Angel for 1,500 feet to a 13,400-foot saddle to the south of the summit. Then follow Shavano's south ridge for 800 more vertical feet to the summit.

DESCENTS

1. ***The Angel of Shavano.*** ■ / ◆ Leave the summit to the south. Ski the broad south and southeast slopes of Shavano to reach the top of the Angel. The Angel's northernmost arm likely will provide a connection from the summit snowfields to the body of the Angel itself. Descend the main body of the Angel, which never exceeds 35 degrees. Views of the Arkansas Valley and the Sangre De Cristo Range to the south provide spectacular backdrops.

ALTERNATIVES

Tabeguache Peak 14,155 feet: ■ / ◆ In a good snow year, the connecting ridge leading north to Tabeguache will allow you to traverse and ski both peaks. Tabeguache's southeast face and east ridge offer nice turns. There are also several north-facing lines and gullies heading down into Browns Creek from the top of Tabeguache. Ski to the Browns Creek Trailhead (see Mt. Antero north and east approach for trailhead access).

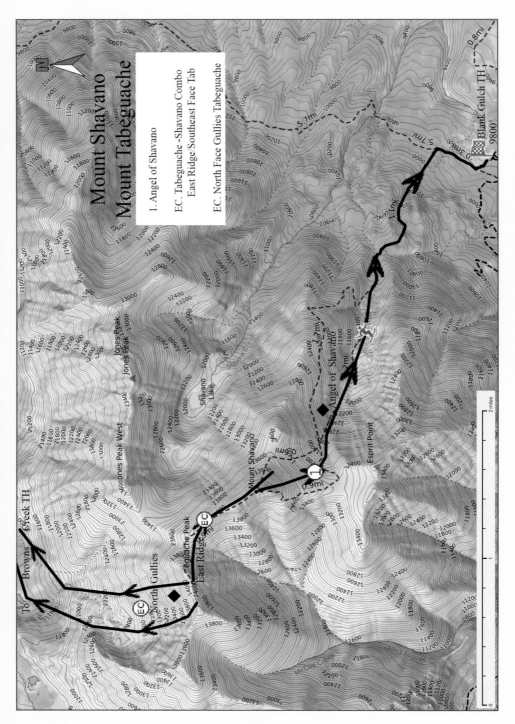

Mount Shavano
Mount Tabeguache

1. Angel of Shavano

EC. Tabeguache -Shavano Combo
East Ridge/Southeast Face Tab

EC. North Face Gullies Tabeguache

MT. SHAVANO

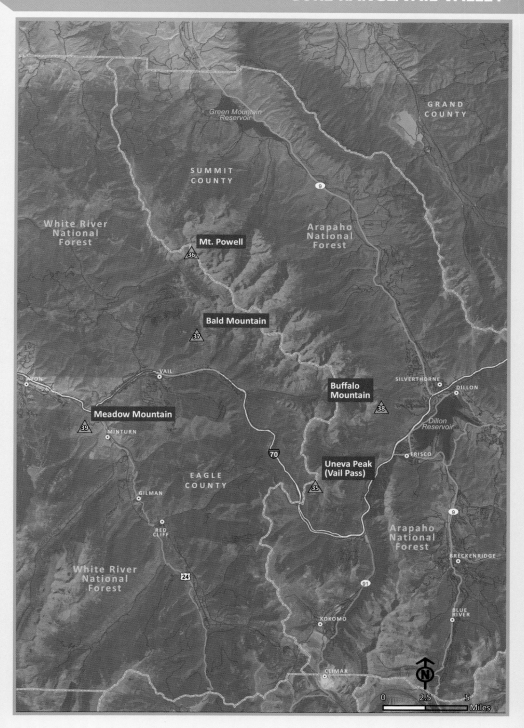

35. Uneva Peak (Vail Pass)
12,522 feet/3817 meters

SKIABLE VERTICAL:	2322 feet/708 meters
ROUND-TRIP DISTANCE:	5.2 miles/8.4 kilometers
TRAILHEAD:	Vail Pass (10,200 feet) at Exit 190 off Interstate 70
DIFFICULTY RATINGS:	■ / ◆
SKI TERRAIN:	Tree glades and moderate faces
OPTIMAL SEASON:	January through May. March and April are ideal.
MAPS:	Trails Illustrated Numbers 108 and 149, Vail Pass, White River National Forest

COMMENT: A spectacular setting with easy access to low angle ski terrain, Uneva Peak has something for everyone. The peak provides an outstanding place for a group outing, and the terrain is ideal for beginner ski mountaineering as well as a place to practice avalanche assessment and training skills. The top of Uneva offers spectacular 360-degree views of the Gore Range, northern Sawatch, Front Range, and Tenmile/Mosquito Range.

Stunning views of the Gore Range en route to skiing Uneva Bowl. Photo by John Fielder

John Fielder enjoys the cruiser terrain at the base of Uneva Bowl.

GETTING THERE

Vail Pass Trailhead. About 80 miles west of Denver on I-70, take Exit 190 from just east of the summit of Vail Pass. There is ample parking on the south side of I-70 located along the frontage road and the designated Vail Pass Recreation Area. *A $6 fee is charged for the day per person, and a $40 season pass from November through May can be purchased.* For more information, see www.fs.usda.gov/recarea/whiteriver/recreation/wintersports/recarea/?recid=40891&actid=89.

THE CLIMB

South Ridge (Class 2). Walk across the I-70 bridge to the north side of the interstate from the parking area. Once across the bridge you will see a well-defined snowshoe/skin track trail angling to the left (northeast) into the trees and away from the highway. Follow the trail for about 0.4 mile through thick trees that eventually give way to flat meadows and the Corral Creek drainage. Continue north along Corral Creek for 0.5 mile or less before crossing the creek to the east side and leaving the meadows behind. While along the creek you will be able to see the ridgeline for Uneva Peak and the southern false summit of Uneva at 12,340 feet, which is situated above the gladed South Uneva Bowl. Angle northeast for a good 0.75 mile to gain the timberline through the trees toward the bowl and the ridgeline just to the right (south and east) of the highest point you can see. Near timberline at 11,700 feet find the lowest-angle terrain to skin up. Once you are above treeline it is easy to zigzag on a southwest-facing slope for about 0.25 mile to gain the south ridge of Uneva at about 13,100 feet. From here, follow the ridge for about 0.5 mile to reach its top. On the ridge, follow gentle slopes over the false 12,340-foot south summit of Uneva, and continue north into a saddle at 13,180 feet. From the saddle travel north for another 0.25 mile to the true summit of Uneva. Use caution along the ridge and stay to the west (windward side) of the ridgeline as you travel along it to avoid the cornice wind-slab that usually develops during winter and can be a dangerous hazard.

Ascending South Uneva Bowl in the early morning light.

DESCENTS

1. *Southwest Face/Uneva Bowl* ◆ Leave the summit to the west on gentle slopes and follow the western end of gentle terrain to the edge of steeper terrain. Angle southwest and look down into Uneva Bowl. There are several options; the farther east the line, the steeper it is to ski. Avoid this bowl after big snows in February or March, and make sure there has been slide activity in April before trying to ski any lines in the bowl. Once back into the trees below, the terrain is flat and funnels back to the south and eventually to Vail Pass.

2. *South Uneva Bowl* ■ / ◆ This is probably the safest and best option for a fun outing with friends that this book has to offer. South Uneva Bowl is starts as more of an open snow face and descends into an excellent glade. Ski south from the 12,340-foot south summit of Uneva, then angle to the southwest after several hundred feet of open powder skiing. A steep section in the trees is usually safe from avalanches any time during winter or spring. This line can be enjoyed multiple times in a day, especially once you've established an excellent skin track.

ALTERNATIVES

1. *East Face* ◆◆ From the 13,180-foot saddle on the south ridge of Uneva, chose any of the chutes that drop to the east off Uneva's steep and generally wind loaded east/southeast face. By late April or early May the eastern aspects are safe from avalanches, but before that time use caution. For a great tour, head southeast from Uneva, drop east into the bowl, and ascend moderate slopes to Peak 12,363 feet. From the top of Peak 12,363 feet there are many options for skiing southwest back to Vail Pass.

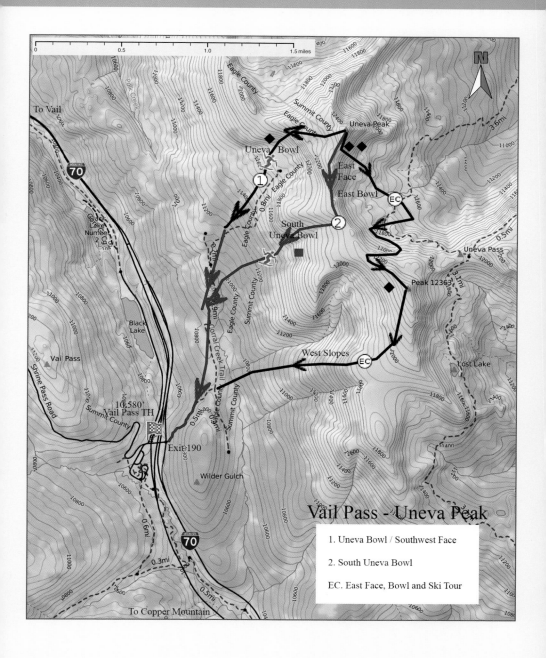

Vail Pass - Uneva Peak

1. Uneva Bowl / Southwest Face

2. South Uneva Bowl

EC. East Face, Bowl and Ski Tour

UNEVA PEAK (VAIL PASS)

36. Mt. Powell
13,580 feet/4140 meters

SKIABLE VERTICAL:	4130 feet/1259 meters
ROUND-TRIP DISTANCE:	12 miles/19.5 kilometers
TRAILHEAD:	Piney Lake (9,450 feet)
DIFFICULTY RATINGS:	◆ / ◆ ◆
SKI TERRAIN:	Steep couloirs, tree glades, and steep faces.
OPTIMAL SEASON:	March through June. May is ideal.
MAPS:	Trails Illustrated Numbers 107, 108, and 149, Eagle's Nest Wilderness, White River National Forest

COMMENT: Ranked 198 out of 200, Mt. Powell barely qualifies as one of Colorado's 200 highest or bicentennial peaks. But this highest peak in the Gore Range has incredible ski lines in a wild and isolated setting. If you visit Mt. Powell in winter, you'll need a snowmobile to access the area, but once the road opens to the Piney Trailhead (sometimes as early as May 1st), you can be out with your party on the peak and won't see another soul, because the Gore Range is devoid of 14ers. Enjoy skiing and earning your turns in this wild and scenic place!

Peering down the powder filled South Couloir on Powell with Peak C and the rest of the Gore Range looming large. Photo by Andrew Warkentin

GETTING THERE

Piney Lake Trailhead. The trailhead is located about 11 miles north of Vail on Red Sandstone Road. Take Interstate 70 Exit 176 from Vail Pass. From the main Vail exit roundabouts, travel on North Frontage Road west along I-70. After 0.5 mile you will cross under the pedestrian bridge that spans I-70. About 200 yards after crossing under the bridge take a right on Red Sandstone Road. This road is paved at its beginning. After two switchbacks, take a left before the third switchback onto Forest Service Road 700, which is dirt. Follow the winding road for 11 miles to Piney River Ranch. Even though the ranch is private at the lake, there is public parking at the trailhead. Park near the gate to access Piney Lake and the trail beyond.

THE CLIMB

Southwest Couloir /SW Ledges (Class 2+). This is a spectacular climb. Start at Piney Lake and follow the Upper Piney Lake Trail along the vast Piney

Gary Smith making nice turns high on Powell with the Vail Ski resort and Mount of the Holy Cross visible to the south. Photo by Andrew Warkentin

River and basin for 3.25 miles. The trail is very flat and after the first 1.5 miles you'll enter trees, where the trail switches back but elevation gain is minimal. If you are in this area before mid-May, the trail may be buried under snow. There is a significant turn off at 9800 feet that is cairned in the melted-out months. Prior to melt-out, after navigating some large boulders and granite slabs along the river, take a sharp left turn and continue northeast into a steeper basin. Follow the creek up, crossing it twice near the 10,500-foot level and reach sparse tees and a flat area just below tree line in a gorgeous basin at 11,200 feet. Mt. Powell and the southwest face will be directly ahead to the northeast of you. At about 11,350 feet, take a sharp left turn (north) in the relatively flat basin and look for an obvious couloir on the central face of Powell. Head north toward the pass. There are two couloirs here; choose the left (northernmost) couloir. At about 11,800 feet enter the couloir and angle northeast again, climbing for 1000 feet. The southwest face opens up above the narrow sections and you can gain the broad and obvious shoulder of Powell's west ridge at about 13,000 feet. From the shoulder wrap around to the north and into a west facing bowl of Powell, doing an ascending traverse for 400 feet to gain the flat area near the summit. Travel east for 250 yards and up another 180 feet and the summit is yours.

Approaching the summit of Powell deep in the heart of the Gore Range.
Photo by Andrew Warkentin

DESCENTS

1. *Southwest Couloir* ◆ / ◆◆ Leave the summit to the west on gentle slopes and retrace your steps to the western end of gentle terrain to the edge of steeper terrain. Angle skier's left (southwest) into the upper western bowl. Ski the bowl for 400 feet to the broad shoulder of Mt. Powell's west ridge. From here ski the spectacular southwest couloir that you ascended. The couloir is narrow in a few places but for the most part is consistent. The steepest sections below 12,600 feet should not exceed 40 degrees. Once into the basin, follow the creek and the river valley to get back into the upper Piney River Basin.

2. *West Couloir* ◆ / ◆◆ This option is just slightly more difficult than the Southwest Couloir, and even more classic and direct, in my opinion. Follow the Southwest Couloir route to the summit as described above. Leave the summit to the west on gentle slopes and retrace your steps to the western end of gentle terrain to the edge of steeper terrain. Instead of angling southwest into the upper western bowl, ski the west bowl, which below 13,000 feet narrows into the West Couloir. The couloir is slightly steeper than the Southwest Couloir and makes this ski line almost 1,500 feet. You will end up down in Cataract Creek Basin to the north of the pass, so you will have to ascend 150 to 200 feet to gain the pass and then ski out to the south toward Piney Lake and the trailhead.

ALTERNATIVES

1. *South Couloir* ◆◆ From the summit, leave the 150-foot summit crest and drop southwest to the vast flat area below the top. Once on the flat area, travel south for a short distance to the steep south face of Powell. Find a steep couloir that can be skied directly south and into a basin to the east of Knee Knocker Pass (12,300 feet). There are pros and cons to this route. The 1250-foot ski line is steep and amazing. But the bottom of the couloir opens into a tempting basin which is to the east of Knee Knocker Pass, requiring you to climb west and back up at least 250 feet to be able to return to the west back toward Piney Lake.

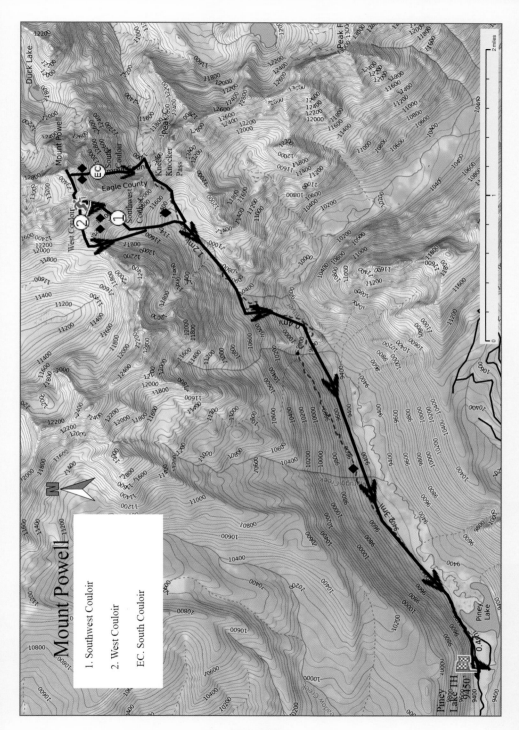

MT. POWELL

37. Bald Mountain
12,136 feet/3700 meters

SKIABLE VERTICAL:	3656 feet/1114 meters
ROUND-TRIP DISTANCE:	10 miles/16.1 kilometers
TRAILHEAD:	Spraddle Creek (8,480 feet)
DIFFICULTY RATINGS:	■ / ◆
SKI TERRAIN:	Ridgelines, tree glades, open meadows, and forest roads
OPTIMAL SEASON:	December through May. March and April are ideal.
MAPS:	Trails Illustrated Numbers 108 and 149, Vail East, Vail West

COMMENT: Easily accessible from the Vail Valley, Bald Mountain is an excellent intermediate peak. The elevation gain combined with the open meadow slopes gives you plenty of vertical to ski, the views are impressive, and the terrain is manageable for most skiers. It's a rewarding feeling to stand high atop Bald Mountain on a warm and sunny spring day in March or April when the hordes of spring-breakers are clogging the slopes of Vail Resort across the valley. You can enjoy solitude and spring powder as you click in and ski meadows, with the Gore Range to your north as an awesome backdrop.

The Eisemann Hut is the best lodge in the Gore Range to launch winter and spring ski tours from and it also provides access to the Northwest Bowl on Bald Mountain.

GETTING THERE

Spraddle Creek Trailhead. Take Interstate 70 Exit 176 at the main Vail exit. Spraddle Creek Road is an immediate right turn from the roundabout on the north side of the interstate. Follow Spraddle Creek Road as it climbs steeply above the valley through a few switchbacks for 0.75 mile until you reach the Spraddle Creek Estates entrance gate. Before entering the gate, take a sharp right up a narrow dirt road for 0.1 mile where you will reach horse stables and a parking area with a pit toilet. This is the trailhead.

THE CLIMB

Southwest Ridge (Class 1). Start at the stables and follow the Spraddle Creek jeep road as it switches back through the aspens. The trail will enter the Spraddle Creek Basin and leave the Vail Valley behind after about 1 mile. At mile 2.2, leave the road by taking a left turn and follow a series of meadows to the north. At times you will be able to see Bald Mountain's southwest ridge. Aim to the west side of the ridge, ascend some moderate slopes with spaced out trees, and eventually gain the ridge at about 11,800 feet. Leave the trees behind and travel northeast for the last 0.25 mile to reach the summit.

DESCENTS

1. *Southwest Ridge/South Glades* ■ / ◆
    Leave the summit to the southwest on gentle ridgeline and retrace your path to treeline. Once in the trees, angle south into a valley that funnels back toward Spraddle Creek. Take the most delightful line down open meadows.

Skiing easy meadows of the South Glades on Bald Mountain. Photo by Tara Nichols

John Fielder approaching the Eisemann Hut on a stormy day.

It's a scenic tour up Bald Mountain through the aspens.

John Fielder skiing deep powder below the Eisemann Hut.

Once back near the Spraddle Creek jeep road, angle left and contour the creek basin to make it easier to get back to the road and eventually the trailhead.

2. **_South Face_** ◆ / ◆◆ This variation is more direct, but can be avalanche prone in mid-winter, so use your best judgment. Leave the summit travelling southwest along the ridge and stop about halfway between the summit and the timberline on the ridge. From this point you are standing at about 12,000 feet on the southwest ridge and can choose any number of lines down the south face of Bald. The skiing at first is steep and open, then you will enter the woods and eventually meet up with the South Glades Route described above.

ALTERNATIVES

Northwest Bowl ◆◆ Any number of lines can be explored to the northwest from the summit. Just remember that these routes will finish in the Middle Creek Basin, and it's a long way down the Middle Creek drainage to return to Vail. Some people ski this face when they are staying in the comforts of the Eisemann 10th Mountain Division hut further to the northwest.

Sunset comes early in the winter at the Eisemann Hut.

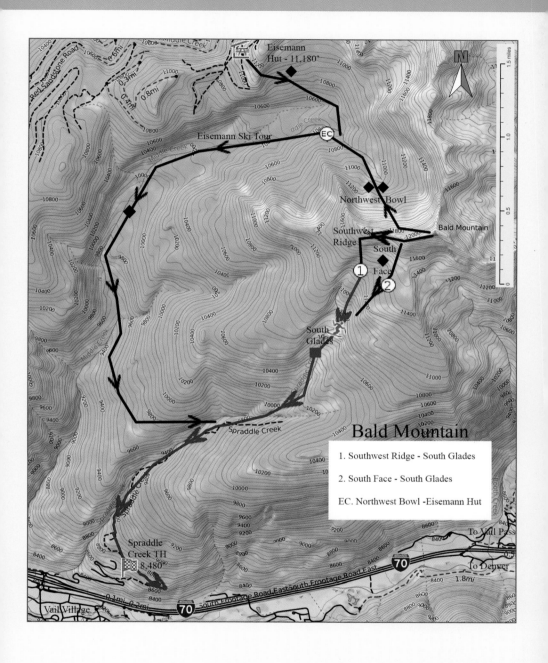

BALD MOUNTAIN

38. Buffalo Mountain
12,777 feet/3894 meters

SKIABLE VERTICAL:	Up to 3200 feet/975 meters
ROUND-TRIP DISTANCE:	8 to 9.5 miles /13 to 16.1 kilometers
TRAILHEAD:	Ryan Gulch (9,600 feet)
DIFFICULTY RATINGS:	■ / ◆
SKI TERRAIN:	Couloirs and moderate faces
OPTIMAL SEASON:	March through June. April through June are ideal.
MAPS:	Trails Illustrated Numbers 108 and 149, White River National Forest

COMMENT: Buffalo Mountain is a 12,000-foot peak close to Silverthorne, and is a reasonable drive from the Denver metro area. The mountain is a great way to hone ski mountaineering skills. It offers a couple of options, depending on conditions. Avalanches have scarred the mountain after big snowstorms, most notably in 1986 after a 5-foot snowfall created unstable conditions resulting in a large slab avalanche down the Silver Couloir that leveled a number of large trees. Buffalo Mountain is generally safe, but it's always a good idea to ski this peak in stable spring conditions.

Climbing the Silver in spring conditions provides firm snow for good steps.
Photo by Anne Marie Migl

Skiing the Silver as it starts to narrow two-thirds of the way down. Be sure to exit the couloir to the skier' right near the base before skiing too far down to avoid missing the route back to the trailhead. Photo by Jason Gebauer

GETTING THERE

Ryan Gulch Trailhead (9,600 feet). Travel west of Denver on Interstate 70 to Exit 205, Silverthorne. Turn north on Highway 9 and take the first left near some outlet stores on a road that becomes Ryan Gulch Road. The road parallels I-70 westbound as it climbs a hill and enters a residential area. Follow Ryan Gulch Road for 3.6 miles to a prominent arching switchback on the road. The parking for the trailhead is on the south side of the road. The Ryan Gulch Trail is to the right (east) of the parking lot. Do not get confused with the Lilly Pad Lake Trail, which is to the left on the west side of the parking area.

THE CLIMB

The standard route follows the corridor of the Buffalo Mountain Trail for 3.2 miles to the summit. Travel east from the trail through the woods. Follow the trail to the four-way junction for the Mesa Cortina Trailhead and the Gore Range Trail. For the Buffalo Mountain Trail, turn left and follow the branch that leads to Buffalo Cabin. After 0.5 mile pass the remains of Buffalo Cabin. From just to the left of the cabin the new Buffalo Mountain Trail begins switchbacking up the steep slope above. From here, zigzag skin up the eastern face to the upper ridge and eventually the summit. The slope soon relents for the final 400 feet as the trail passes through some of the last crooked trees.

In the Silver, turns are delightful and are sustained at 35 degrees for a nice long run.
Photo by Jason Gebauer

If you want to climb and ski the Silver Couloir, you can climb the couloir directly. Instead of turning left to Buffalo Cabin, continue straight on the South Willow Creek Trail. This trail wraps around to the north side of the mountain. You will descend slightly while traversing around and to the base of the couloir at about 10,300 feet. Once in the couloir, ascend for more than 2000 feet to the summit.

DESCENTS

1. *Silver Couloir* ◆ Leave the summit directly to the north and then angle to the northeast to ski the broad and steep couloir. The Silver Couloir is more northeast facing than north. It is broad and reaches 48 degrees at its steepest, but averages 40 degrees overall. Turns for 2000 feet can be exhilarating, and the northeastern aspect sometimes yields stable powder conditions into late May. Above 11,800 feet the couloir has a "Y" shape and you can choose which arm to drop into.

2. *East Face* ■ Leave the summit and ski relatively gentle slopes to the east and back toward the Buffalo Mountain Trail. This is fun skiing for an outing with folks who aren't quite ready for the steepness of the Silver Couloir.

ALTERNATIVES

Sacred Buffalo to Salt Lick Drainage East ◆ Climb south from the summit of Buffalo to the southern sub-summit known as Sacred Buffalo. From here it is possible to ski and explore either the southeast face and glades carved out by an avalanche years ago, or drop into the steeper and more technical Salt Lick Cirque to the east that bisects the sub-summits. Return to the east and northeast once down in the trees to find the Ryan Gulch Trailhead.

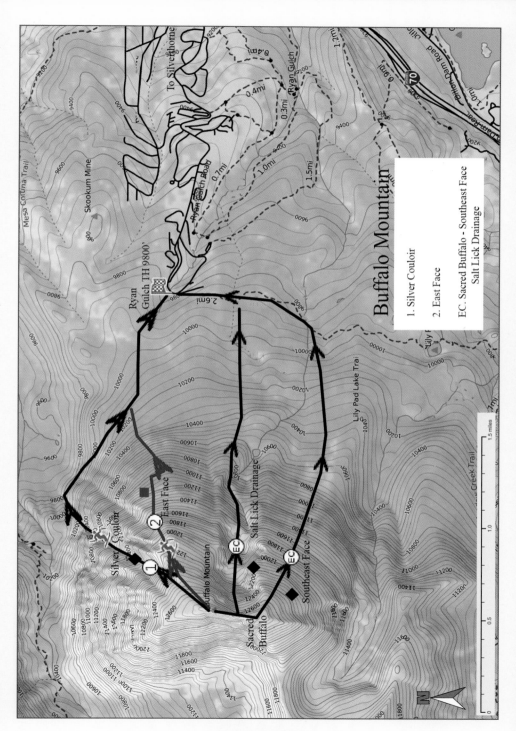

BUFFALO MOUNTAIN

39. Meadow Mountain
9,756 feet/2974 meters

SKIABLE VERTICAL:	2006 feet/611 meters
ROUND-TRIP DISTANCE:	9.0 miles/14.5 kilometers
TRAILHEAD:	Meadow Mountain Forest Service (7,750 feet).
DIFFICULTY RATINGS:	● / ■
SKI TERRAIN:	Tree glades, open meadows, and forest service roads
OPTIMAL SEASON:	December through April. March is ideal.
MAPS:	Trails Illustrated Numbers 108 and 149, Minturn, White River National Forest

COMMENT: Meadow Mountain is a great place to explore for an afternoon, evening, or moonlight adventure. It offers easy access, a beautiful setting, and opportunities to teach friends, family, little kids, and beginners how to ski mountaineer. This is also a great place to dial in your new backcountry gear for larger ski trips.

GETTING THERE
Meadow Mountain Trailhead. Take Interstate 70 Exit 171, which is 105 miles west of Denver and 5 miles west of Vail. Travel east on US Highway 24 for a short

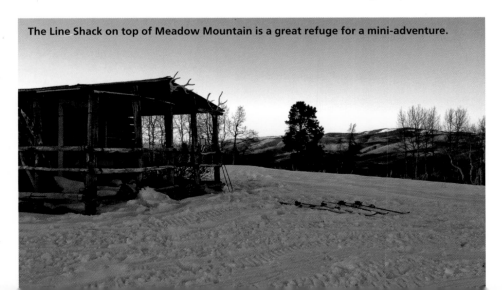
The Line Shack on top of Meadow Mountain is a great refuge for a mini-adventure.

distance from the interstate and the large US Forest Service building with a significant parking area is immediately on your right.

THE CLIMB
Line Shack Cabin (Class 1). The Meadow Mountain Trail (Number 748) begins through a gate at the south end of the parking lot. The trail switches back and follows an old road up through meadows and aspen forests. This is a popular area for hikers, snowshoers,

Clicking in for a sunset ski down Meadow Mountain.

and snowmobilers in the winter. If you follow the road it eventually leads to the Line Shack Cabin after 4.5 miles and numerous switchbacks. Snowmobilers often shortcut the road and following their winter tracks is a good way to shave some distance from the route to the Line Shack Cabin.

DESCENTS
1. *East/Northeast Slopes* ● / ■ Leave the Line Shack Cabin and follow the open meadows and slopes of the former ski area. You will generally cross and follow the snowmobile trail along the main road and trail finishing in a northerly direction back at the trailhead. Enjoy the powder, especially right after a storm cycle!

ALTERNATIVES
Western Viewpoint Slopes ● / ■ Travel west from the Line Shack Cabin for about 0.5 mile across the wide-open expanse of Meadow Mountain. After gradually rising about 300 feet, you will arrive at an obvious viewpoint in the meadow. From here enjoy views of the Gore Range as well as an outstanding view of the lower Vail Valley and Beaver Creek Ski Resort to the west. Ski gentle slopes back to the Line Shack Cabin. Some folks choose to enjoy an evening in the Line Shack Cabin, so consider packing a sleeping bag and snacks to enjoy a gorgeous sunset. Then greet the sunrise with a morning ski down the East/Northeast Slopes route described above!

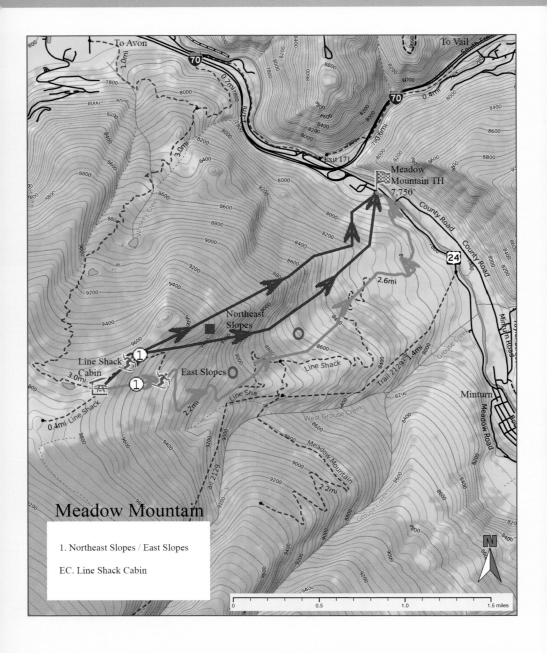

Meadow Mountain

1. Northeast Slopes / East Slopes

EC. Line Shack Cabin

MEADOW MOUNTAIN

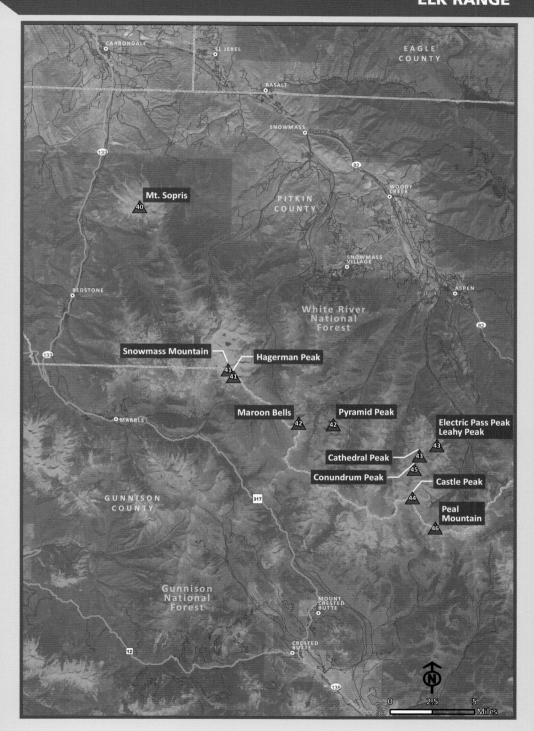

40. Mt. Sopris

12,953 feet/3948 meters

SKIABLE VERTICAL:	4853 feet/1479 meters
ROUND-TRIP DISTANCE:	15.5 miles/25 kilometers
TRAILHEAD:	Thomas Lakes (8,100 feet) (also referred to as the Dinkle Lake Divide, Prince Creek Divide, or West Sopris Creek Trailhead)
DIFFICULTY RATINGS:	■ / ◆ / ◆ ◆
SKI TERRAIN:	Steep couloirs, tree glades, moderate bowls, and steep faces
OPTIMAL SEASON:	March through June. May is ideal.
MAPS:	Trails Illustrated Numbers 128 and 143, Mt. Sopris, White River National Forest

COMMENT: Mt. Sopris dominates the view from the Roaring Fork Valley near Carbondale and Glenwood Springs. This peak will inspire any ski mountaineer who lays eyes on it to climb and ski its alluring slopes!

The Nellie Creek Cirque and the Laundry Chutes are steep and imposing features on Sopris. Photo by Torrey Udall

GETTING THERE

Thomas Lakes Trailhead/Dinkle Lake Divide/West Sopris Creek Trailhead (8,100 feet) From the town of Carbondale (west of Aspen and southeast of Glenwood Springs) travel south on Highway 133 for approximately 1.4 miles. Turn left on Prince Creek Road (which turns to dirt after the first mile) and go 6 miles to a fork in the road. Take a right at the fork and follow it for 2 miles. The trailhead is 0.25 mile before Dinkle Lake. The road generally melts out by the end of April.

THE CLIMB

West Sopris Creek to Thomas Lakes to Thomas Lakes Bowl and the Northeast Ridge (Class 2). From the trailhead at Dinkle Lake Divide, look for the Forest Service trailhead signs a few hundred feet south of the road; your trail starts up an obvious cut behind these signs and is usually packed by snowmobiles and skiers. Sometimes mountaineers snowmobile up the trail corridor to Thomas Lakes and the nearby wilderness boundary. Follow the old roadcut as it makes a long climbing traverse west, then switchbacks and climbs east to pass around a shoulder at 9,200 feet. Follow the obvious roadcut for a few hundred yards. When the roadcut swings left (east), leave the road and climb 250 yards directly up the shoulder to

Multiple lines exist on the northeast aspect of Sopris leading into Thomas Lakes Bowl—pick your favorite!

the right of a small avalanche bowl at the head of an open area. This little detour avoids taking the roadcut around a long and inefficient traverse to the east. Once you've arrived at the shelf above the avalanche slope (9,600 feet), locate the Thomas Lakes Trail and follow its obvious cut through aspen and conifer to another open area at 10,000 feet. Continue southwest up a small gulch to the vicinity of lower (northern) Thomas Lake (10,200 feet).

Southeast of the lakes there is a prominent wide ridge that rises to the east subsidiary summit of the mountain. The crest of this ridge is safe from avalanches, and much of it is skiable. From the upper (southern) lake, head to the northeast and take an ascending traverse onto the northeast ridge, gaining the broad ridge top at about 10,400 feet. Once on the ridge, climb through a glade to a broad saddle (10,800 feet) near timberline. Above timberline the terrain steepens. To avoid avalanche danger, stay left and stick to the scrub-covered ridge crest, which leads to a lower-angled area at 11,400 feet. Continue up the low-angled terrain to a narrow, corniced section of the ridge. Beware of the cornice, and walk to the right (northwest) side of the ridge to another headwall, which

Transitioning and waiting for the spring corn to soften up with a nice view of the Elks and Capitol Peak on the horizon. Photo by Jake Marty

is usually snow covered. To avoid avalanche danger, take the rocky ridge to the left of the headwall (this may require crampons and ice ax), and stick with the ridge to the east summit. Follow the ridge from the subsidiary east summit west to the main summit and Sopris' highest point. There is also a summit further west that is nearly as high.

Climb Thomas Lakes Bowl direct. After avalanche danger stabilizes in the spring, head up the center left (south side) of the bowl. At 11,100 feet, push to the right (north) and climb a final pitch to a major saddle (12,300 feet) that separates the lower east subsidiary summit from the main summit to the east. Take the wide ridge 0.5 mile northwest to the main summit.

DESCENTS

1. ***Thomas Lakes Bowl*** ◆ Ski from the summit of Sopris by angling east on the gentle ridgeline toward the top of Thomas Lakes Bowl, which you climbed. Once in the bowl, ski down for 2000 feet into the enjoyable basin and back to the Thomas Lakes. Follow the trail corridor back to the trailhead.

2. ***East Ridge Route*** ◆ From the eastern subsidiary summit, ski the east ridge to a small shoulder at 12,300 feet. There are numerous choices here that are slightly steeper than the Thomas Lakes Bowl heading down to the vicinity of Thomas Lakes to the northeast.

ALTERNATIVES

Laundry Chutes ◆◆ In a big snow year in early May, it is possible to find any number of steep and dangerous ski lines directly off the summit to the east and into the basin below Sopris' northeast face. Named for Chris Landry, the Laundry Chutes demand your respect. A rappel may be necessary into the Purex Chute, East Laundry Chute, and the Main Chute.

Nettle Creek Cirque ◆ From the west main summit, ski north and then east into the glacial valley known as the Nellie Creek Cirque. Terrain here includes The Cone, the Alaska Face, and The Elbow Chute.

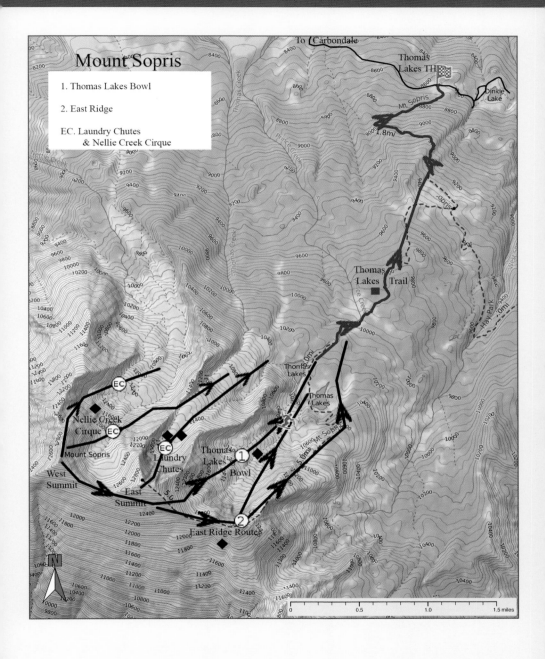

MT. SOPRIS

41. Snowmass Mountain
14,092 feet/4295 meters

SKIABLE VERTICAL:	Up to 5700 feet/1738 meters
ROUND-TRIP DISTANCE:	21 miles/33.9 kilometers
TRAILHEAD:	Snowmass Creek (8,400 feet)
DIFFICULTY RATINGS:	■ / ◆ / ◆ ◆
SKI TERRAIN:	Moderate slopes, tree glades, steep faces, and narrow trail corridors
OPTIMAL SEASON:	March through July. May and June are ideal.
MAPS:	Trails Illustrated Number 128, Snowmass Mountain, White River National Forest

The author carefully cutting turns into the top of the Southwest Couloir.
Photo by Tara Nichols

COMMENT: Snowmass is one of Colorado's most spectacular snowy peaks, located deep in the heart of the Elk Range. Most years it skis very well into July, and sometimes even August. Snowmass is isolated and a long distance from the trailhead, so this adventure may be best enjoyed with an overnight camp either at Snowmass Lake or a couple of miles below the lake at the infamous "Log Jam."

GETTING THERE

Snowmass Creek Trailhead (8,400 feet). From the town of Glenwood Springs, take Colorado Highway 82 south for 28 miles to the small town of Snowmass, located at a small gas station and lone stop light right on Colorado Highway 82. Or travel north on Colorado

Highway 82 for 13 miles from the Maroon Creek Road on Aspen's north side.

Charging onto the top of the namesake Snowmass East Face. Photo by Tara Nichols

At the stoplight in Snowmass, turn west on Snowmass Creek Road and travel 1.7 miles to a "T" junction. Turn left and continue up the road for 7.3 miles where the road turns to dirt. You will pass several ranches in a gorgeous mountain valley along the way. At 10.7 miles cross Snowmass Creek on a bridge; the road is usually plowed to the bridge until it melts out in late April or early May. At 10.9 miles turn right at another "T" junction. Proceed to the gate for Snowmass Falls Ranch at 11.3 miles and find a good-sized parking area and a trailhead kiosk..

THE CLIMBS

Snowmass East Face (Class 3, Moderate Snow). The classic namesake east face of Snowmass is climbed from Snowmass Lake. From the trailhead follow the Maroon-Snowmass Trail for 8 miles to Snowmass Lake. At about

The crew surveying the East Face of Snowmass from Snowmass Lake just before sunrise.

4 miles catch a stellar view of Snowmass Massif up the Bear Creek Basin (Pierre Lakes Basin) to the west. At 6 miles you will reach the second of two lakes and an interesting crossing on a logjam. Continue up the trail through some thicker pinewoods for the final 1.5 mile, reaching the lake at 11,000 feet. Skirt around the south side of the lake to access the snowfield and the upper portion of the peak. In a strong snow year it is possible even into early June to skin around the edge of the frozen lake and then use ski crampons or boot pack for the first 500 feet above the lake to ascend a shallow gully. The gully affords access to the main snowfield and much gentler slopes on Snowmass. Ascend slopes on skins from 12,400 to 13,400 feet before climbing to a notch at 13,700 feet on Snowmass' southeast ridge. Wrap around the west side of the ridge for 400 feet to reach the top of Snowmass.

DESCENTS

1. *Southeast ridge to notch to Snowmass East Face* ■ / ◆ Leave the summit by angling east on the ridgeline, staying on the southwest aspect of the peak toward the top of the notch on the ridge. Once at the notch, navigate any cornices and ski east down the face directly onto the spectacular Snowmass Snowfield. The first 100 feet are steep. Enjoy turns for nearly 2,500 feet back to Snowmass Lake at 11,000 feet. Many hoots and hollers of pure exhilaration have been heard on this route, one of the best to backcountry ski in all of North America!

2. *East Snowmass Face Direct* ◆◆ Descend the initial steps of the southeast ridge for about 100 feet to an even smaller notch on the ridge. From here you can look northeast and down directly onto the face. Depending on how much snow is there, you can delicately side slip onto the top of the face and ski directly down the east face and beyond, eventually reaching the lake below. In a huge snow year, a direct descent from the summit to the east might also be possible. This descent could start at up to 60 degrees, but after the first 100 feet, the angle rapidly eases onto the snowfield below.

ALTERNATIVES

Southwest Couloir and West Face ◆◆ The famous "S" ridge on Snowmass divides these two amazing ski options, which can be enjoyed with a little research and effort. To get into the southwest couloir, ski off the summit to the south. The beginning of the southwest face on the south side of the "S" ridge funnels into an excellent couloir that skis up to 45 degrees for almost 2000 feet down into the upper reaches of Geneva Basin. Alternatively, find a pair of gullies to the west of the summit on the north side of the "S" ridge. These gullies also lead into Geneva Basin and eventually Lead King Basin. These basins are approached from the town of Marble to the west, so do your research before attempting these runs.

North Snowmass ◆◆ There is a small connecting saddle between Snowmass at 14,092 feet and its northern sub-peak 14,061 feet, North Snowmass. The saddle is accessible from the northwest reaches of Snowmass' permanent snowfield. It is possible to ski from the top of North Snowmass.

Centennial Hagerman Peak ◆◆ Seldom skied Hagerman Peak (13,841 feet) is a centennial with numerous options that are worth exploring. While ascending the Snowmass east face from Snowmass Lake, examine the possibilities of a couple enticing couloirs on Hagerman's northeast face. There are also a handful of excellent lines off the peak's southwest aspects.

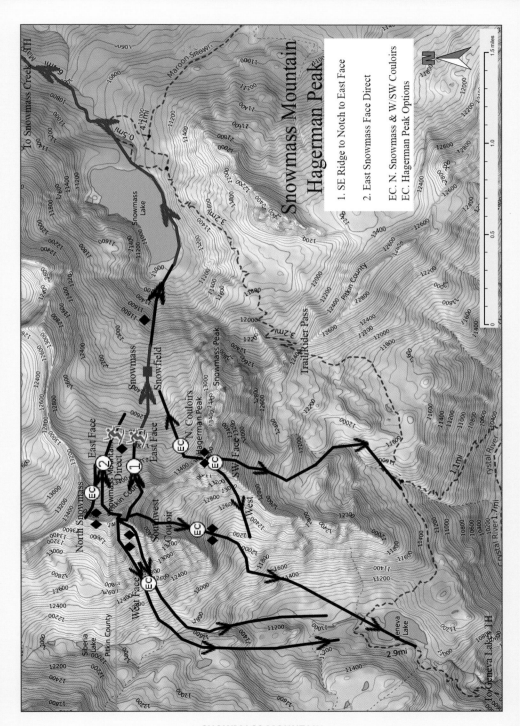

SNOWMASS MOUNTAIN

42. Maroon Bells
14,156 feet/4315 meters
(South Maroon Peak and North Maroon Peak Alternatives)

SKIABLE VERTICAL:	4556 feet/1389 meters
ROUND-TRIP DISTANCE:	8 to 9 miles/15 to 17 kilometers
TRAILHEAD:	Maroon Lake (9,600 feet)
DIFFICULTY RATINGS:	◆ / ◆ ◆
SKI TERRAIN:	Steep couloirs and steep faces
OPTIMAL SEASON:	March through June. May is ideal.
MAPS:	Trails Illustrated Number 128, Maroon Bells, Hayden Peak, White River National Forest

COMMENT: The Elk Range is rugged and well known for its 14ers. The Maroon Bells are likely the most famous mountains in all of Colorado. They offer three ski lines that are difficult and dangerous, yet rewarding and exhilarating. Ski these peaks once and you might just be hooked forever. Ascending them while they are snow-covered is preferable to climbing the loose and unstable sedimentary mudstone that reveals itself in summer.

The northeast ridge of Pyramid provides views to North Maroon, Sleeping Sexton, Snowmass, and Capitol (left to right).

Climbing into the bottom of the Y-Couloir before the sun rises.

Skiing the upper portion of the Y-Couloir.
Photo by Brad Burgtorf

GETTING THERE

<u>*Maroon Lake*</u> (9,600 feet). From the town of Aspen, take Maroon Creek Road from the roundabout on Colorado Highway 82 on the northwest side of town. This roundabout is shared with Castle Creek Road. Follow paved Maroon Creek Road for 9.5 miles to Maroon Lake and a paved parking area. Until early May, the road is only open for 3.0 miles, from Colorado Highway 82 to just past the T-Lazy-7 Ranch.

From Memorial Day weekend through Labor Day weekend (and sometimes through early October) the road is closed from 8:30 a.m. until 5 p.m., but a shuttle bus runs from the Aspen Highland Ski Resort to Maroon Lake. For more information call the White River National Forest Ranger Station in Aspen at (970) 925-3445.

THE CLIMBS

<u>*Bell Chord Couloir (Class 4)*</u>. Before May, park near the T-Lazy-7 Ranch and skin nearly 6 miles up the Maroon Creek Road to reach the summer trailhead. Snowmobiles are helpful in April and May and in early May before the road opens, a bike might be a good option too! From the Maroon Lake Trailhead, walk or skin west for 1.5 miles to Crater Lake. From the east end of the lake pass willows and large pine trees before turning west and northwest toward the basin between South Maroon and North Maroon Peaks. Enter the straight and direct couloir at 12,000 feet and climb to the 13,780-foot saddle between South Maroon and North Maroon Peaks. The nearly 2,000-foot long couloir does not exceed 45 degrees. From the saddle climb a class 4 cliff and some class 3 ledges (which likely will be heavily snow covered) for 250 yards to reach the summit.

Casey Rietz slashing a turn on the perfect east wall of Maroon Peak next to the Bell Chord Couloir. Photo by Drew Warkentin

Southeast Couloir and Ridge (Class 3). From the base of the Bell Chord Couloir, at about 12,000 feet, angle southwest and into the Garbage Chute, a slot couloir. Ascend the chute to a small flat area and then continue up either of two separate couloirs, the "Y" Couloir. The right (northern) branch is the best and most direct route to the 13,660-foor notch on the south ridge. From the saddle follow the south ridge by traversing a pair of gullies along South Maroon's west aspect. Climb directly on the ridge reach the true summit.

DESCENTS

1. *East Face/Bell Chord Couloir* ◆◆ Leave the summit of South Maroon skiing the first 150 feet by angling east on the ridgeline toward the east face. To cleanly access the Bell Chord, you must descend a steep and exposed face for about 200 vertical feet. Your goal is to ski onto a prominent ledge at 13,700 feet, then take a left turn to access and ski into the Bell Chord. The Bell Chord never exceeds 45 degrees and runs 2,500 feet to the valley floor.

2. *South Ridge/"Y" Couloir* ◆◆ Descend the steps of the south ridge to the initial broad shoulder of South Maroon, leaving the summit to your west and northwest. From here you can look southwest and traverse to the southwest along the south ridge route. Cross a pair of gullies in the process; at

times skiing close to the south ridge is best. Traverse to the notch/saddle at 13,660 feet below a point at 13,763 feet on the south ridge. From the top of this notch you can look into the southeast couloir, which forms the northern branch of the "Y." Ski the southeast facing chute (up to 40 degrees) for 1,500 feet to get into a basin that meets the bottom of the Bell Chord. From here ski another 1,000 feet or so down

Carefully assessing the ski line on the north face of North Maroon.

either the Garbage Chute (skiers right) or some intermediate faces (skiers left) that access the valley below and the vicinity of Crater Lake.

ALTERNATIVES

North Maroon, North Face Direct ◆◆ Mid- to late May is the best time to ski a well-covered North Maroon Peak by its classic north face. The route is a maze of cliff bands that can be carefully navigated and skied in the right snow conditions; the slope is north and northeast facing, so it can be descended between 9 a.m. and 11 a.m. in stable snow conditions. The biggest crux is navigating the "Punk Rock" band, which is on the crest of the northeast ridge. Near the lower west end of the face, angle to the northwest to avoid the bottom cliff bands and ski into the basin below. Access this ski line by crossing Minnehaha Gulch above Crater Lake and climbing to the base of the north face via the basin that holds a prominent rock glacier to the north of North Maroon. You can either climb the face directly or navigate up a hidden couloir that gains the northwest ridge on the west end of the north face (See photo).

North Maroon West Face Gully ◆◆ Leave North Maroon to the northwest along the ridge and look for one of the more prominent shallow gullies that will ski directly down for almost 2,000 feet into the upper Snowmass Creek Basin. The only drawback is you will have to climb over Buckskin Pass to get back to Maroon Lake!

Sleeping Sexton 13,460 feet ◆ A smaller but prominent objective stands to the north of the Maroon Bells, but is not often skied.

Pyramid Peak 14,018 feet ◆◆ This steep and dangerous neighbor of the Maroon Bells can be considered one of Colorado's toughest ski objectives. With careful research, you can ski the Landry Line, the Amphitheatre, or West Ridge.

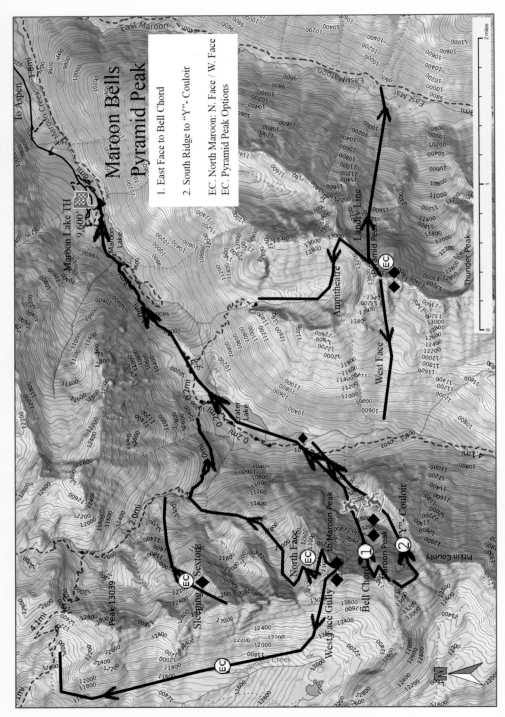

Maroon Bells
Pyramid Peak

1. East Face to Bell Chord

2. South Ridge to "Y" - Couloir

EC. North Maroon: N. Face / W. Face
EC. Pyramid Peak Options

MAROON BELLS (SOUTH AND NORTH)

43. Cathedral Peak
13,943 feet/4250 meters

SKIABLE VERTICAL:	4043 feet/1232 meters
ROUND-TRIP DISTANCE:	9 miles/15.5 kilometers
TRAILHEAD:	Cathedral (9,900 feet)
DIFFICULTY RATINGS:	◆ / ◆ ◆
SKI TERRAIN:	Steep couloirs, tree glades, and steep faces
OPTIMAL SEASON:	March through June. May is ideal.
MAPS:	Trails Illustrated Numbers 127 and 148, Maroon Bells, Hayden Peak, Pearl Pass, White River National Forest

COMMENT: Near the shadow of the highest peak in the Elk Range, Castle Peak, lies Cathedral, a gem that is just shy of 14,000 feet. A tour into this part of the Elk Range is spectacular, marked by solitude, amazing skiing in deep snowpack, and stellar summit views.

Ascending the Pearl Couloir you begin to understand how Cathedral got its name.

Skiers admiring the Pearl after descending.

Looking down the Pearl from the top of the crest on the east ridge.

GETTING THERE

Cathedral Trailhead (9,900 feet). From the town of Aspen, take Castle Creek Road from the roundabout on Colorado Highway 82 on the north side of town. This roundabout is shared with Maroon Creek Road. Follow paved Castle Creek Road for 11 miles to Ashcroft. Until late April or early May, the road will only be open as far as Ashcroft. After early May, continue past Ashcroft 1 mile to a marked road leading to Cathedral Trailhead. Turn right onto this dirt road and follow it as it switches back through aspen forests for 0.75 mile and reaches the Cathedral Trailhead and parking area.

THE CLIMBS

Pearl Couloir (Class 3). Before May, you'll have to park in Ashcroft and skin nearly 2 miles up the Castle Creek Road and the Cathedral Trailhead access road to reach the summer trailhead. From the trailhead, follow the Cathedral Trail for 3.25 miles to Cathedral Lake at 11,866 feet. The trail corridor follows the right side (north) of the basin and the creek all the way up the valley, so if it's snow covered you should be able to find your way. The trail steepens right below the lake, so mitigate avalanche danger accordingly.

Approaching the Pearl and the dramatic east face of Cathedral.

The final 250 yards to the summit along the east ridge with Castle Peak (left). Beware of cornices on the south side of the ridge!

Look at Cathedral Peak from the lake and find the sharp southeast ridge coming directly toward you. Find the Pearl Couloir by following the lake on its north side and skinning north into the basin to the right (east side) of Cathedral's prominent southeast ridge. After about 0.5 mile, you will be to the east of the southeast ridge; look to your left and spot the Pearl Couloir tucked into the ridgeline amongst the stunning "cathedral towers". It's a gorgeous line that you can climb in a westerly direction to near the summit ridge for about 1600 feet. Ascend the couloir. Halfway up there is a choke point where the couloir cuts between the ridgeline and east face; climb to the top to a prominent notch within 150 feet of the top. From the notch turn left on the sometimes bony and difficult east ridge and follow the ridge for 250 yards to the west toward the summit.

South Ridge (Class 3). If the Pearl Couloir isn't your cup of tea, head for Cathedral's south ridge. From the west end of the lake, look to the west/northwest and spot the Cathedral Massif. Hike around to the north end of the lake and begin to ascend up an old rock glacier to the west. In spring the rock glacier is buried under plenty of snow and you can zigzag skin up into the broad and deep basin to the west and northwest of the lake. Stay west of the southeast ridge in the basin and aim for an obvious couloir that leads to your west and to Cathedral's south ridge at a 13,000-foot saddle. Ascend this couloir. It's steep near the top, but by April or May it should be solid and safe from avalanche. From the saddle, follow Cathedral's south ridge for 0.25 mile and 900 feet vertical to the summit.

DESCENTS

1. **Pearl Couloir** ◆ / ◆◆ Leave Cathedral's summit by skiing the 150 steep feet, angling east on the ridgeline toward the top of the Pearl Couloir. Once

Sweet turns down the center of the Pearl.

in the couloir, ski (east) down the couloir for 1500 feet to 12,300 feet. Then turn right and ski through the enjoyable basin back to Cathedral Lake.

2. *South Ridge/East Couloir* ◆◆ Descend the steps of the south ridge to the 13,000-foot saddle. From here you can look east and down into the basin toward Cathedral Lake. Ski down the couloir into the basin below and head east and southeast toward Cathedral Lake. The couloir is steep (up to 40 degrees) and narrow and the top.

ALTERNATIVES

Southeast Face Direct or West Face Direct ◆◆ In a big snow year in early May, it is possible to find any number of ski lines directly off the summit to the south and into the basin below Cathedral's south face. Start early to avoid the wet-slab avalanches that can occur after 10 a.m. in late spring. Or ski the west face of Cathedral into Conundrum Basin and back toward the Conundrum Trailhead.

South Face Electric Pass Peak ■ / ◆ Not feeling up to the challenges of the mighty Cathedral? Admire it from a distance and ascend 13,621-foot Electric Pass Peak and ski it's relatively gentle south face toward Cathedral Lake. This is a fun and avalanche-safe option.

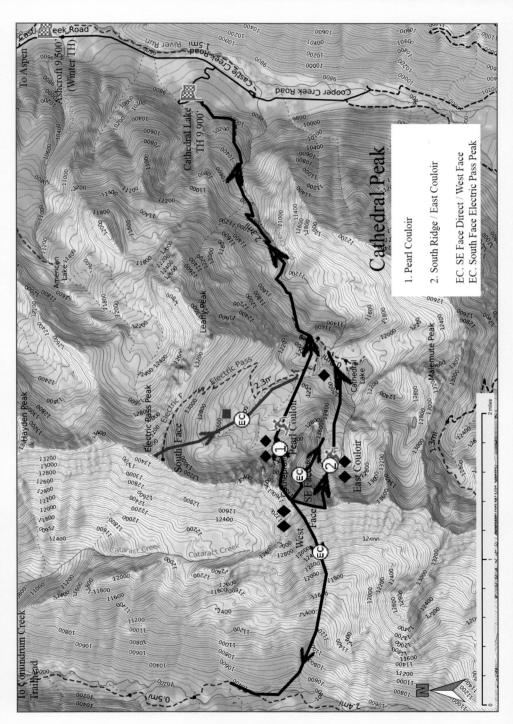

Cathedral Peak

1. Pearl Couloir

2. South Ridge / East Couloir

EC. SE Face Direct / West Face
EC. South Face Electric Pass Peak

CATHEDRAL PEAK

44. Castle Peak

14,265 feet/4348 meters

SKIABLE VERTICAL:	4765 feet/1452 meters
ROUND-TRIP DISTANCE:	12 miles/19.3 kilometers
TRAILHEADS:	Ashcroft (9,500 feet), Castle Creek (9,900 feet).
DIFFICULTY RATINGS:	■ / ◆ / ◆ ◆
SKI TERRAIN:	Steep couloirs, steep faces, bowls, basins, and four-wheel-drive roads
OPTIMAL SEASON:	January through June. March through May are ideal.
MAPS:	Trails Illustrated Numbers 127 and 148, Hayden Peak, Pearl Pass, White River National Forest

COMMENT: An opportunity to climb and ski Castle Peak, the monarch of the Elk Range, could be one of the most incredible ski descents in a ski-adventurer's career. The views of the Elk Range are un-paralleled, and the descents offer extreme yet classic lines.

GETTING THERE
Ashcroft Trailhead (9,500 feet). From the town of Aspen, take the Castle Creek Road from the roundabout on Colorado Highway 82 on the north side of town. This roundabout is shared with Maroon Creek Road. Follow paved Castle Creek

Follow the correct turn to the right above Ashcroft to access Castle Peak.

Climbing near the summit to Castle Peak on the northeast ridge.

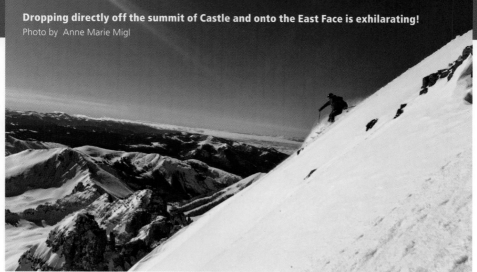

Road for 11 miles to Ashcroft. Until late April or early May, the road will only be open to Ashcroft.

Castle Creek (9,900 feet). After early May, continue past Ashcroft for 2 miles to a marked road leading to Montezuma Basin. There is plenty of parking at this road fork and an information sign marks the trailhead/road toward Pearl Pass. If you like rougher roads, turn right onto a dirt road and follow it along the creek as it winds through a small aspen forest for 0.5 mile and reaches campsites and small places to park before the road get steeper and much rougher. Depending on time of year, you can drive as far as you'd like as long as you don't value your vehicle!

THE CLIMB

Northeast Ridge (Class 2+). Before May, you'll have to park in Ashcroft and skin nearly 2 miles up the Castle Creek Road and the Castle Trailhead access road to reach the summer trailhead. From the summer trailhead at the fork in the road, follow the four-wheel-drive road for 2.25 miles to another fork at 11,000 feet, which is right after some significant switchbacks. On the way you will cross Castle Creek twice. At this 11,000-foot point the road splits; most of the tracks in the snowy months will likely head left (south) toward Tagert and Green-Wilson Huts. Take the right (north) fork and continue up into Montezuma Basin. Right below treeline you will cross into the north side of the basin, follow a few switchbacks, and take a turn to the northwest. The road then gains elevation along the south aspects of the basin and finally ends after 2 more miles at almost 13,000 feet. From a flat part of the basin, looking southwest to see Castle's summit tucked into and almost behind some peaks. Ascend a moderately steep basin to 13,400 feet where you will be able to look directly at Castle (left) and Conundrum (right). From here there is an obvious snow slope that you can sometimes skin up on the summer trail (if the snow has not been blown away by strong winter winds), and reach the northwest ridge at a notch at 13,750 feet. Follow the ridge by climbing a mix of rocks, snow cornices, and powder for almost 0.5 mile and 500 feet to reach the summit. You are off route if the terrain becomes harder than Class 3.

DESCENTS

1. *North Couloir* ■ / ◆ / ◆◆ Leave the summit of Castle skiing the first steep 250 feet by angling southeast on the ridgeline toward the top of the east face and then turning toward the northeast ridge that you climbed. Once at the top of a saddle below the summit pitch on the northeast ridge, look north down the couloir. Drop in and ski for nearly 1000 feet to 13,400 feet, then turn right and ski into the enjoyable Montezuma Basin back toward timberline and the trailhead.

2. *East Face /East Couloir* ◆◆ Head southeast for 50 yards on the flat and small summit of Castle. The east face drops immediately from the top, and is often crowned and wind-loaded, so use caution. The start of the triangular face fans out into an obvious couloir (skier's left), or out on to the direct portion of the face (skier's right). You can follow part of the south ridge of Castle (right) until some steep towers and pinnacles force you to drop in. Depending on how caked and deep the face is, you can pick any number of lines and ski down for about 1200 feet. Near the bottom of the face a big 100 to 150-foot cliff band blocks access to the valley below. To get through this portion, rejoin the East Face Couloir that started way up near the top of the face. At the bottom the narrow chute cuts through the cliff band and spits you out into the broad glacially carved basin below. The couloir will be steep and narrow at the top (up to 45 degrees) and narrows again 400 feet down before it gets wider. If you choose to stay on the face until the cliff band and head more toward skier's right, you can also wrap around the cliffs to skier's right (south) into a gully and down into the basin below. Follow the basin down the drainage into the vicinity of Green-Wilson and Tagert Huts.

ALTERNATIVES

West Face Direct ◆ Leaving the summit to the west takes you into Conundrum Basin and toward the Conundrum Hot Springs. Return down the basin by way of the Conundrum Trailhead.

King's South Notch Couloir ◆◆ Descend the northeast ridge route to the 13,750-foot notch on the northeast ridge. This is where the climber's trail on the ridge meets the ridgeline. From here find the obvious south facing King's Couloir. It's a steep and spectacular ski line fit for a king that travels to the base of Castle's east face.

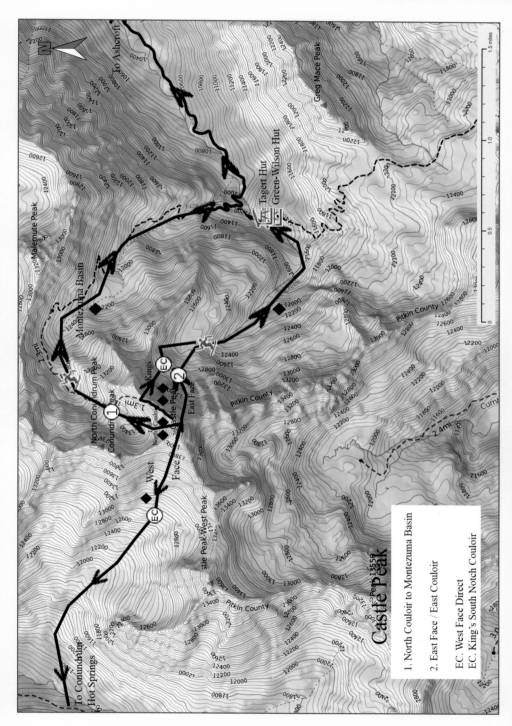

Castle Peak

1. North Couloir to Montezuma Basin

2. East Face / East Couloir

EC. West Face Direct
EC. King's South Notch Couloir

CASTLE PEAK

45. Conundrum Peak
14,060 feet/4285 meters

SKIABLE VERTICAL:	4560 feet/1390 meters
ROUND-TRIP DISTANCE:	12 miles/19.3 kilometers from Ashcroft Trailhead; 9.5 miles round-trip from Castle Creek Trailhead.
TRAILHEADS:	Ashcroft (9,500 feet), Castle Creek (9,900 feet).
DIFFICULTY RATINGS:	◆ / ◆ ◆
SKI TERRAIN:	Steep couloirs, steep faces, bowls, basins, and four-wheel-drive roads
OPTIMAL SEASON:	January through June. March through May are ideal.
MAPS:	Trails Illustrated Numbers 127 and 148, Hayden Peak, Pearl Pass, White River National Forest

Descending the steep "4th of July Couloir" with the North Face of Castle and North Couloir visible (left). Photo by Andrew Warkentin

COMMENT: The Elk Range offers so many options for the ski mountaineer. While the peaks are often skied in late winter or early spring conditions, Conundrum Peak is well known for its namesake couloir that sometimes skis very well on the 4th of July. If you are eager to ski summer snow, grab a few friends and head up Montezuma Basin to let the fun begin!

GETTING THERE
Ashcroft Trailhead (9,500 feet) See Castle Peak. Take Colorado Highway 82 to Aspen. *Castle Creek* (9,900 feet). See Castle Peak.

THE CLIMB
Conundrum Couloir (Class 3). Sometimes nicknamed the "4th of July Couloir," this couloir faces southeast but often holds excellent skiable snow from top to bottom until mid-July. Before May, you'll have to

Conundrum from the south, Conundrum—4th of July Couloir seen to the left.

park in Ashcroft and skin nearly 2 miles up the Castle Creek Road and the Castle Trailhead access road to reach the summer trailhead. From the summer trailhead at the fork in the road, follow the four-wheel-drive road for 2.25 miles to a fork in the road at 11,000 feet, which is right after some significant switchbacks. On the way you will cross Castle Creek twice. At this 11,000-foot point the road splits; most of the tracks in the snowy months will likely head left (south) towards Tagert and Green-Wilson Huts. Take the right (north) fork and continue up into Montezuma Basin. Right below treeline you will cross into the north side of the basin, follow a few switchbacks, and take a turn to the northwest. The road gains elevation along the south aspects of the basin and finally ends after 2 more miles at almost 13,000 feet. From a flat part of the basin, ascend a moderately steep slope to 13,400 feet where you will see Castle (left) and Conundrum (right). Find an obvious couloir that you can climb for 600 feet to reach the summit. Be aware of the cornices near the top of the couloir.

DESCENTS

1. ***Conundrum Couloir*** ◆ / ◆◆ Leave the summit of Conundrum by skiing the first 100 feet, angling west into the top of the Conundrum Couloir. Carefully assess the snow conditions at the top of the couloir. Once in the couloir, ski southeast down 600 steep feet to 13,400 feet, then turn left and ski through the enjoyable basin back toward Ashcroft. The couloir is about 47 degrees near the center choke and steepest portions.

ALTERNATIVES

West Face Direct Couloirs ◆◆ In a big snow year in early May there are any number of ski lines directly off the summit to the west and into the basin near Conundrum Hot Springs. For a challenging tour, ski these west lines off Conundrum into Conundrum Basin and stay overnight at the hot springs. This tour requires heavy overnight gear. Return by skiing back toward the Conundrum Trailhead.

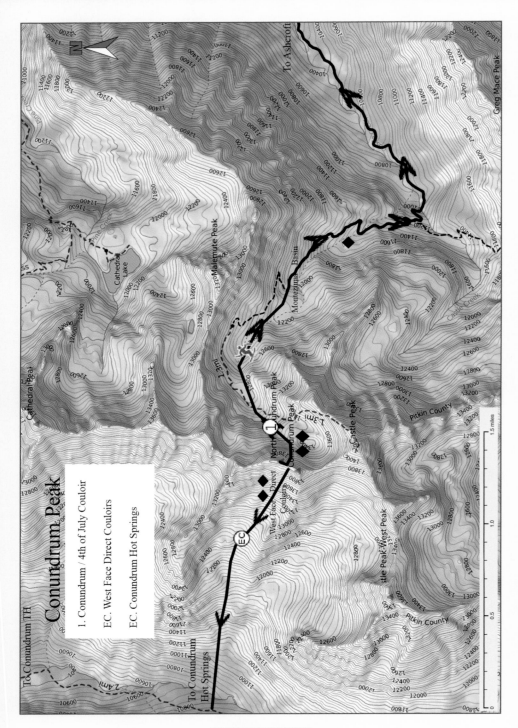

CONUNDRUM PEAK

46. Pearl Mountain
13,362 feet/4073 meters

SKIABLE VERTICAL:	4765 feet/1452 meters
ROUND-TRIP DISTANCE:	13 miles/20 kilometers
TRAILHEADS:	Ashcroft (9,500 feet), Castle Creek (9,900 feet).
DIFFICULTY RATINGS:	■ / ◆ / ◆ ◆
SKI TERRAIN:	Moderate faces, bowls, basins, and four-wheel-drive roads
OPTIMAL SEASON:	January through June. March through May are ideal.
MAPS:	Trails Illustrated Numbers 127,131, and 148, Pearl Pass, Gunnison National Forest

COMMENT: The 13er Pearl Peak is a hidden and secluded gem in the deepest corner of the Elk Mountains. It is seldom skied from its summit. While the mellower basins nearby see plenty of visitors to the nearby huts, the extra effort to summit Pearl will reward you with amazing views and great skiing! This peak is best combined with a hut trip to the Green-Wilson or Tagert Huts.

GETTING THERE
Ashcroft Trailhead (9,500 feet). See Castle Peak.
Castle Creek (9,900'). See Castle Peak.

THE CLIMB
Northeast Bowl (Class 2+). Before May, you'll have to park in Ashcroft and skin nearly 2 miles up the Castle Creek Road and the Castle Trailhead access road to reach the summer trailhead. From the summer trailhead at the fork in the road, follow the four-wheel-drive road for 2.25 miles to a fork in the road at 11,000 feet, which is right after some significant switchbacks. On the way you will cross Castle Creek twice.

Pearl's North Bowl is scenic and fun.
Photo by Anne Marie Migl

John Fielder skiing powder in the basin below Pearl Mountain near Green-Wilson and Tagert Huts.

At this 11,000-foot point the road splits; most of the tracks in the snowy months will likely head left (south) toward Tagert and Green-Wilson Huts. Continue south to the Tagert and Green-Wilson Huts and skin up the established road above the huts and into the large basin to your south. Above timberline after ascending some benches, reach a very flat area that offers great views of Castle Peak to your northwest. At 12,200 feet near a flat saddle, you will see Mace Peak to your east. Looking south from here across a broad expanse of relatively flat and barren terrain, Pearl Mountain, with its jagged northwest ridge, will beckon you. Travel south for 1 mile up a narrowing bowl toward the summit.

DESCENTS

1. *North Bowl* ■ / ◆ Leave the summit of Pearl by skiing the first steep portion, angling northwest on the ridgeline toward the top of the north bowl. Drop in and ski northeast down the bowl for 800 feet to 12,500 feet, then take a slight left turn and ski in the flatter basin back down toward timberline and the Green-Wilson and Tagert Huts. Above timberline in the basin there are unlimited options on low angle terrain.

2. *East Face Direct* ◆ ◆ Head southeast for 50 yards on the narrow and long summit of Pearl. The east face drops immediately from the top and is often wind-loaded, so use caution. Part way down the 800 foot face there are a few rocky outcroppings that you should and can avoid; these outcroppings often fracture and can be avalanche prone. The face widens near the base and skis nicely into the basin. Take a left (north) turn to ascend to the saddle between the jagged northeast ridge of Pearl and Mace Peak to ski down the drainage north into the vicinity of Green-Wilson and Tagert Huts.

ALTERNATIVES

South Face ◆ Leaving the summit to the south takes you down into the Middle Brush Creek Basin and toward Crested Butte. Combining a ski of Pearl's south aspects with a stay at the Friends Hut near timberline at 11,400 feet is a brilliant way to spend a few days skiing in this corner of the Elk Range. Consider exploring 13,500-foot Star Peak to the northeast of the Friend's Hut.

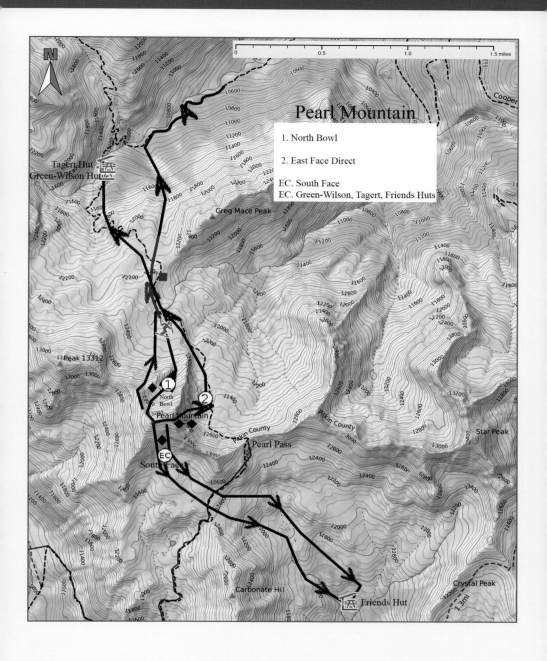

1. North Bowl

2. East Face Direct

EC. South Face
EC. Green-Wilson, Tagert, Friends Huts

PEARL MOUNTAIN

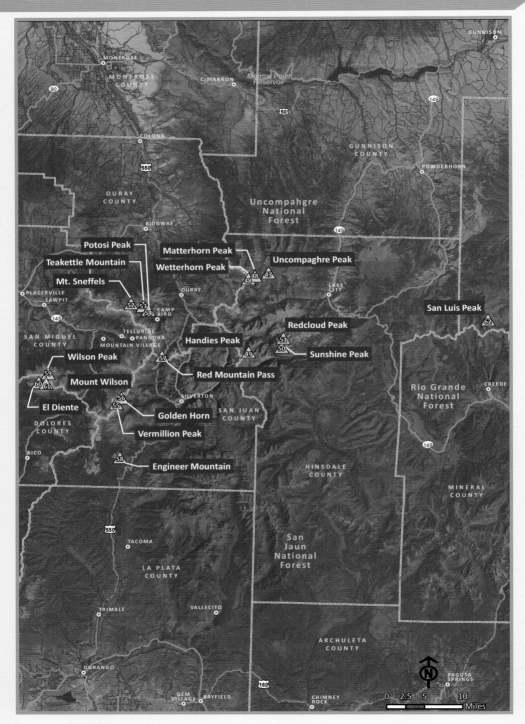

Potosi Peak

Teakettle Mountain

Mt. Sneffels

Matterhorn Peak

Wetterhorn Peak

Uncompaghre Peak

Redcloud Peak

San Luis Peak

Handies Peak

Sunshine Peak

Wilson Peak

Mount Wilson

Red Mountain Pass

El Diente

Golden Horn

Vermillion Peak

Engineer Mountain

47. Uncompahgre Peak
14,309 feet/4361 miles

SKIABLE VERTICAL:	5009 feet/1526 meters
ROUND-TRIP DISTANCE:	15.5 miles/25 kilometers
TRAILHEAD:	Nellie Creek (9,300 feet)
DIFFICULTY RATINGS:	■ / ◆
SKI TERRAIN:	Four-wheel-drive road, wide trail, tree glades, moderate faces, and couloirs
OPTIMAL SEASON:	January through May. March, April, and May are ideal.
MAPS:	Trails Illustrated Number 141, Uncompahgre Peak, Wetterhorn Peak, Uncompahgre National Forest

COMMENT: The mighty 14er Uncompaghre Peak in the San Juan Range offers a couple of excellent options on several slopes that are relatively avalanche free during most seasons. Standing on the summit clicking into your skis on Colorado's sixth highest peak feels like a true accomplishment. This is one of Colorado's finest mountains to make turns down.

GETTING THERE
Nellie Creek (9,300 feet). This trailhead is accessed from the town of Lake City. Traveling from Gunnison, take US Highway 50 west until you reach Colorado Highway 149 near Blue Mesa Reservoir. Travel south on Colorado Highway 149 for 45 miles to the scenic and isolated town of Lake City. When driving

Sunrise ascending Uncompahgre.

Powder awaits on the West Face with Wetterhorn visible in the distance.

through the small downtown area of Lake City, look for scenic byway signs pointing toward Engineer Pass. Turn right (west) onto Second Avenue and begin measuring your distance. After two blocks, turn left turn onto Hensen Creek Road (dirt). Continue to follow the scenic byway signs, leaving Lake City behind as you drive up a narrow canyon for 5.0 miles, passing the old Hensen town site at about 4 miles. Just before crossing Nellie Creek, make a right turn on Nellie Creek Road and follow this dramatically rougher four-wheel-drive road up Nellie Creek Basin. In the winter Hensen Creek Road is plowed to this junction with Nellie Creek Road where there is also camping and a pit toilet. After about mid-May, Nellie Creek Road is passable, but the distance you can drive up the road (up to 4 miles total to the summer trailhead) depends on the seasonal snowfall and melt-out situation. The ski route for this entry begins at the junction of Hensen Creek Road and Nellie Creek Road, which is where the majority of ski attempts on Uncompahgre start.

THE CLIMB

East Slopes (Class 2). The Nellie Creek four-wheel-drive road is a long ski-skin for 4 miles and 2,110 feet to the start of the summer trailhead and the Uncompahgre Wilderness boundary near timberline at 11,440 feet. Along the road you will cross Nellie Creek from east to west after about 2 miles; take a sharp left into an upper valley just after crossing the creek. Once past the wilderness boundary, travel west and into upper Nellie Basin, leaving the trees behind. The stone sentinel Uncompahgre Peak dominates the view to the west. Follow the easiest slopes up toward the peak and at about 12,800 feet turn left (south) to gain the south ridge at 13,250 feet. Follow the ridge north for 0.25 mile. Between 13,750 feet and 14,100 feet you may have to boot pack up the steepest slopes on the ridge. Avoid the steepest cliffs by climbing some steep gullies for about 100 feet on the ridge's left (west) side. By March, the snow should be settled and firm enough for kicking excellent steps in the snow. You might want crampons here. Once past the steepest portion of the small gully, reemerge on the south ridge, click back into your skis, and follow gentle slopes and the summit plateau north for 200 yards to the flat and broad summit.

DESCENTS

1. *West Face* ◆ Leave the summit to skier's right and follow the western end of the summit plateau to the edge of the cliffs. Travel south along the edge of the summit cliffs to look for your entrance onto the west face. If you bring a rope with you, it's possible to rappel into the top of the center of the west face for about 60 feet. If you choose not to rappel, sim-

Creamy turns down the West Face.

ply travel farther south along the cliffs until a steep gully allows you the choice of skiing a couple of short couloirs to access the west face. Once at the top of the face, a pair of broad gullies provides a nearly 2,000-foot ski run into the Cimarron Basin below. Once at 12,400 feet in the Cimarron Basin, you can turn skier's left and ascend the southwest shoulder of Uncompahgre for nearly 1000 feet to ski over and back down the Nellie Creek Basin to the trailhead.

2. *South Ridge /East Slopes* ■ / ◆ Leave the summit and basically retrace the route you climbed. Just below the summit ridge there is a steep but short couloir on the ridge's west side that you likely booted up; this couloir provides excellent skiing from 14,100 feet down to 13,900 feet. Just remember to stay to skier's left (southeast) of the ridge when you drop below 13,900 feet. Once you wrap back around the peak's south ridge below 13,800 feet and head east, you can drop directly into Nellie Creek Basin and enjoy easy snow slopes all the way back to timberline. Follow the Nellie Creek four-wheel-drive road back to your vehicle.

ALTERNATIVES

1. *Southwest Couloir* ◆ From 13,500 feet on the south ridge of Uncompaghre, there is a prominent notch, leading to a narrow couloir through the cliffs and then the broadening southwest face. Reach this notch by skiing the south ridge route down from the summit. Drop down this excellent ski line for almost 1,000 feet, reaching the upper portion of the Cimarron Basin. Once the descent is over, you can turn skier's left and ascend the southwest shoulder of Uncompaghre for nearly 1000 feet to ski over and back down the Nellie Creek Basin to the trailhead. Alternatively, make a long scenic loop over a 12,450-foot pass toward the southwest near Colorado's Matterhorn and down to the Matterhorn Creek Trailhead and upper Hensen Creek Road. Make your way back to the Nellie Creek Trailhead (see Wetterhorn Peak further details on traveling down the basin).

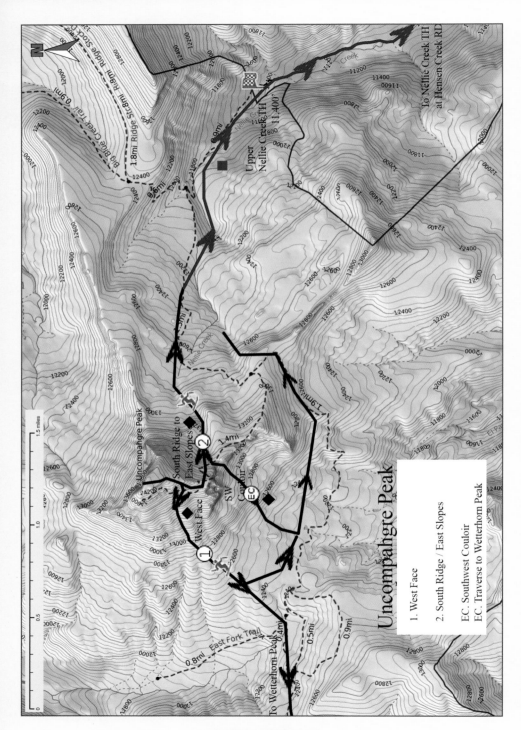

UNCOMPAHGRE PEAK

Uncompahgre Peak

1. West Face

2. South Ridge / East Slopes

EC. Southwest Couloir

EC. Traverse to Wetterhorn Peak

48. Wetterhorn Peak

14,015 feet/4268 meters

SKIABLE VERTICAL:	4715 feet/437 meters from Nellie Creek Trailhead 4315 feet/1315 meters from Capitol City Trailhead 3615 feet/100 meters from Matterhorn Creek Trailhead
ROUND-TRIP DISTANCE:	8 miles/13 kilometers from Matterhorn Creek Trailhead
TRAILHEADS:	Matterhorn Creek (10,400 feet), by May 1; Capitol City (9,700 feet), sometime in April; Nellie Creek (9,300 feet), all winter. Follow Hensen Creek Road toward Matterhorn Creek Trailhead during the winter months, typically until early May.
DIFFICULTY RATINGS:	◆ / ◆ ◆
SKI TERRAIN:	Four-wheel-drive road, wide trail, tree glades, and steep faces
OPTIMAL SEASON:	January through May. March, April, and May are ideal.
MAPS:	Trails Illustrated Number 141, Uncompahgre Peak, Wetterhorn Peak, Uncompahgre National Forest

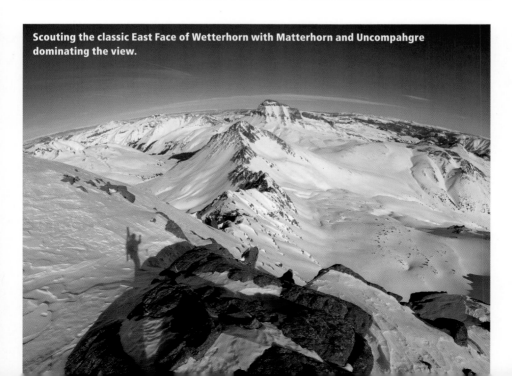

Scouting the classic East Face of Wetterhorn with Matterhorn and Uncompahgre dominating the view.

The East Face of Wetterhorn in prime conditions.

COMMENT: Wetterhorn Peak means "Weather Peak" in German. Isolated deep in the San Juan Mountains west of Lake City, Wetterhorn is relatively difficult to access in the winter, and it remains to be seen if a full ski descent from the true summit is possible, given the moderately technical and rocky nature of the 150-foot summit pitch on the peak's southeast ridge. Snow would have to entirely cover and stick to the summit pitch for it to be truly skiable. Nevertheless, the best place to start your ski descent is from the base of the summit pitch, in a flat spot near the prominent Ship's Prow. Regardless of your descent route, the snow is generally deep in the San Juans and the skiing from the mighty Wetterhorn is as good as it gets.

GETTING THERE

Matterhorn Creek (10,400 feet). This trailhead is accessed from the town of Lake City. If traveling from Gunnison, take US Highway 50 west until you reach Colorado Highway 149 near Blue Mesa Reservoir. Travel south on Colorado Highway 149 for 45 miles to the scenic and isolated town of Lake City. When driving through the small downtown area of Lake City, look for scenic byway signs pointing toward Engineer Pass. Turn right (west) onto Second Avenue and begin measuring your distance. After two blocks, turn left onto Hensen Creek Road (dirt) and continue to follow the scenic byway signs, leaving the town of Lake City behind as you drive up a narrow canyon for 5 miles, passing the old Hensen town site at about 4 miles. Reach the Nellie Creek Road at mile 5.1. In the winter Hensen Creek Road is plowed to this junction with Nellie Creek Road and there is also camping and a pit toilet here. Before April you will need to park here and continue up the road on skis or a snowmobile. After about April 10th, Hensen Creek Road is passable, but the distance you can drive up the road (up to 6 miles total to the Matterhorn Creek Trailhead) depends on the seasonal snowfall and melt-out situation. Travel up Hensen Creek Road for 4 miles to the old Capitol City town site, which is a little over 9 miles from Lake City. By early May you can turn right (northwest) on North Hensen Creek Road (FR 870) and travel 2 miles to the Matterhorn Creek Trailhead at 10,400 feet.

THE CLIMB

Southeast Ridge (Class 3). Consider using a snowmobile to avoid the 6 mile, 1,100-foot elevation gain skin on Hensen Creek Road to the start of the summer trailhead for Matterhorn Peak.. From the Matterhorn Creek Trailhead, follow a four-wheel-drive road for 0.5 mile to a forest service gate. Pass through the forest service gate and travel up to a basin and meadows after 0.75 mile. You can zig-zag up a basin to the right (north) through a few groves. Wetterhorn and Matterhorn will be visible as you exit the trees at 11,600 feet just past the wilderness boundary. From here take a direct line up some slopes in the southeast basin below the Matterhorn, but turn toward Wetterhorn once you can see the saddle on the peak's southeast ridge. You can skin all the way to the start of the southeast ridge at 13,000 feet by staying on low-angled terrain below Wetterhorn's dominating east face. Once on the ridge, travel northwest along the ridge toward the summit. In late spring, when snow conditions are the best, the steeper sections of the ridge between 13,500 feet and 13,750 feet will become steep snow climbs via some narrow couloirs. Stay to the east of the prominent Ship's Prow and climb with skis on your back up the final sections of the ridge to the base of the cliff, which seems impassable at just above 13,800 feet. The key to the summit is finding a prominent notch at the base of the southern summit cliffs. When you pass through the notch, wrap around to the left (west) and climb up 150 feet of stable rock and ice and/

Passing the Ship's Prow on the left as the ridge tops out on a small flatter snowfield.

The steep summit pitch is typically close to snow free.

or snow to the tiny flat summit. By March, April, or May, the summit pitch rock usually gets enough sunlight to become bare rock.

DESCENTS

1. ***East Face*** ◆◆ More than likely you won't be able to ski the summit pitch, so downclimb or rappel the pitch to the flat area just east of the Ship's Prow. From here you are just above the east face, which is nearly 1500 feet and is usually loaded with snow. This face is not recommended before April when snow conditions stabilize. (The author skied it once in mid-March after a week of sunny weather). The face is sweeping with a perfect line right down the center and steepness of up to 50-degrees in several places. Once down to 12,500 feet in the basin, enjoy turns in the southeast basin and ski back down the Matterhorn Basin to the trailhead.

2. ***Southeast Ridge/Southeast Basin Slopes*** ■ / ◆ Leave the summit and basically retrace your route to the southeast ridge and southeast basin slopes. Just below the Ship's Prow on the ridge skier's left there is a nice steep but short couloir angling to the south side that you likely booted up. This couloir provides excellent skiing from 13,700 feet down to 13,500 feet. Just remember to stay to skier's left (east) side of the ridge when you drop below 13,100 feet. There is also a variation higher up on the ridge at about 13,300 feet where you can ski part of the east face to get into the Matterhorn Basin. Once you wrap back around the peak's east face below 13,000 feet and head east, you can drop directly into Matterhorn Creek Basin and enjoy easy snow slopes all the way back to timberline. Follow the Matterhorn Creek four-wheel-drive road back to your vehicle.

ALTERNATIVES

1. ***Southwest Face*** ◆ From 13,750 feet on the southeast ridge of Wetterhorn, ski the broad but steep couloir that hugs the base of the Ship's Prow. After a few hundred feet the southwest face of the peak opens up. You can ski down into a basin that reaches West Matterhorn Creek at 12,000 feet. Follow the creek back down to the east to meet the Matterhorn Creek Trail in a meadow 0.75 mile above the forest service gate.

2. ***Matterhorn Peak*** ◆ Matterhorn Peak at 13,573 feet is an outstanding objective. The broad south ridge is a relatively straightforward climb and ski that rewards with incredible views of Uncompahgre to the east and Wetterhorn to the west.

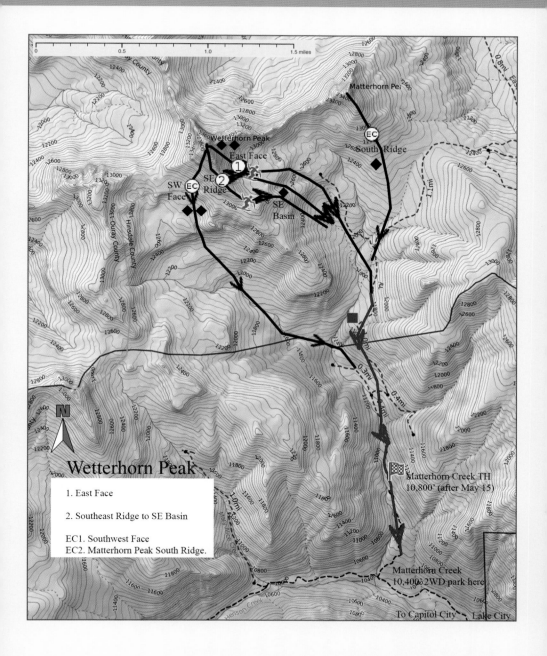

Wetterhorn Peak

1. East Face

2. Southeast Ridge to SE Basin

EC1. Southwest Face
EC2. Matterhorn Peak South Ridge.

WETTERHORN PEAK

49. Handies Peak 14,048 feet/4282 meters
50. Redcloud Peak 14,034 feet/4278 meters
51. Sunshine Peak 14,001 feet/4267 meters

SKIABLE VERTICAL:	3650 feet/1112 meters
ROUND-TRIP DISTANCE:	8 miles/13 kilometers for Handies, 9 to 10miles (16.2 kilometers) for Redcloud and Sunshine
TRAILHEADS:	Silver Creek/Grizzly Gulch (10,400 feet), by May 1; Cinnamon Pass Road junction (9,600 feet) all winter.
DIFFICULTY RATINGS:	■ / ◆ / ◆ ◆
SKI TERRAIN:	Four-wheel-drive road, wide trail, tree glades, and steep faces
OPTIMAL SEASON:	January through May. March, April, and May are ideal.
MAPS:	Trails Illustrated Number 141, Handies Peak, Redcloud Peak, Uncompahgre National Forest

COMMENT: This trio of 14ers provides excellent touring in a lost corner of the San Juans. While many people hike these 14ers in summer, winter access to these peaks is difficult but very rewarding with a little extra effort. One April I was able to ski all three peaks in a day with a small team, and we never saw another person during the entire adventure.

Ascending the east slopes of Sunshine peak on a bluebird morning.

Climbing up the East Slopes of Handies from Grizzly Gulch.

Skiing the North Ridge of Handies.

GETTING THERE

Silver Creek/Grizzly Gulch (10,400 feet). This trailhead is accessed from the town of Lake City. If traveling from Gunnison, take US Highway 50 west until you reach Colorado Highway 149 near Blue Mesa Reservoir. Travel on Colorado Highway 149 south for 45 miles to the scenic and isolated town of Lake City. Measuring from the bridge at Hensen Creek in Lake City, continue south on Colorado Highway 149 for 2.2 miles and turn right (southwest) onto Lake San Cristobal Road. The road is paved as you travel around Lake San Cristobal, but turns to dirt near the west upper end of the lake. Pass the Williams Creek Campground at 9 miles, and reach the Mill-Creek Campground bridge turnoff at 13 miles. Continue another 1.3 miles to the Cinnamon Pass turnoff (mile 14.3). Park here during winter. After mid-May, continue up the Cinnamon Pass shelf road (right) as it climbs to the northwest for an additional 4 miles to reach the trailhead, which has a pair of outhouse pit-toilets.

THE CLIMB

Handies East Slopes/North Ridge (Class 2). Before Cinnamon Pass Road is clear for driving, skin for 4 miles and 800 feet up to the start of the spring/summer trailhead for Handies/Sunshine and Redcloud Peaks at 10,400 feet. Consider using a snowmobile for easier winter access to save several hours on the approach. *Handies*: From the Grizzly Gulch Trailhead, follow a trail corridor on the southern aspects (north side of the gulch) of the basin for 2 miles to timberline at almost 2,000 feet. Continue into the upper basin up northeast facing slopes to gain a 13,460-foot saddle on Handies' north ridge. Climb south up steep slopes for 0.5 mile to reach Handies' summit.

Summit of Sunshine. Photo by Anne Marie Migl

The author skis the east aspect of the north ridge of sunshine en route to Redcloud in the distance.

Redcloud and Sunshine: From the start of the Silver Creek Trailhead, follow the trail corridor for 1.5 miles as it climbs on the north side of the creek along the south aspects. Reach a junction with the south fork of Silver Creek at 11,300 feet. Skin/climb up the south-fork trail corridor on the east side of the creek and enter a deep gully that opens up into a basin below Redcloud's west face. There are two gullies to climb from here; the northern gully/shallow couloir is steeper and more direct, while the southern gully is a bit longer from the basin but is a gentler climb to the top. Most people consider skiing the north ridge of Redcloud to skin/ski to Sunshine's summit.

DESCENTS

1. _Handies North Ridge/East Slopes /NE Couloir_ ◆ / ◆◆ Follow the gentle north ridgeline of Handies for 200 yards to where it gets steep and reach a drop off point. The north ridge face is nearly 400 feet and can be skied well. The northeast aspect of the ridge drops into a couloir (northeast couloir) that empties into the basin below Handies' east face. This couloir is not recommended until at least May when snow conditions stabilize. (The author skied it once in mid-April after a week of sunny weather). Instead, take the north ridge back to the saddle at 13,460 feet and then enjoy a gentle cruise of the east slopes of Handies into Grizzly Gulch. Once down to 12,500 feet in the basin, you can continue to enjoy turns in the basin and ski back to the Silver Creek-Grizzly Gulch Trailhead.

2. _Handies West Face/Southwest Slopes_ ■ / ◆ Leave the summit and ski the moderately steep terrain of the west face of Handies into American Basin.

Skiing into Silver Creek Basin, Handies Peak in   Redcloud's Northeast Ridge.
the distance to the east. Photo by Anne Marie Migl

For easier terrain, ski southwest off the summit. Just remember to stay to skier's right side of the basin when you drop below 13,000 feet. These descents require you to work your way down American Basin to the northeast and east to wrap back around Handies Peak heading east, and then follow the four-wheel-drive road corridor back to the Silver Creek/Grizzly Gulch Trailhead.

ALTERNATIVES

Redcloud Peak ◆ From Redcloud's summit, ski the west face gullies into south-fork basin and back to the Silver Creek Trailhead. Redcloud's northeast ridge also delivers a nice descent and a spectacular ski into the upper reaches of Silver Creek Basin.

Sunshine Peak ◆ Ski the south ridge of Redcloud Peak to reach Sunshine Peak's summit and explore the bowl/basin to the northwest of Sunshine Peak that also exits into South Fork Basin and back to the Silver Creek Trailhead.

Handies Peak /South Bowl ◆ From Handies' summit ski south along the ridge and enter an aesthetic and rarely skied bowl that descends southeast into Boulder Gulch. To return to the bottom of the Cinnamon Pass shelf road and the vicinity of Sherman, ski out of Boulder Gulch to the east via Cottonwood Creek Road on this wild and scenic tour.

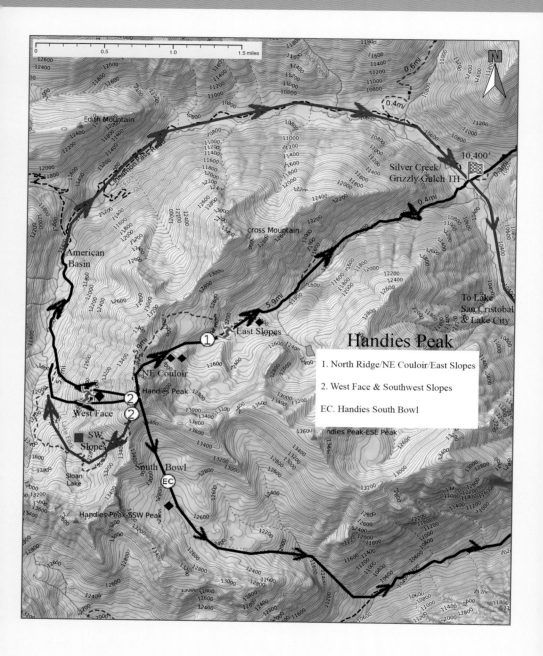

HANDIES PEAK

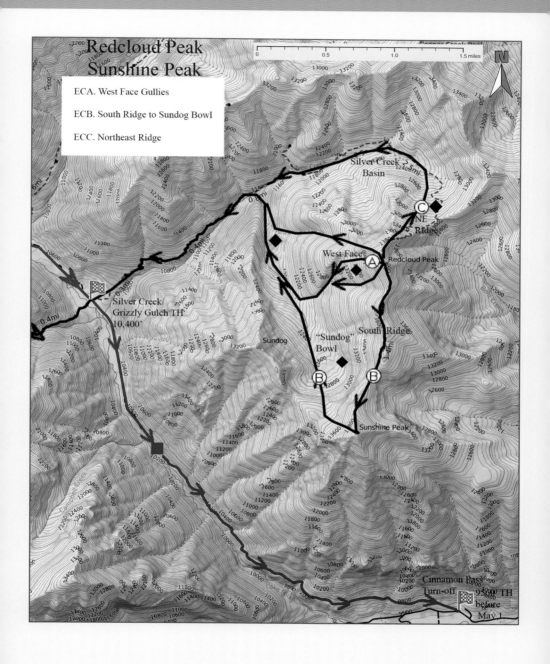

Redcloud Peak
Sunshine Peak

ECA. West Face Gullies

ECB. South Ridge to Sundog Bowl

ECC. Northeast Ridge

52. Mt. Sneffels
14,150 feet/4313 meters

SKIABLE VERTICAL:	4810 feet/1466 meters
ROUND-TRIP DISTANCE:	10 miles/16.1 kilometers
TRAILHEAD:	East Dallas Creek (Blaine Basin/Blue Lakes) (9,340 feet).
DIFFICULTY RATINGS:	◆ / ◆ ◆
SKI TERRAIN:	Steep couloirs, tree glades, and steep faces
OPTIMAL SEASON:	March through June. May is ideal.
MAPS:	Trails Illustrated Numbers 141 and 146, Mt. Sneffels, Telluride, Uncompahgre National Forest

COMMENT: This monarch of the San Juans commands impressive views from the top with ultra-classic couloir skiing. Sneffels offers several options for ambitious ski mountaineers, and the northern end of the San Juan Range gets a lot of snow that is often skiable above timberline into late June. Choose between narrow couloirs, or broad and less intimidating couloirs; there is something for everyone here.

Even on the lower reaches of the South Face Direct, the Wilsons (right-center), and Dallas Peak (right-13,809') are dramatic.

Sneffels viewed from Blaine basin to the northeast. The exit to the Snake Couloir is visible to the upper right center of the face.

The access to Lavender Col also known as Scree Col as seen from the lower East Slopes. From the col at top, the skier can chose either the East Slopes to Blaine Basin, or ski south into Yankee Boy Basin.

GETTING THERE

East Dallas Creek Trailhead (9,340 feet) (sometimes referred to as the Blaine Basin/Blue Lakes Trailhead because two trails start from here) From the town of Ridgeway, travel west on Colorado Highway 62 for 5 miles from the Colorado Highway 62/US Highway 550 junction in Ridgeway. Turn left (south) on Ouray County 7 (East Dallas Creek Road) and follow the dirt road for 9 miles to the trailhead; stay left at 0.3 mile, stay right at 2 miles, and enter the Uncompahgre National Forest boundary at 7 miles. Upon entering the National Forest, the views of Sneffels beckon. Usually by mid-April you can drive on the road until at least the National Forest boundary and may only have to skin up the road for 2 miles or less to reach the summer trailhead.

THE CLIMBS

Given the nature of couloir skiing, it is good practice to climb the line you are going to ski. Two climbing routes are discussed here that match the recommended ski lines. For both lines, follow the Blaine Basin Trail for 3 miles up the Wilson Creek drainage to a meadow at 10,800 feet. The Blaine Basin Trail crosses East Dallas Creek almost immediately upon leaving the trailhead and contours to the left toward a separate drainage. Once into the Wilson Creek drainage you will cross the creek several times before contouring past steep terrain on the east side of the basin while heading south and into Blaine Basin. From Blaine Basin you have a neck-bending view of Sneffels.

East Slopes/Scree Col (Class 2+). From the Blaine Basin meadows at 11,000 feet, climb south for 1 mile and pass underneath and to the east of Sneffels' east face.

The top of the Snake Couloir is loaded with snow!

At 12,500 feet you will reach a flat spot where you will see a few couloirs and insurmountable walls to the south, including Kismet Peak. Turn right (west) and ascend a broad snow face that steepens near the top. It is generally possible to skin zigzags about 0.75 mile up this face. At 13,500 feet you will reach the flat Scree Col, which is to the southeast of Sneffels' summit. Take another right and follow this glacial trough couloir known as Lavender Col for about 500 feet until it tops out at a prominent notch. From the top of this notch look off the other side to the north and down into the top of the Snake Couloir. On the south side of the notch, about 25 feet below the top, there is a 30 foot exit crack that you can climb and scramble to gain the finishing 200 feet along the south face. The exit crack is the route's crux and key to making the summit.

Snake Couloir (Class 3). This deeply inset couloir is one of Colorado's finest couloir climbs. From timberline in Blaine Basin climb southwest for 1 mile to the base of the north face, entering the couloir at about 13,000 feet. The first half of the couloir (500 feet) faces northeast and is steep and narrow at 40 degrees. At 13,550 feet the couloir narrows, steepens to about 50 degrees, and takes a sharp left turn. The upper portion of the couloir is less inset, faces northwest, and ends at a cliff at 13,900 feet. The cliff leads directly to the summit. From here you have two choices: 1) you can climb low 5th class rock, snow, and some ice and finish directly on the summit. In the right snow conditions, the snow cliffs can be ideal and an incredible climb is rewarded. 2) If the step finish isn't your jam, angle east for a short distance to the top of the couloir (and the ski line), meeting the top of the East Slopes/Scree Col route described above and follow that route and exit crack notch on the south side of Sneffels to the summit.

DESCENTS

1. **Scree Col to East Slopes** ■ / ◆ Leave the summit of Sneffels skiing the first steep 150 feet by angling southeast toward the Scree Col and exit crack you climbed. Once to the entrance to Lavender Col, depending on snow depth, you can choose among a few ways to get into the top of Scree Col (Lavender Col). Once in the couloir, ski south for 500 feet to 13,500 feet, then turn left turn and ski 1,000 feet of the broad but relatively steep east slopes of Snef-

fels. When you reach the basin below at 12,500 feet take another left turn and ski down into Blaine Basin and back toward the trailhead at East Dallas Creek.

2. *Snake Couloir* ◆◆ This is a fun and classic ski line in the right conditions. To reach the top of the Snake Couloir, ski off the summit to the south, and wrap around to the southeast (skier's left) to the exit crack leading to the top of the notch at 14,020 feet that marks the top of both Scree Col and the Snake Couloir. It is also possible to rappel directly off the summit to the north and down 100 feet to get into the top of the couloir. From the top of the Snake Couloir, drop in, first veering skier's left (northwest) for the first 500 feet. Before the Snake Couloir gets steep near its right turn, there is often a safe place on skier's left at about

Peering down into the Lavender Couloir from the top of the 'exit crack' on the summit ridge.

13,550 feet to stop, look down, and assess the rest of the couloir. The steepest part of the inset couloir starts here, but in the right snow, the skiing is impressive. It's a wild setting, and you are skiing down one of the finest lines in all of North America! When you finally drop into the lower 500 feet of the northwest facing couloir, you will exit onto broad slopes at about 13,000 feet and can then enjoy another 1,500 to 2,000 feet of delightful turns all the way to timberline in Blaine Basin. Follow Blaine Basin Trail along Wilson Creek back to your vehicle at the East Dallas Creek Trailhead.

ALTERNATIVES

South Face Direct ◆◆ From the 14,150-foot summit of Sneffels, ski south and take a direct line down the south face of the peak. At about 13,600 feet a series of cliffs can prove difficult, but in the deep and stable snow conditions of early May, you can choose any of 3 or 4 narrow couloirs that empty into Yankee Boy Basin to the south. If the south face is too dicey, consider skiing the Scree Col, and then instead of following the East Slopes route, ski the face below the bottom of the Lavender Col. Once into Yankee Boy Basin, you will need to ascend west to Blue Lakes Pass for 300 to 400 feet to travel down to Blue Lakes and eventually reach the East Dallas Creek Trailhead, a true circumnavigation of Sneffels.

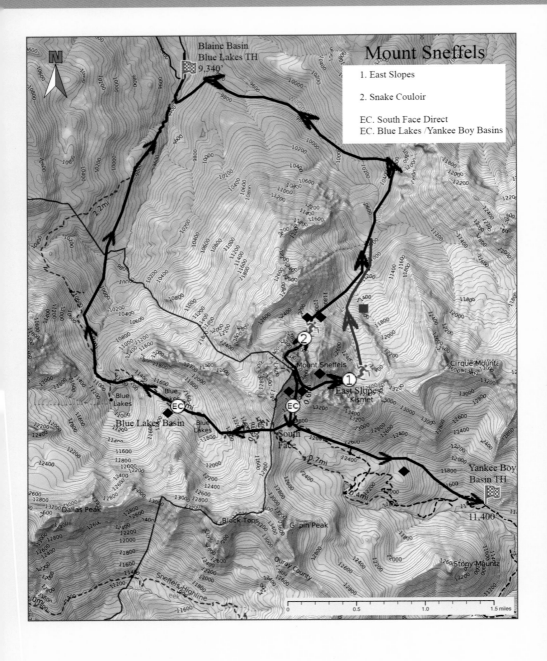

MT. SNEFFELS

53. Teakettle Mountain 13,819 feet/4212 meters
54. Potosi Peak 13,786 feet/4202 meters

SKIABLE VERTICAL:	3119 feet/950 meters
ROUND-TRIP DISTANCE:	4.5 miles/7.25 kilometers
TRAILHEAD:	Yankee Boy Basin (10,700 feet; four-wheel-drive at 11,300 feet).
DIFFICULTY RATINGS:	◆ / ◆ ◆
SKI TERRAIN:	Steep couloirs and steep faces
OPTIMAL SEASON:	March through June. May is ideal.
MAPS:	Trails Illustrated Numbers 141 and 146, Mt. Sneffels, Telluride, Uncompahgre National Forest

COMMENT: Teakettle is a 13er across the ridgeline from Sneffels. It is an iconic San Juans gem that is often admired from a distance but rarely skied. But it is quite easy to access. From the four-wheel-drive parking at 11,300 feet in Yankee Boy Basin, the peak is straight up and relatively direct to reach through a series of gullies. Potosi, Teakettle's neighbor to the southeast, boasts one of Colorado's best and relatively unknown lines: the north couloir.

Traversing a ridgeline exploring the unlimited terrain with Potosi (left) and Teakettle (right). Photo by Steve House

Heading towards the black gully along the ledges past 'Coffeepot' while ascending to Teakettle (left). Photo by Steve House

GETTING THERE

Yankee Boy Basin Trailhead (10,700 feet). This is the popular access from Ouray to Sneffels and Teakettle's south side. The trailhead is often plowed to 11,300 feet by mid-May and in some years it is kept open all year. From Ouray, follow US Highway 550 southwest above town for 0.5 mile. Turn right (south) on Ouray County Road 361, which is marked for Yankee Boy Basin. Follow 361 (Yankee Boy Basin Road) for 6.7 miles into Canyon Creek. While following the road, stay right at mile 4.7, continue west and straight at mile 6, and reach a short side road at mile 6.7 where plenty of parking is available on the left side road. The road beyond the parking at 10,700 feet becomes much rougher. Four-wheel-drive vehicles can continue right up the road for another 1 mile to the closed gate, outhouses, and parking for several cars at 11,300 feet.

THE CLIMBS

Southeast Ridge/Face (Class 5.3+). This route to the true summit of Teakettle is above class 5 only because of the 40-foot summit tower. The tower is not skiable, but many climb the tower and then rappel to the start of the gully to ski. From the 4WD parking at 11,300 feet, you can look north and see parts of the mountain. Leave the road and climb 0.2 mile north up a steep slope that takes you past the first cliff band to 11,800 feet. Next ascend another 0.2 mile north/northeast up more steep terrain until reaching a relatively flat area at 12,300 feet. From here you can see Teakettle's upper cliffs and the ridgeline between you and 13,568-foot Coffeepot to your right. Stay to the right to avoid cliff bands while ascending and follow the right side of the ridge for 0.3mi to the base of Coffeepot at 13,440 feet. It may also be possible to reach the ridgecrest slightly to the east of Coffeepot before taking a left (west) and skinning or climbing to the base of the Coffeepot. Once on the southwest side of Coffeepot you can view the rest of the route. From this point, descend 150 feet following around the south end of a cliff band that blocks a direct descent from the viewpoint. Contour northwest toward the base of what is known as the "black gully". In April or early May the snow will be firm enough for crampons, and the ski descent of this gully will be steep but good. For 300 feet climb the gully, then angle toward the western branch to exit and continue toward the summit up to the northwest through a series of small gullies that, in snow,

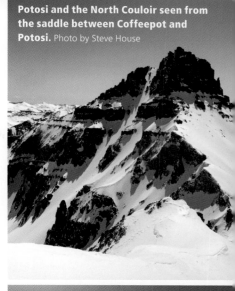

Potosi and the North Couloir seen from the saddle between Coffeepot and Potosi. Photo by Steve House

offer excellent passage for a great ski descent. Just below the summit tower, be sure to access and look through the circular 8-foot arch that is south of the summit tower; this is one of Colorado's great photo opportunities. The skiing begins from right near this location, or you can choose to climb the summit tower.

DESCENTS

1. *Black Gully/South Face* ◆ / ◆◆ Leave the summit of Teakettle by rappelling or downclimbing the summit tower. From the base of the tower click in and carefully ski the upper gullies and ledges to reach the black gully/couloir. From here descend the black gully. The lower face of Teakettle has a series of cliff bands that must be avoided by traversing skiers left to below Coffeepot. Then choose from a couple of lines, all of which lead back to the south and the trailhead. Be aware of cliff bands at 11,800 feet and make sure you know where the slopes lead so you can safely descend. In good snow years its possible to ski the south couloir from the base of the tower directly down the south face of the peak into the basin.

ALTERNATIVES

Potosi Peak, North Couloir ◆◆ From Yankee Boy Basin, climb the prominent gully on the south side to the 13,100-foot

Carving turns high in the North Couloir on Potosi. Photo by Steve House

saddle between Coffeepot and Potosi peaks. From the saddle drop in between a couple of cornices and ski a line to the north for about 600 feet, which will put you at the base of the North Couloir. From near the base of the couloir it is about 1,300 vertical feet up to a small col, where a snowy ramp wraps around the back (east side) and up to the flat but spacious summit. For your ski descent, simply retrace your route. This is a challenging day with three climbs and descents. It may be possible to ski from the southeast aspect (class 2+), but this rocky climb often doesn't hold enough snow for skiing.

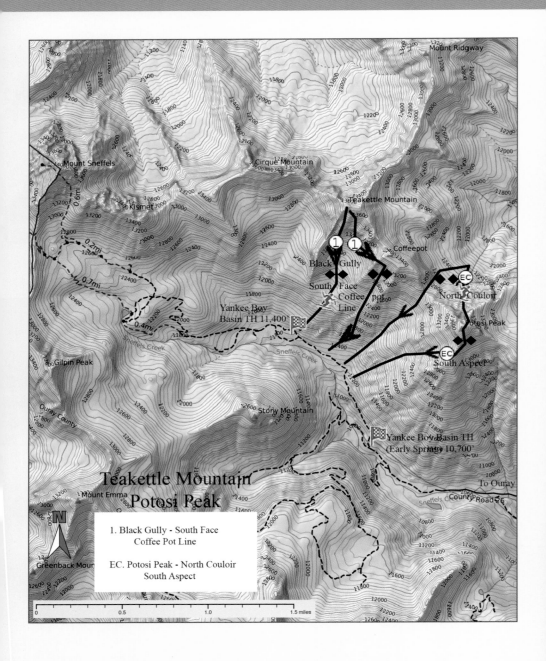

TEAKETTLE MOUNTAIN / POTOSI PEAK

55. Vermillion Peak 13,894 feet/4235 meters
56. Golden Horn 13,780 feet/4200 meters

SKIABLE VERTICAL:	4074 feet/1242 meters
ROUND-TRIP DISTANCE:	10 miles/16.1 kilometers
TRAILHEAD:	South Mineral (9,820 feet; four-wheel-drive at 10,360 feet).
DIFFICULTY RATINGS:	◆ / ◆ ◆
SKI TERRAIN:	Steep couloirs, steep faces, and open basins
OPTIMAL SEASON:	March through June. May is ideal.
MAPS:	Trails Illustrated Numbers 140 and 141, Ophir, San Juan National Forest, Uncompahgre National Forest

COMMENT: Located in a spectacular setting, Vermillion Peak is one of Colorado's most under-rated backcountry ski descents. In the summer hundreds flock to the Ice Lake Basin to see Island Lake and the stunning wildflowers, but in the winter and spring, you can approach these peaks on skis and have them all to yourself.

GETTING THERE
South Mineral Trailhead (9,820 feet). This is the popular access from Silverton to Ice Lake, Island Lake, and Vermillion's east side. From Ouray, follow US Highway

Vermillion (left) and Golden Horn (right) from the summit of Fuller Peak with the Wilson Massif in the distance.

Fuller, Vermillion and Golden Horn viewed from the east on the approach. The Vermillion Dollar Couloir is visible on the right side of the face.

550 south to Red Mountain Pass. Go 7.8 miles south on US Highway 550 from the top of Red Mountain Pass or 2 miles northwest on US Highway 550 from Silverton. Turn south on San Juan County Road 7, which is marked for South Mineral Basin. Follow 7 (South Mineral Creek Road) for 4.4 miles. You can park along the road anywhere on the straight (left) fork after 3.7 miles, up until the road ends at mile 4.4. The right fork at mile 3.7 gets steep; later in the spring four-wheel-drive vehicles can drive 1 mile from here to get up to the 10,360-foot parking on Clear Creek Road. The road beyond the parking at 9,820 feet becomes much rougher.

THE CLIMBS

Vermillion Dollar Couloir (Class 3). Climb the prominent couloir that splits the mountain's east face and tops out at a notch just 100 feet below the summit to the southeast. From the South Mineral Trailhead, travel west up the Ice Lake Basin to Fuller Lake at 12,585 feet. You will pass lower and upper Ice Lake Basins. From Fuller Lake the Vermillion Dollar Couloir will be obvious. Climb on.

DESCENTS

1. *Vermillion Dollar Couloir* ◆ / ◆◆ Leave the summit of Vermillion by skiing 100 feet to your southeast to the top of the couloir. Dropping in, the couloir is narrow and usually has a small cornice on the top. The first 100 feet is the steepest, then after 300 feet the couloir opens onto the east face. Lower down, be careful to avoid a small cliff band to skier's right (south).

ALTERNATIVES

Golden Horn ◆◆ From near Fuller Lake's north side, climb up the basin to your northwest. Some people will traverse from 13,500 feet after skiing the top of the Vermillion Dollar Couloir and take advantage of the elevation gain to climb Golden Horn's southwest ridge. From the summit of Golden Horn there are several options off the south aspect of the peak. If you are really motivated, go for the Trifecta: add Fuller Peak (13,761 feet), which is Vermillion's southern neighbor. Fuller's north face is rarely skied but offers some spectacular ski lines.

VERMILLION PEAK / GOLDEN HORN

57. Red Mountain Pass
11,018 feet/3358 meters

SKIABLE VERTICAL:	2300 feet/702 meters
ROUND-TRIP DISTANCE:	4 to 5 miles/7-9 kilometers
TRAILHEAD:	Red Mountain Pass (11,018 feet).
DIFFICULTY RATINGS:	■ / ◆
SKI TERRAIN:	Moderate faces, couloirs, tree glades, and open basins
OPTIMAL SEASON:	March through June. May is ideal.
MAPS:	Trails Illustrated Number 141, Ophir, San Juan National Forest, Uncompahgre National Forest

COMMENT: Red Mountain Pass is a relatively easy place to get to along US Highway 550. There are three cabins near the pass, all within a mile or less of the highway, which can make your adventures that much more enjoyable and accessible. See Skihuts.com for booking the Addie S, Mountain Belle, and Artist Cabins, which can be reserved for an outstanding backcountry ski experience.

GETTING THERE
Red Mountain Pass (11,018 feet). This is the popular access directly on the Pass and there is ample parking for snowmobile trailers as well. Red Mountain Pass is 10 miles north of Silverton and 14 miles south of Ouray on US Highway 550 and is open year-round.

Great views and easy access make the ski potential unlimited at Red Mountain Pass.

THE CLIMBS
Trico Peak (Class 2+). Located to the west/northwest of Red Mountain Pass, this 13,321-foot peak is climbed directly from the Pass. Travel west and northwest into a flat area of evergreens before ascending further above the trees on steeper terrain. A deep but prominent creek basin offers

a moderate snow climb from 11,600 feet for 800 feet into a hanging basin below Trico's northeast face at 12,400 feet. Approach the summit by climbing the northeast ridge. The final 500 feet to the summit are steep. **_Red Mountain Number 3 (Class 2)._** Follow four-wheel-drive roads and a series of old mining roads to the south and then circle around to the northeast. Pass Carbon Lake at 11,600 feet and continue up a prominent ridgeline to the northeast. From above 12,000 feet it is possible to skin to the summit of Red Mountain Number 3 at 12,890 feet.

There are many historical sites, cabins, and mine ruins in the area to see while ski touring.
Photo by John Fielder

DESCENTS

1. **_Trico Peak_** ◆ Leave the summit of Trico Peak by following its steep northeast ridge for 200 to 300 feet. You can choose to stay on the ridge crest or traverse skier's right (southeast) and ski a portion of the northeast face for nearly 500 feet into the gentler bowl below. The basin above treeline is gentle, but be aware of the minor cliff bands and steeper terrain to the east as you descend back to Red Mountain Pass. There are multiple options to explore here and the skiing is always tremendous.

2. **_Red Mountain Number 3 Southwest Ridge_** ■ / ◆ The southwest ridge and bowls of Red Mountain are at a relatively low angle and there are stunning mountains in all directions. Use mining roads to create excellent skin tracks and you might just enjoy this descent so much that laps in good weather and perfect snow can keep you and your party occupied all day long.

ALTERNATIVES

Red Mountain Number 3, Northwest Couloir ◆ From the top of Red Mountain Number 3, ski northwest down into the northwest couloir. This classic ski descent will take you all the way back to US Highway 550 to the north of Red Mountain Pass, but a vehicle shuttle may be required. For the even more adventurous, check out Champion Basin to the northeast off of the summit.

Trico Peak, South Face ◆ From the summit of Trico Peak's steep south face enjoy an exciting descent into Mineral Creek Basin. Be sure to traverse skier's left (to the east) on a prominent bench at 12,500 feet to get back to Red Mountain Pass. Snowmobile tracks in this area might grant you easy access back to the Pass.

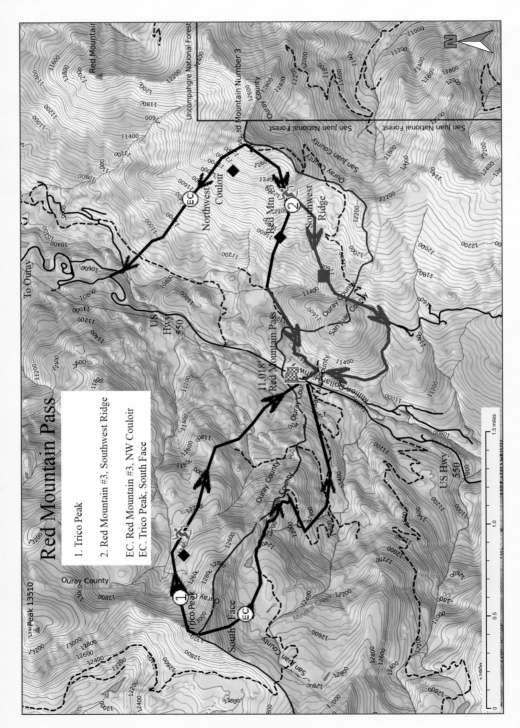

Red Mountain Pass

1. Trico Peak

2. Red Mountain #3, Southwest Ridge

EC. Red Mountain #3, NW Couloir
EC. Trico Peak, South Face

RED MOUNTAIN PASS

58. Engineer Mountain
12,968 feet/3953 meters

SKIABLE VERTICAL:	2328 feet/710 meters
ROUND-TRIP DISTANCE:	6.5 miles/10.5 kilometers
TRAILHEAD:	Coal Bank Pass/Pass Creek (10,640 feet).
DIFFICULTY RATINGS:	◆ / ◆ ◆
SKI TERRAIN:	Tree glades, open meadows, and steep faces
OPTIMAL SEASON:	December through May. April or May are ideal.
MAPS:	Trails Illustrated Number 140, Weminuche Wilderness, Engineer Mountain

COMMENT: An easy to access peak in the southern San Juans, Engineer Mountain is steep and brief, providing a very challenging ski mountaineering objective. First climbed in 1873 by H.G. Prout, the peak has been routinely climbed for decades. In 2004, Matthias Giraud ski/BASE jumped off Engineer Mountain's very steep and sheer south face cliffs—not a recommended feat, as there are excellent normal ski options.

GETTING THERE

Coal Bank Pass/Pass Creek Trailhead. This trailhead is located right at the summit of Coal Bank Pass on US Highway 550, 35 miles north of Durango and 13.5 miles south of Silverton. During winter, park at the lot on the east side of the highway at the restrooms. In the spring after snowmelt, you can also park on

Looking north on the flat slopes near Engineer Mountain into a sea of peaks in the San Juans.

Engineer Mountain and the Southeast Face ski line with reasonable coverage into June. Ideally ski the peak in prime conditions in April or May.

the west side of the highway on a dirt road near where the summer trailhead begins.

THE CLIMB

Northeast ridge (Class 3). The Pass Creek Trail begins in evergreen trees just north of Coal Bank Pass. The trail crosses an avalanche slope heading east across the slope and eventually gains the broad plateau to the north and then heads back west toward the mountain in a series of open meadows. You will see the obvious bulging prominence of Engineer's northeast ridge. Aim for the base of the ridge, skinning to its start, where you can transition into crampons on steeper terrain. Follow the ridge for 800 feet to the summit. Stay away from the north side of the ridge, as the north face drops off abruptly. There is a ridge section near 12,500 feet that requires a scramble and climb (depending on snow conditions) up a small chimney for 50 to 75 feet to stay on the ridge crest and continue to the summit.

DESCENTS

1. *Northeast Ridge/Southeast Face* ◆◆ Excellent snow coverage is a must on this very step and exposed ski descent. Leave the summit and ski the southern aspect of the northeast ridge crest for the first 300 feet to reach a very tiny flat col below the summit pyramid. Here you have two choices: 1) ski a direct line down the southeast face for several hundred feet. In deep snow you can ski through the cliff bands and onto slopes below before skiing east out onto flat portions and glades below the mountain; 2) traverse the south aspect of the northeast ridge down to 12,400 feet before skiing the lower portions of the southeast face.

ALTERNATIVES

Southwest Face ■ / ◆ Travel west/northwest from the summit for about a hundred yards and explore the southwest aspects of the peak, which get easier the farther west you traverse. There are lines here that lead down to timberline and into the Cascade Creek drainage all the way down to US Highway 550. You can also traverse just to the south of Engineers western 12,600 feet summit and ski the moderately steep west face of this sub-summit.

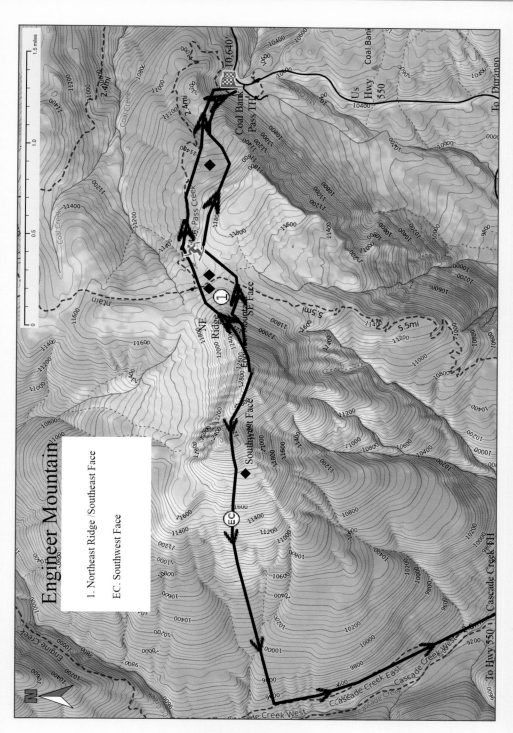

1. Northeast Ridge /Southeast Face

EC. Southwest Face

ENGINEER MOUNTAIN

59. Wilson Peak
14,017 feet/4272 meters

SKIABLE VERTICAL:	3,634 feet/1108 meters
ROUND-TRIP DISTANCE:	9.5 miles/15.3 kilometers
TRAILHEAD:	Silver Pick/Rock of Ages (10,383 feet)
DIFFICULTY RATINGS:	■ / ◆ / ◆ ◆
SKI TERRAIN:	Four-wheel-drive road, wide trail, tree glades, moderate faces, and couloirs
OPTIMAL SEASON:	January through June. April and May are ideal.
MAPS:	Trails Illustrated Number 141, Mt. Wilson, Delores Peak, San Juan National Forest, Uncompahgre National Forest

COMMENT: Wilson Peak, famously seen from Telluride Mountain Village, is one of Colorado's iconic postcard views. It's "the peak that's on the Coors beer can." The famous east face of the peak is classic, but skied by few. Wilson boasts a few ski lines that are excellent descents. Approach this peak with caution and care, but enjoy the experience of "tapping the Rockies."

Deep powder on the summit of Wilson Peak. 13er Gladstone (left), Mt. Wilson (center), and El Diente (right).

GETTING THERE

Silver Pick/Rock of Ages. Rock of Ages is a newer and slightly more scenic trailhead than Silver Pick. Rock of Ages passes the old Silver Pick Trailhead and reroutes the trail to Wilson Peak to detour around private land.

If travelling from the north or west, go 6.7 miles east from Placerville on Colorado Highway 145 and Colorado Highway 62. You can reach

The iconic Wilson Peak from the east featuring the Coors Face / East Face. Photo by John Fielder

Placerville by driving over Dallas Divide from Ridgeway. From Telluride, head west on Colorado Highway 145 from the Telluride spur roundabout. After 6 miles, turn south onto the Silver Pick Road (dirt) and cross the San Miguel River. Continue south on the road as it climbs a small canyon. At 3.3 miles stay left. At 4.0 miles from Colorado Highway 145 turn right and take the middle of three roads. At this fork there is a sign showing the correct direction toward Wilson Peak and Silver Pick Basin on road 59H. Enter the Uncompaghre National Forest at mile 6.3, stay left at 6.4 miles, and reach a flat area where the road forks again at mile 7.2. There are good campsites here and generally by May 15th the road is melted out to this point. From here, the road straight ahead (left fork) is blocked by a gate, beyond which is private property. Go right instead and continue on the road as it contours to the west. Descend to Big Bear Creek at mile 8 and reach the well-marked Rock of Ages parking area at the end of the road around mile 9.4.

THE CLIMB

Northwest Couloir (Class 3). Follow the Rock of Ages Trail (Number 429) through the woods to the west. Above timberline, the trail winds back north on a switchback, then crosses a scree slope and turns south into upper Silver Pick Basin. From 12,400 feet in Silver Pick Basin, follow the prominent creek bed by skinning up the center of the basin. You will see Wilson Peak straight ahead to your south. Ascend the north and northwest facing slopes of Wilson Peak, which are about 35 degrees. Aim for a narrowing portion of the slope and an obvious couloir to the west of the summit. Enter the couloir, which has steep walls at about 13,500 feet. Climb to the notch in the face and then head climber's left up the steeper portion of the final summit pitch, reaching the summit ridge about 100 feet from the true summit.

Looking down the Northwest Couloir.

DESCENTS

1. *Northwest Couloir* ◆ Leave the summit to the west, angle skier's right, and follow the western end of the summit ridge to the edge of the cliffs. You can retrace your steps by skiing down the west/northwest aspect of the ridge to enter the couloir. The first 150 feet are steep and narrow, but once you get to the main part of the couloir at a small flat spot below the steep cliffs, you can enjoy 200 feet of narrow turns, and at 13,500 feet open things up on the northwest face of the peak to ski all the way into the basin below.

2. *Coors Face* ◆◆ The east face of Wilson is one of Colorado's classics. A bit of careful side-slipping and traversing off the summit will eventually get you into the central narrow couloir in the face, but you can only ski this face safely and completely in a big snow year.

ALTERNATIVES

West Ridge/South Face ◆ / ◆◆ If you start very early (about 4 a.m.) you can ski Wilson Peak, El Diente, and Mt. Wilson in one 12-hour day from the Rock of Ages Trailhead. To get to El Diente and Mt. Wilson, descend the initial 150-foot summit pitch on Wilson Peak. Ski the west ridge and south aspects of the west ridge to traverse to Navajo Basin. From the true summit of Wilson Peak, you can also ski the south face of Mt. Wilson, but use caution as the face is steep, complex, and has many cliff bands. If you ski the south face, the upper Bilk Basin will leave you a long way from your vehicle.

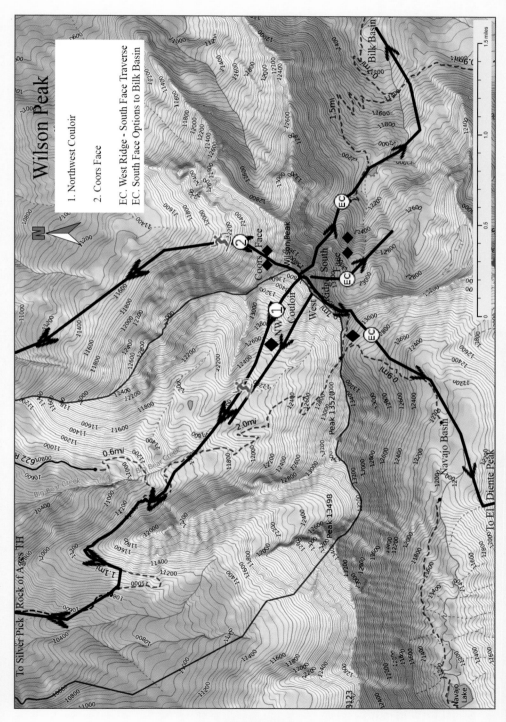

Wilson Peak

1. Northwest Couloir

2. Coors Face

EC. West Ridge - South Face Traverse
EC. South Face Options to Bilk Basin

WILSON PEAK

60. El Diente Peak
14,159 feet/4316 meters

SKIABLE VERTICAL:	5,600 feet/1108 meters
ROUND-TRIP DISTANCE:	12 miles/19.5 kilometers
TRAILHEAD:	Silver Pick/Rock of Ages (10,383 feet)
DIFFICULTY RATINGS:	■ / ◆ / ◆ ◆
SKI TERRAIN:	Four-wheel-drive road, wide trail, tree glades, steep faces, and couloirs
OPTIMAL SEASON:	January through June. April and May are ideal.
MAPS:	Trails Illustrated Number 141, Mt. Wilson, Dolores Peak, San Juan National Forest, Uncompahgre National Forest

Preparing to drop off the summit of El Diente into the Northwest Couloir en route to the Fox Face. Wilson Peak on the horizon to the left.

COMMENT: There is sometimes debate about whether El Diente—the Tooth—is an official 14er. Regardless, the ski lines on the north face are classics and will test even the most seasoned ski mountaineer. Approach this peak from Rock of Ages saddle to reach the two best ski lines on the peak for a big and rewarding day in the mountains.

GETTING THERE
Silver Pick/Rock of Ages. See Wilson Peak.

THE CLIMB
Northwest Couloir/Fox Face (Class 3). Follow the Rock of Ages Trail (Number 429) through the woods to the west. Above timberline the trail winds back north on a switchback, then crosses a scree slope and turns south into upper Silver Pick Basin. From 12,400 feet in Silver Pick Basin, follow the prominent creek bed by skinning up the center of the basin. You will see Wilson Peak straight ahead to your south. Ascend the 13,060-foot saddle to the west of Wilson Peak. From here you can see

Mt. Wilson and El Diente. Ski into upper Navajo Basin to your south and travel southwest down the basin. At about 12,000 feet, traverse along the north face of El Diente and past a significant buttress that comes down the north face. Once past the buttress, the very long north/northwest couloir comes into view. Ascend the couloir. Skin about the first 500 feet. When the steepness increases, you'll have to boot

Two climbers part way up the snowy Northwest Couloir at 13,875' just above the Fox Traverse.

pack. At about 13,200 feet it looks like the couloir will end. Turn left here and ascend an even narrower couloir for another 400 feet. This smaller couloir ends at a tiny saddle on El Diente's north face. The next feature you will traverse is known as the Fox, which is visible from a distance on El Diente's north face. Traverse the Fox to the northeast for 100 yards and gain an upper couloir for the final 300 feet to the top. The finishing couloir ends directly on the summit. Take care to not foolishly fall off the steep cornices on the north face.

DESCENTS

1. *Fox Face/Luttrell Line* ◆◆ Retrace your booted steps from the Fox Traverse. Drop into the couloir immediately below the summit and ski the narrow gully to the top of the Fox. Then traverse west/northwest across the Fox to the tiny saddle at 13,800 feet. From here ski an exhilarating 2,000 feet all the way down to the valley floor. Enjoy!
2. *Hanging Traverse/North Face* ◆◆ On descent, instead of funneling down into the Fox Traverse, traverse the north face along the ledges (the summer route) and ski east across the traverse to a small saddle at 13,900 feet. From here you can ski down the north face into Navajo Basin.

ALTERNATIVES

South Face ◆◆ From the 13,900-foot saddle described in the hanging travers route, descend the south face of El Diente, which is initially a narrow and steep snow filled couloir. This line exits into Kilpacker Basin, so plan your trailhead parking accordingly. Depending on time of year, a Snowmobile is required to reach the Kilpacker Trailhead.

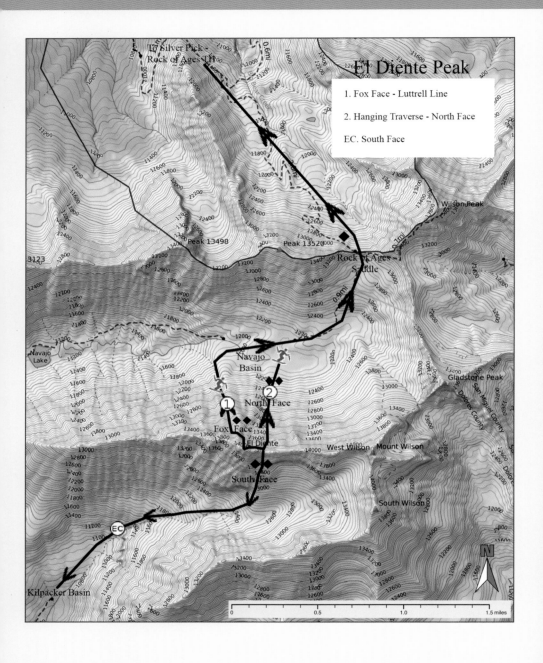

EL DIENTE PEAK

61. Mt. Wilson
14,246 feet/4342 meters

SKIABLE VERTICAL:	4,300 feet/1310 meters
ROUND-TRIP DISTANCE:	12 miles/7.5 kilometers
TRAILHEAD:	Rock of Ages (10,383 feet); Lizard Head Pass/Cross Mountain Trailhead (10,039 feet)
DIFFICULTY RATINGS:	◆ / ◆ ◆
SKI TERRAIN:	Wide trail, tree glades, steep faces, and couloirs
OPTIMAL SEASON:	January through June. March, April, and May are ideal.
MAPS:	Trails Illustrated Number 141, Mt. Wilson, Lizard Head Pass, San Juan National Forest, Uncompahgre National Forest

COMMENT: Mt. Wilson is the highest of the Wilson group of 14ers and provides outstanding lines that will test even the best ski mountaineers. In good snow years, you can ski right off the summit from the south portion of the summit block and into both Slate Creek Basin to the east and Kilpacker Basin to the west. Enjoy this peak; it's rewarding.

GETTING THERE
Silver Pick/Rock of Ages. See Wilson Peak.

Mt. Wilson (14,246') the highest summit of the Wilson Massif that includes El Diente (left) and Wilson Peak (right). All three peaks can be skied in one day with the right conditions, weather and fitness.

Cross Mountain. From 4 miles west of Telluride at the Telluride spur roundabout highway intersection, travel south on Colorado Highway 145 for 10 miles to the top of Lizard Head Pass. Continue for another 2 miles on the southwest side of the Pass. Turn right into the Forest Service parking lot located on the northwest side of the highway. You can also reach Lizard Head Pass by traveling north on Colorado Highway 145 for 10 miles from Rico. The Cross Mountain Trailhead is about 2 miles southwest of Lizard Head Pass. There is also parking with restroom facilities at the top of Lizard Head Pass, but the direct access is on the southwest side of the Pass at Cross Mountain.

THE CLIMBS

North Face (Class 4). Follow the Rock of Ages Trail (Number 429) through the woods to the west. Above timberline the trail winds back north on a switchback, then crosses a scree slope and turns south into upper Silver Pick Basin. From 12,400 feet in Silver Pick Basin, follow the prominent creek bed by skinning up the center of the basin. You will see Wilson Peak straight ahead to the south. Ascend the 13,060-foot saddle to the west of Wilson Peak. From here you can see Mt. Wilson and El Diente. Ski down into upper Navajo Basin to your south and travel south in the basin, aiming for an elevated portion of the basin that ascends toward the north face of Mt. Wilson. Climb the face and ascend a gully to your right (west) to reach a col at 14,100 feet. From this small saddle, the summit is in front of you, at the top of a challenging 150-foot steep snow and/or rock pitch to the summit.

Slate Creek /Box Car Couloir (Class 3). Follow the Cross Mountain Trail through the woods to the northwest for nearly 2 miles to reach 11,100 feet. Turn left, leaving the trail corridor, and make your way west through the forest. Your goal is to reach Slate Creek by contouring without losing too much elevation. Do not drop directly to the creek; instead, continue northwest through the forest while staying above 11,000 feet for a mile. After the final of two significant creek crossings, near 10,900 feet, exit the thick forest and continue northwest to timberline. Near 11,000 feet catch your first view of Gladstone Peak and the east side of Mt. Wilson. Leave the trees to meet upper Slate Creek.

Turn north and follow the obvious drainage up an easy headwall to reach 12,000 feet and a spectacular view of Gladstone Peak. Continue north toward Gladstone, picking your line to skin up. If your goal is to climb Boxcar Couloir, the entry is off to the left, near 12,400 feet. Otherwise, continue north/northwest toward Gladstone until you reach 12,900 feet, where you can see Mt. Wilson's east face directly to the west.

Continue west-southwest toward the east face. As you approach the difficulties of the east face, locate the summit and a small couloir (upper Boxcar

In order to get to the Boxcar Couloir, carefully ski directly off the summit for 150 feet to a small saddle just south of the summit.

Couloir) that leads up to Wilson's south ridge. This couloir is the key to gaining the ridge, just below the summit. Climb steepening snow to reach the defined couloir, near 13,700 feet. The angle of the couloir exceeds 40 degrees briefly but does not get much steeper. Climb to reach the col on Wilson's south ridge.

From the col, you can see some of the final summit pitch. Drop 10 feet into a gully on the west side, turn right at a large rock, and climb the final 150-foot pitch up steep snow in a good spring snow year, or rock in meager years, to reach the top.

DESCENTS

1. *North Face* ◆◆ Dropping off the northeast aspect of the summit block can be challenging, but is possible in deep snow conditions. After the steep initial 100 feet, aim north toward a small flat col at 14,100 feet. From here you can look down Wilson's north face for many ski options. You can funnel to your right into a narrowing gully below a broad rock tower that leads to the open north face, or you can take a skier's left onto the north face, which is steeper initially. Either option provides almost 2,000 feet of skiing into the upper reaches of Navajo Basin. Skin back up to the Rock of Ages saddle to return via the Silver Pick/Rock of Ages Trail.

2. *Box Car Couloir* ◆◆ This is the best ski line off of Mt. Wilson. Carefully ski 150 feet of the south face to reach the saddle at 14,090 feet. From this saddle, ski east and down into the upper couloir. At 13,700 feet, where the upper

Looking down into the upper reaches of the Boxcar couloir from the saddle 150 feet south of the summit. The entrance to the lower Boxcar Couloir is at the 'v-notch' in the upper center of the photo.

couloir ends and allows easy passage to skier's left into the basin below, traverse east along the north aspect of the slope and enter the aesthetic Boxcar Couloir. The couloir is wider at the top and then about 200 feet down it narrows into a box-canyon or box-car style opening for a short distance. At 12,900 feet it opens up into the upper Slate Creek Basin. Enjoy wide turns as the Slate Creek Basin angles southeast and then south down to timberline. Once in the trees, you will have to ascend a few hundred feet in the timber (east/southeast) skier's left to reach the Cross Mountain Trail corridor, which provides an easy ski for 1.5 miles back to the Cross Mountain Trailhead.

ALTERNATIVES

Kilpacker Basin ◆◆ Mt. Wilson's Kilpacker Y Couloir has two arms that meet just to the west of Mt. Wilson's summit at 13,500 feet. For the south arm, which is west facing, carefully ski 150 feet from the summit of the south face to reach the saddle at 14,090 feet. Instead of skiing east into the Box Car Couloir, ski west into a 35 to 40 degree couloir. After the first 150 feet make sure to stay skier's right (a bit northwest) and down to meet the northern arm of the couloir (skier's left near the top is cliffed out). At 13,400 feet, ski back to your southwest and open things up into Kilpacker Basin. For the north arm of this couloir, descend off the summit to the northeast (combo Number 1 above), staying on the east side of the north ridge. After the steep initial 100 feet, aim north to a small flat col at 14,100 feet. From this col, a southwest descent into the northwestern arm of this couloir is steep and obvious, and exhilarating. At 13,500 feet you'll meet the south arm of the couloir. This line exits into Kilpacker Basin, so plan your trailhead parking accordingly.

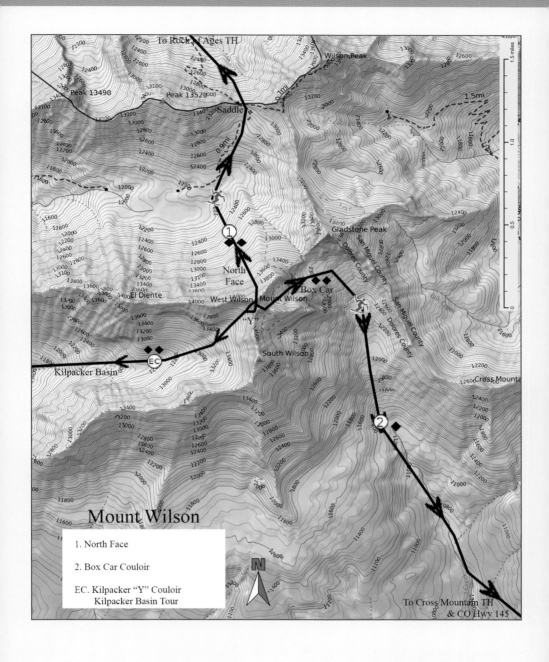

Mount Wilson

1. North Face

2. Box Car Couloir

EC. Kilpacker "Y" Couloir
   Kilpacker Basin Tour

MT. WILSON

62. San Luis Peak
14,014 feet/4271 meters

SKIABLE VERTICAL:	4500 feet/1372 meters
ROUND-TRIP DISTANCE:	Up to 18.5 miles/30 kilometers
TRAILHEAD:	Allens Crossing (10,500 feet); West Willow Creek (11,000 feet)
DIFFICULTY RATINGS:	■ / ◆
SKI TERRAIN:	Four-wheel-drive road, wide trail, tree glades, moderate faces, and couloirs
OPTIMAL SEASON:	January through May. March, April, and May are ideal.
MAPS:	Trails Illustrated Number 139, San Luis Peak, Stewart Peak, Gunnison National Forest

COMMENT: San Luis Peak in the San Juan Range is the most isolated 14er but provides a spectacular spring skiing tour in a wild and scenic setting. Use snowmobiles to the La Garita Wilderness boundary just beyond the Equity Mine in the West Willow Creek drainage to shorten this approach to the peak.

San Luis from the 12,300' ridgeline near the Colorado Trail. The Southwest Face/Yawner Gullies and South Ridge are clearly visible.

GETTING THERE

West Willow Creek (10,500 to 11,000 feet). This trailhead is accessed from the town of Creede on Colorado Highway 149. On the west and southwest side of town in Creede on Colorado Highway 149, look for three roads leading west (right). Turn west onto the northernmost of the three roads, which is initially paved. Follow the road as it ascends above Creede and passes the Creede cemetery at 0.5 mile. Turn left (west) at a T-junction at 1.2 miles. The road turns to dirt and passes the southern turnoff for the Rat Creek/West

The South Ridge of San Luis near the summit. The Southwest Face/Yawner Gullies ski line drops off to the left.

Willow Creek four-by-four loop road at 3.3 miles and reaches Allens Crossing over West Willow Creek at mile 6.3. The road will be plowed in the winter to just beyond Allens Crossing, marking the winter trailhead at 10,500 feet. There is adequate parking here, including for snowmobile trailers. After mid-May, turn left (north) and continue up the road for another 2.3 miles to parking near the Equity Mine at 11,000 feet. In a four-wheel-drive vehicle you can continue up the road for an additional 1 mile, but the road is rough and must be snow free.

THE CLIMB

South Ridge or West Face (Class 2). From near the Equity Mine, go north on the Rat Creek/West Willow Creek four-wheel-drive road for 1.5 miles to 11,500 feet. In March and April, the road will likely be packed down by snowmobile tracks and/or a snow cat. Before the road leaves the valley and heads steeply to the west, continue north into the basin. Even when snow covered, you might be able to see remnants of an old four-wheel-drive road that crosses Willow Creek on its east side and then fades away as it climbs up a shoulder to the northeast toward a saddle to the right of Point 12,540. Southeast of Point 12,540, after another 1.5 miles, you will arrive at a 12,300-foot saddle near the Colorado Trail (identified by one or two wooden poles marking the trail along the tundra). While standing on the saddle, look to the northeast and get your first glimpse of San Luis. Pull skins and descend into the basin to your north and northeast. Be aware of the snow-loaded cornice along the saddle's eastern ridgeline, which might have to be avoided by skiing initially to the northwest and then dropping into the basin and heading east. When you descend to your east and get to timberline, you have two choices:

1) Follow the Colorado Trail by skiing east into an 11,900-foot low point in some timber. Skin and climb back up to the east toward a basin and reach a saddle at 12,400 feet in the upper Spring Creek drainage. Continue east as it contours around a second basin, then ascend north to a 12,620-foot saddle between San Luis Peak and Point 13,155 feet, which is the start of the south ridge of San Luis, 1.5 miles from the summit. Skin/climb the final 1.2 miles of the south ridge to reach the summit.

2) From timberline to the northeast below the 12,300-foot saddle, continue to ski northeast down into the upper Spring Creek drainage. Descend to 11,200 feet and contour around the north end of Point 12,562 to the base of San Luis' southwest face. Boot pack up the face and choose one of the three "yawner gullies." The southernmost gully follows the best classic ski line directly to the summit. The central gully is not quite as steep (about 30 degrees) and reaches the western ridgeline of San Luis. See you on the summit!

DESCENTS

1. *Southwest Face/Yawner Gullies* ◆ Leave the summit directly to the southwest to ski the 35 to 38 degree southernmost yawner gully. This classic line is fun and not as steep as it looks. If you drop right off the top of the peak, you will achieve close to 3,000 feet of vertical skiing all the way to the trees in the basin below. If you don't want to ski quite as steep terrain, consider either the central or northern yawner gully, which can be accessed from the western flank of San Luis' summit ridge. Once back in the basin, skin west then southwest back up to the 12,300-foot saddle near the Colorado Trail, then return to the Equity Mine/Allens Crossing Trailheads by skiing south back down the Willow Creek Basin.

2. *South Ridge* ■ / ◆ Ski south from the summit along the ridgeline, which is sharp and narrow initially but becomes broad and safe from avalanche danger after about 200 feet. This is likely the easiest and safest ski line off the peak. Retrace your skin tracks to traverse and return back to the 12,300-foot saddle toward Equity Mine/Allens Crossing on this excellent ski tour.

ALTERNATIVES

East Face/Stewart Creek Drainage ◆ Leave the summit to the east and ski several hundred feet of excellent terrain. Traverse to the east then northeast to drop into the Stewart Creek drainage. This basin funnels down to the Stewart Creek Trailhead after 6 miles. This trailhead is accessed from Gunnison and can be approached with snowmobiles. The road will be clear by early June. (This is the east slopes standard climbing route for San Luis Peak in the summer).

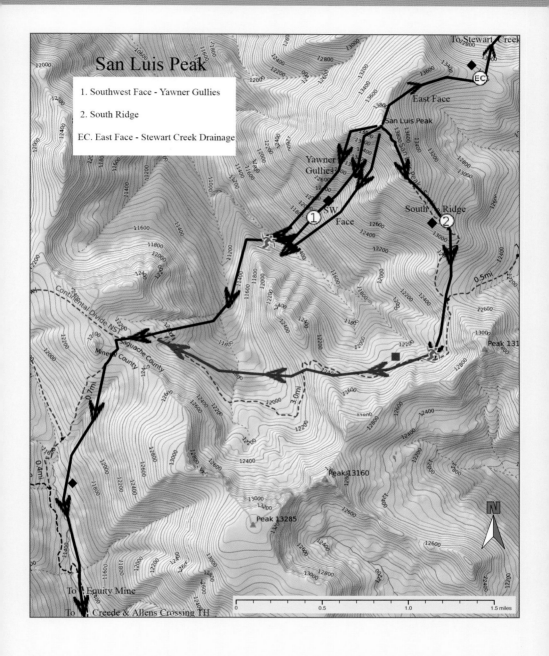

San Luis Peak

1. Southwest Face - Yawner Gullies

2. South Ridge

EC. East Face - Stewart Creek Drainage

SAN LUIS PEAK

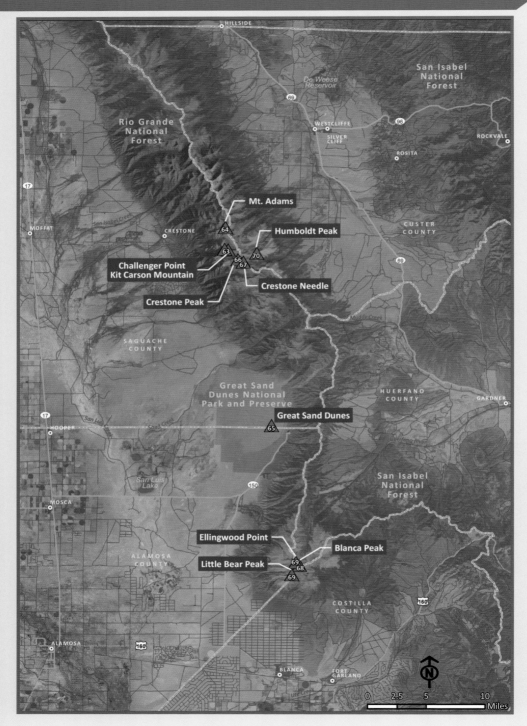

Mt. Adams

Humboldt Peak

Challenger Point
Kit Carson Mountain

Crestone Needle

Crestone Peak

Great Sand Dunes

Ellingwood Point

Blanca Peak

Little Bear Peak

63. Kit Carson Peak
14,165 feet/4317 meters

SKIABLE VERTICAL:	5905 feet/1800 meters
ROUND-TRIP DISTANCE:	11 miles/17.75 kilometers
TRAILHEAD:	Spanish Creek (8,260 feet)
DIFFICULTY RATINGS:	◆ / ◆ ◆
SKI TERRAIN:	Narrow trail, downed timber, tree glades, steep faces, and couloirs
OPTIMAL SEASON:	January through May. April and May are ideal.
MAPS:	Trails Illustrated Number 138, Crestone, Crestone Peak, San Isabel National Forest

COMMENT: Kit Carson Peak in the Sangre de Cristo Range is a 14er that is steep on all sides. The famous Prow is a well-known and sharp rock buttress that gives the Kit Carson massif a distinct shape when viewed from the San Luis Valley. Kit Carson Peak includes Challenger Point to the west (14,081 feet) and Kat Carson to the east, which is only a shade below 14,000 feet. The Sangre de Cristos can be very windy, dry, and bitter cold in the winter. Strong winds that scour the peak above timberline keep it almost devoid of snow for most of the winter season. Therefore, the best way to descend this peak is from several couloirs that hold snow.

GETTING THERE
Spanish Creek Trailhead
(8260 feet). Only a few miles south of the town of Crestone, this trailhead is on private property, but with proper Leave No Trace ethics, permission to use the trailhead from the parking area is permitted. From the North (Salida), drive over Poncha Pass by traveling south on US Highway 285.

Approaching Kit Carson and the Prow from the southwest in the Spanish Creek drainage.

Steep and technical conditions at 13,500' leading into the South Couloir. Crestone Peak's north couloir provides the backdrop.

Climbing close to the top of the OB Couloir and past the cornice that guards the top. Photo by Garrett Eggers

From the US Highway 285/Colorado Highway 17 junction, take Colorado Highway 17 south for 13.8 miles, passing through the small town of Moffat. When you are 0.4 mile south of Moffat, turn left (east) on a paved road, and head toward the town of Crestone. From Alamosa in the south, travel north on Colorado Highway 17 and travel through the town of Hooper. From the Colorado Highway 112/Colorado Highway 17 junction in Hooper, drive 16.8 miles and turn right (east) on the paved road from Moffat. Travel 12 miles east to the entrance of the Baca Grande Chalets Grants.

Turn right (south) into the Baca Grande Chalets Grants following the paved Camino Baca Grande. If you somehow end up in the town of Crestone, you missed this turn. Proceed south, crossing Crestone Creek at 0.8 mile, and cross Willow Creek at 2.2 miles. The road will turn to dirt after 3.5 miles at Spanish Creek and the trailhead. There is parking on the north and south side of the creek. The trailhead begins on the north side of the creek heading east.

Willow Creek Trailhead (8900 feet). From the center of the town of Crestone, take Galena Street east, following a dirt road for 2.3 miles to the well-marked trailhead (also called North Crestone Trailhead) and pit toilet.

APPROACH

Spanish Creek. Travel 3.5 miles, initially along the north side of Spanish Creek. The trail is often difficult to follow but crosses the creek a few times. Stay on the south side of the creek at the mouth of the canyon to gain passage into the lower valley. Approaching 10,000 feet, you will cross over to the north side of the creek, reach a burn area, and then get into the upper basin where the valley opens up and flattens out at 10,500 feet. Above 10,500 feet Kit Carson and the Prow come into view. Travel up to about 11,000 feet near timberline and find meadows, which provide a safe haven for winter camping as well as some great views of Kit Carson to the northeast and Crestone Peak to the southeast. The toughest part of this approach can often be the downed timber, especially when the snow isn't very deep.

THE CLIMB

South Couloir (Class 3, moderate snow).

Once you travel east through the trees and reach timberline at 11,800 feet, Kit Carson will be directly north of you. On gentle slopes that get steeper, you can skin up the basin toward the narrow inset couloir. At a couple hundred feet below the base of the couloir, transition to carrying your skis on your back and boot packing. As you head north the couloir angles slightly to the northeast and climbs from 12,250 feet to 13,620 feet. In ideal conditions, ascend to the 13,260-foot saddle between Kit Carson and Kat Carson. With enough snow, you can leave the couloir early and climb north and west in a broader class 3 snow-filled gully, just below the saddle, toward the summit ridge. Gain the summit ridge and climb west for 150 yards to the small summit.

DESCENT

1. **South Couloir** ◆ / ◆◆ This narrow ski line is usually in the best condition by mid-May. Catching the south couloir in December or January in a low snow year can also eliminate avalanche danger. Always be aware of potential

Getting ready to carefully ski right off the top of Kit Carson. Blanca Massif in the distance.

Quick precise jump turns are required through the narrow 'finger' sections of the South Couloir.

Ascending the steep and narrow South Couloir

Big turns with a view down into the San Luis Valley before the South Couloir narrows at 13,400 feet.

avalanche hazards at the top of this route. Snow near the summit ridge and in the highest parts of the upper gullies above 14,000 feet can create large crowns, especially 24 to 48 hours after a big storm. If you trigger a slide, it will funnel all the way down the couloir. Most of this route never exceeds 40 degrees, and strong ability to jump turn in the narrow portions of the couloir is an asset. Once leaving the couloir at the bottom, turn west into Spanish Creek Basin and follow your skin tracks back to the Spanish Creek Trailhead.

ALTERNATIVES

Outward Bound Couloir ◆◆ (If you chose to ski the north side of Kit Carson a vehicle shuttle may be necessary): From the 13,620-foot connecting saddle between Kit Carson and Kat Carson, ski north down the steep and narrow Outward Bound Couloir (**A**). Unfortunately, this option takes you north and into the Willow Creek Basin, but the deep inset ski line is extreme and rewarding. From the base of the route ski west out of Willow Creek Basin passing Willow Lake and down to the Willow Creek Trailhead at 8900 feet, which is 2.3 miles east and southeast of the town of Crestone on Galena Street. Alternatively, ski the Kirk Couloir (**B**), which is the steep chute leading north and down from Challenger Point and the Kit Carson connecting saddle at the end of the ledge known as Kit Carson Avenue.

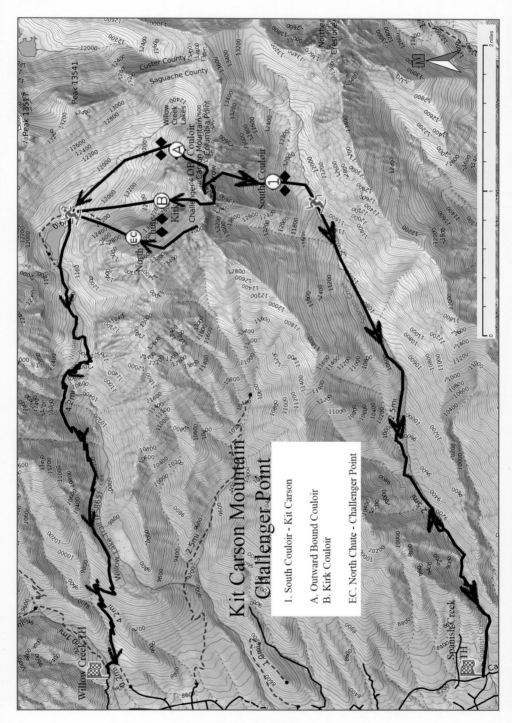

Kit Carson Mountain – Challenger Point

1. South Couloir - Kit Carson

A. Outward Bound Couloir
B. Kirk Couloir

EC. North Chute - Challenger Point

KIT CARSON PEAK

64. Mt. Adams
13,931 feet/4246 meters

SKIABLE VERTICAL:	5031 feet/1533 meters
ROUND-TRIP DISTANCE:	10 miles/16.1 kilometers
TRAILHEAD:	Willow Creek/South Crestone (8,900 feet)
DIFFICULTY RATINGS:	◆ / ◆ ◆
SKI TERRAIN:	Narrow trail, tree glades, steep faces, and couloirs
OPTIMAL SEASON:	February through May. April and May are ideal.
MAPS:	Trails Illustrated Number 138, Crestone, Crestone Peak, Horn Peak, San Isabel National Forest

COMMENT: The Sangre de Cristo's northernmost Centennial 13er, Mt. Adams is a relatively obscure and unknown peak for most mountaineers. It's tucked away only about 2 miles north of Kit Carson, but visited by few. Winter access up Willow Creek is straightforward and the peak has at least four major aspects to ski off of in all directions from the top (west, southwest, east, and north).

Near the summit of Adams which provides some aesthetically pleasing ski aspects in good snow years, most recently in the spring of 2016 and 2017. Photo by Ben Conners

GETTING THERE

Willow Creek Trailhead/South Crestone Trailhead (8900 feet). From the center of the town of Crestone, take Galena Street east, following the dirt road for 2.3 miles to the well-marked trailhead (also called North Crestone Trailhead) and pit toilet. Usually the snow is melted out to the trailhead by late March or early April, and you can drive to within 0.5 mile of the trailhead year-round.

THE CLIMBS

West Ridge (Class 2+). From the South Crestone Trailhead, hike east for 100 yards, turn right (south), cross the creek in the woods, emerge in a meadow, and turn left. Follow the

Descending a couloir towards Willow Lake as a storm approaches.

sandy trail through an initial meadow and the start of the Willow Creek Trail. Hike or skin up the very well defined Willow Lake Trail for 3.5 miles. The trail climbs up a gorgeous basin and you will enter a hanging valley above the gorge and flatter terrain before reaching Willow Lake. About 100 yards below Willow Lake, there is a creek basin that empties into Willow Creek. Follow this creek north as it leaves the timber and gains 600 feet to a small basin under Adam's southwest face at 12,200 feet. Continue north across the basin for 0.5 mile and up to a 12,900-foot saddle west of Adams. Follow the ridge for another 0.5 mile and 1,000 feet to the east and to the summit. Where the ridge is too sharp, traverse easier ledges on the ridge's right (south) side. The final summit pyramid is steep and can be climbed directly up a small couloir on the southwest face, or circle around to the east side of the summit and climb to the top.

West/Northwest Face (Class 2+). From the South Crestone Trailhead, continue straight (east) and follow the Crestone Lake Trail. Cross to the south side of Crestone Creek and then back to the north side of the creek after 3 miles. You will reach South Crestone Lake at 11,780 feet after 3.5 miles. From the lake you will see the west/northwest face of Mt. Adams. Follow the valley southeast for 1 mile to the base of the face at 12,400 feet. Finally, after several hours of approach, climb the center of the west face for 1,500 feet to a small cliff band just below the summit. Navigate the cliff band to the north to gain the ridge, or climb it direct in a good snow year.

Skiing the east face before funneling into the "Sam Adams" Couloir. Left to right: Humboldt Peak, Crestone Needle and Peak adds to the allure. Photo by Ben Conners

DESCENTS

1. **_Southwest Face_** ◆ / ◆◆ Follow a short portion of the summit ridge south to gain access to the southwest face. The initial drop to the face requires you to carefully ski a steep couloir for 100 feet; then the face opens up at angles of less than 40 degrees. You can also choose to stay in the couloir/gully in the center. Ski back to the south into the basin and eventually back to Willow Lake.

2. **_West Face/northwest aspect_** ◆ The northwest aspect of the west face is a safe spring option, especially considering the long approach and the extra time to allow the snow to soften. This option not as steep as the southwest face or the east side of the mountain. Ski off the summit slightly to the north, then take a left (west) turn and drop into the face. The northwest aspect of the face will hug cliff bands above you as you descend, making for an aesthetic ski. Descend to South Crestone Lake.

ALTERNATIVES

East "Sam Adams" Couloir ◆◆ This east-facing line is rarely skied and needs a heavy snow year for clean passage into the couloir. May storms in 2014, 2015, and 2016 all miraculously delivered enough snow to allow for complete ski descents. The very steep east face is initially 40 degrees, and the first 400 feet of the upper portion of the face funnels down into the only reasonable exit couloir. Ski this line down to Horn Lakes to the east and the Rainbow Trailhead.

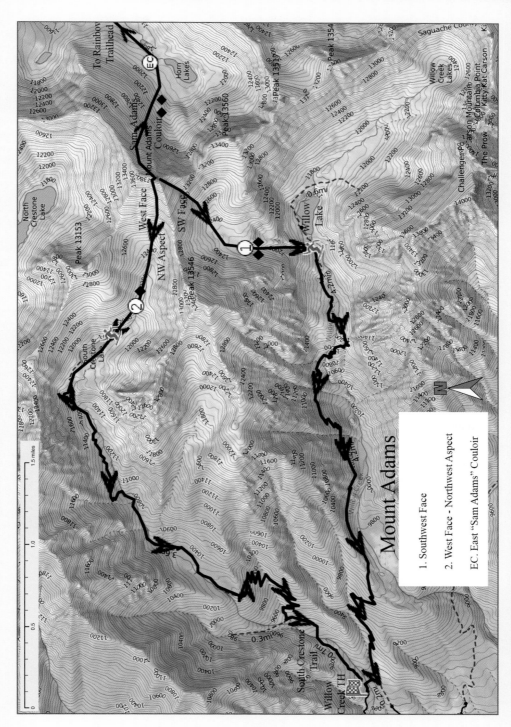

Mount Adams

1. Southwest Face

2. West Face - Northwest Aspect

EC. East "Sam Adams" Couloir

MT. ADAMS

65. Great Sand Dunes National Park
8,175 feet/2492 meters

SKIABLE VERTICAL:	755 feet/230 meters
ROUND-TRIP DISTANCE:	1 to 2 miles/0.6-1.2 kilometers
TRAILHEAD:	Visitor Center (8,175 feet)
DIFFICULTY RATINGS:	■
SKI TERRAIN:	Sand dune skiing, sand boarding, and sand sledding
OPTIMAL SEASON:	Year round in mornings when the sand is coolest. On some occasions, ski on snow on top of sand after the rare large snowstorms occur.
MAPS:	Trails Illustrated Number 138, Great Sand Dunes National Park Map

COMMENT: If you ever have a chance to visit the Great Sand Dunes on the west side of the Sangre de Cristo Range in the San Luis Valley, consider taking your skis or a snowboard! There are many options available for sand boarding or sand sledding. North America's tallest sand dunes are calling, and this is a great way to expand your ski experience with a true novelty.

Charlie Ziskin skiing the dunes at Castle Creek. Photo by Peder Hans Engebretsen

THE CLIMB

While the popular Star Dune (755 feet) and High Dune (699 feet) are two of North America's tallest dunes, the approaches are long and flat, with short runs steep enough to ride off the summits. The sand in Great Sand Dunes National Park is slower than snow and behaves much differently. Use skis with sintered bases and strip off all your wax. The sand will not harm your skis. Skiing uphill is just like skinning. Despite the attraction of the tallest dunes, the best ski descents are found on sustained pitches of 400-500 feet at Castle Creek, about 3 miles north of Pinon Flats Campground on the Primitive Road. For more information on skiing, boarding, or sledding at Great Sand Dunes National Park, visit www.nps.gov/grsa/planyourvisit/sandboardingsandsledding.htm.

Peder Hans Engebretsen skiing the dunes at Castle Creek. Photo by Charlie Ziskin

DESCENTS

The dune directly above the Castle Creek picnic area is a 34-37 degree face of about 400-450 vertical feet, varying a bit as the dunes change shape. The next dune to the north can be as much as 100 feet taller. Go straight down until you feel your momentum overcome the additional friction of sand before you start turning. Don't finish your turns until the last one at the creek, as the transition

Charlie Ziskin skiing the dunes at Castle Creek. Photo by Leif Brown

from 34 degrees to 0 is rather abrupt. Wet sand is faster but hot, dry sand sings when you ski over it. You might want to consider carrying some cold beverages to stay hydrated and toast to this adventure before dropping in!

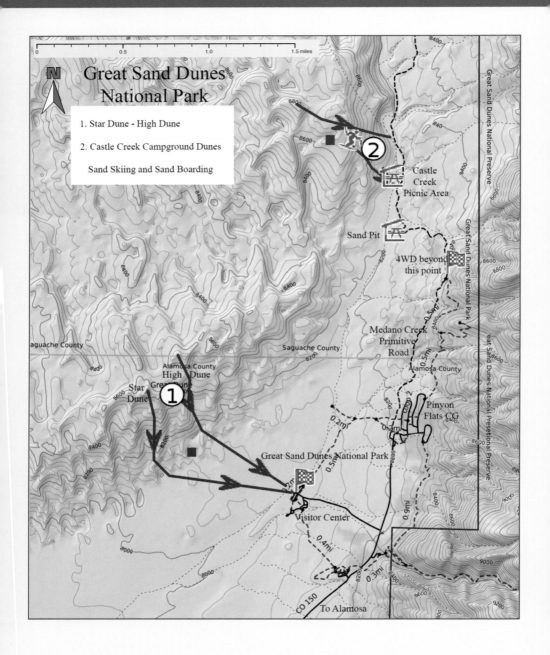

Great Sand Dunes
National Park

1. Star Dune - High Dune

2. Castle Creek Campground Dunes

Sand Skiing and Sand Boarding

GREAT SAND DUNES NATIONAL PARK

66. **Crestone Peak** 14,294 feet/4357 meters
67. **Crestone Needle** 14,197 feet/4327 meters

SKIABLE VERTICAL:	6114 feet/1864 meters
ROUND-TRIP DISTANCE:	17.5 miles/28.2 kilometers (Crestone Peak); 15.5 miles/25 kilometers (Crestone Needle)
TRAILHEAD:	South Colony (8,780 feet)
DIFFICULTY RATINGS:	◆ / ◆ ◆
SKI TERRAIN:	Four-wheel-drive trail, tree glades, steep faces, and couloirs
OPTIMAL SEASON:	February through May. April and May are ideal.
MAPS:	Trails Illustrated Number 138, Crestone, Crestone Peak, San Isabel National Forest

COMMENT: While Crestone Peak and Crestone Needle in the Sangre de Cristo Range are known for their conglomerate rock and challenging climbing in the summer, they are not-to-be-missed ski mountaineering experiences in the snowy months. The steep couloirs fill with snow in good years, and the lines become ultra-classic in the right conditions.

GETTING THERE

South Colony Trailhead (8780 feet). From the Shell gas station on the south end of Westcliffe, travel south on Colorado Highway 69 for 4.5 miles. Turn right (south) on Colfax Lane and follow the road as it turns to dirt for 5.5 miles to a T-junction. Turn right (west) and follow the road as it ascends the valley. There is a parking area 1.5 miles from the T-junction turn. Passenger cars will need to park here. In winter months up until about April, the road is impass-

Crestone Peak's 2,000 foot long classic South Red Gully Couloir.

A storm approaches while skiing the Red Gully on Crestone Peak.

able once you enter the trees 1 mile beyond this parking area. In mid- to late May, depending on snow conditions, you can travel up to another 2.7 miles on the road and into the San Isabel National Forest (1.4 miles up) and to the South Colony Trailhead beyond. Do not park along the road on private property below the National Forest boundary. The road is generally skiable all winter, and you might be able to take advantage of someone's snowmobile tracks.

THE CLIMBS

Crestone Peak, South Red Gully (Class 3). From the South Colony Trailhead in the valley, skin up the road for 2.7 miles to the summer South Colony Trailhead, which is well marked. Cross South Colony Creek to the southwest side and continue up 2.5 miles to the end of the old four-wheel-drive road. In the middle of a small meadow at 11,000 feet near historical kiosk signs, look for a small sign that splits the trails to the south and southwest sides of the basin. It is best to stay right (southwest) at this trail junction and find your way up toward South Colony Lake through the trees. At 11,600 feet you will emerge near the lake with the iconic Crestone Needle above you. From South Colony Lake you will be able to see Broken Hand Pass to your left (southwest). Traverse around the south end of South Colony Lake until you are on the end closest to Crestone Needle. From here at 11,600 feet you can look south while ascending the bowl to your southwest. Aim for the 12,900-foot saddle between Broken Hand Peak (left) and Crestone Needle (right). Climb the bowl to 12,500 feet and ascend a moderate northeast facing couloir for 400 feet to Broken Hand Saddle (12,900 feet). From the saddle descend on skis for 600 feet to your west to Cottonwood Lake (12,300 feet). Ski 0.25 mile farther west from the lake to the base of Crestone Peak. You will clearly see the south couloir, also known as the "red gully" in the summertime. Ascend the couloir for nearly 2000 feet to the 14,180-foot notch saddle between the true summit to the northwest (left) and the false east summit. The couloir is steepest and narrow in the lower third of the couloir, and gets wider and easier near the notch. Carefully assess snow conditions in the couloir because anything that slides from higher up will funnel all the way down the couloir! From the notch, traverse the steep face along ledges and snow and travel west/northwest to reach the summit.

Crestone Needle (Class 3). Follow the same route as described above to reach the 12,900-foot Broken Hand Saddle between Broken Hand Peak and Crestone Needle. From the saddle, traverse northwest on the west side of Crestone Needle's southeast ridge to 13,300 feet. Be careful with your route finding in this section and make your way through minor cliff bands. There is one section with a short 15-foot downclimb that can be tricky. When covered in snow the downclimb can be skied or carefully traversed into a landing zone at 13,300 feet, which then traverses for 100 yards to reach the base of the major south couloir on Crestone Needle's south face. This is where the climb begins. Ascend the eastern and main couloir for 600 feet to reach the upper portion of Crestone Needle's south face. Lower down in the couloir an ice bulge may create problems in low snow years and then half way up the couloir, the steepness reaches almost 50 degrees for a short pitch. Near the top of the couloir the terrain opens up to a wider face, and after a final cliff band, top out on the ridge and triumphantly walk across the rocky ridge and/or stable snow cornices to the summit.

The South Couloir of the Needle is filled in nicely for a ski descent.

DESCENTS

1. *Crestone Peak South Face/Red Couloir* ◆ / ◆◆ Follow the very short portion of the summit ridge southwest to gain access to the south face, which leads into the south couloir/red gully. When you initially drop in to the face, carefully ski some steep but exhilarating turns to get into the couloir. You can also carefully traverse skier's left (east) to the 14,180-foot notch that is at the top of the couloir. From the top of the couloir, drop in and ski 2000 feet of the classic line that you just climbed to get all the way back to the basin below. Traverse east to Cottonwood Lake in the basin and then skin/ boot pack back up to Broken Hand Pass (12,900 feet) before skiing the steep northeast couloir and bowl back to South Colony Lake. Follow the road back to South Colony Trailhead.

2. *Crestone Needle South Couloir* ◆ / ◆◆ It is very rare to get a good snow year in which this entire line is skiable. Descend the short and sharp south-

Just below the narrowest portion of the South Couloir on the Needle. The Great Sand Dunes are visible.

east ridgeline of Crestone Needle from the summit. Where the ridge crest gets ready to drop abruptly directly to the south, ski the wider upper portion of the face until it funnels into the very steep and narrow south couloir. You will have likely climbed this line on your ascent so you were able to assess its skiability. In the narrowest portions of the upper couloir, sideslipping may work best, or if the snow is good, careful jump turns will get you down into the wider portions of the couloir. Just above 13,400 feet a large ice bulge can often be skied and bypassed to the left (east). Once reaching 13,250 feet you have two choices: ski the couloir below you, which opens up and runs down to Cottonwood lake; or if you don't want to have to climb the 600 feet back up to Broken Hand Saddle, traverse the southeast ridge of Crestone Needle, avoiding cliff bands, and make your way back to Broken Hand Saddle. From Broken Hand Saddle, ski the northeast facing couloir and north bowl back to South Colony Lake.

ALTERNATIVES

Crestone Peak Northwest Couloir ◆◆ (See photo of the couloir on page 264, Kit Carson entry) This northwest facing line is rarely skied and needs good snow coverage to allow a clean passage into the couloir and the valley below. You can drop in from the 14,180-foot notch to the east of the true summit at the top of the south facing red gully couloir. Be aware that near the bottom of the northwest couloir you must traverse out and into Bear's Playground before a steep cliff band. From Bear's Playground you can ski some chutes to your east and back down to Upper South Colony Lake to the west of Lower South Colony Lake.

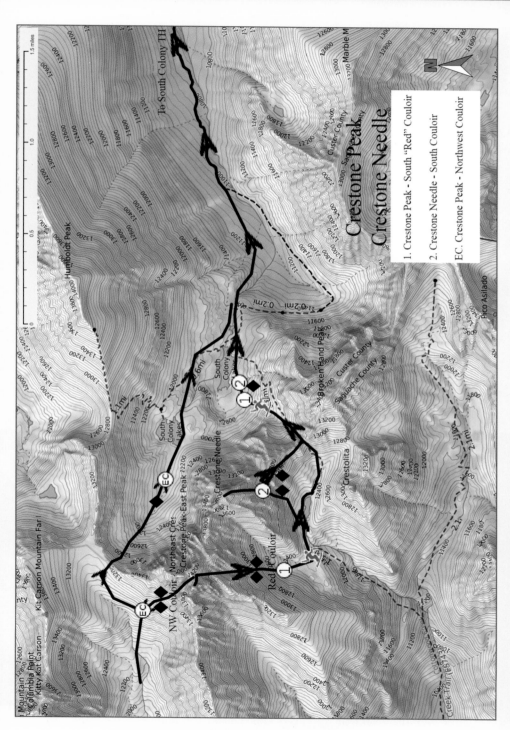

CRESTONE PEAK / CRESTONE NEEDLE

68. Humboldt Peak
14,064 feet/4286 meters

SKIABLE VERTICAL:	4550 feet/1405 meters
ROUND-TRIP DISTANCE:	13 to 14 miles/21 kilometers
TRAILHEAD:	South Colony (8,780 feet)
DIFFICULTY RATINGS:	■ / ◆
SKI TERRAIN:	Four-wheel-drive trail, tree glades, moderate faces, and couloirs
OPTIMAL SEASON:	February through May. April and May are ideal.
MAPS:	Trails Illustrated Number 138, Crestone Peak, San Isabel National Forest

COMMENT: Humboldt Peak is a worthy and rewarding ski objective that stands in the shadow of Crestone Peak and Crestone Needle to the east. The two main ski descent lines discussed here are filled in by April and May nearly every year. Humboldt's summit serves as a vantage point for viewing the stellar Crestones from a safe distance.

Sunrise over Humboldt from the Broken Hand Couloir. The South Face and South Couloir ski line is visible at a 45-degree angle from the summit ridge across the center of the peak.

The summit of Humboldt on a windy winter day. Crestone Needle and Peak as well as Kit Carson (right) provide the scenery.

Making turns in the upper South Colony Basin below Crestone Peak's north face.

GETTING THERE

South Colony Trailhead. See Crestone Peak, Crestone Needle.

THE CLIMBS

West Ridge or South Face & Couloir (Class 2). From the South Colony Trailhead in the valley, skin up the road for 2.7 miles to the summer South Colony Trailhead, which is well marked. Cross the South Colony Creek to the southwest side and continue 2.5 miles up to the end of the old four-wheel-drive road. In the middle of a small meadow at 11,000 feet near historical kiosk signs, find a small sign that splits the trails to the south and southwest sides of the basin. Stay right (west/northwest) at this trail junction and find your way up toward South Colony Lake through the trees. At 11,400 feet you will emerge below the lake with the iconic Crestone Needle above you to the west and Humboldt's relatively steep south couloir gully above you to the north. If snow conditions are stable, climb the south couloir direct for 2,300 feet to reach the summit ridge of Humboldt at 13,900 feet. Then climb or skin east for 200 yards to the summit. If snow conditions are not as stable, proceed to the west up to 11,600 feet and South Colony Lake. Climb toward Upper South Colony Lake to your northwest and reach a 12,800-foot connecting saddle on Humboldt's west ridge. Follow the west ridge east to reach the summit.

DESCENTS

1. *South Face/South Couloir* ◆ Follow a very short portion of the summit ridge west to gain access to the south face, which leads into the south couloir.

A spectacular sunrise en route to Humboldt's West Ridge.

The steepness of the face is 30 degrees where you drop in and it easily funnels into the couloir. You can ski the couloir all the way down into the valley or choose small variations to the west on a shoulder that stays out of the couloir and provides an incredible backdrop of the Crestones. Once back to timberline travel southeast to follow the road back to South Colony Trailhead.

2. **_Southeast Face Gully_** ◆ / ◆◆ This line is only slightly harder than the south face line. Leave the summit and traverse east for 150 yards to reach the crest of the ridge. Drop into a face to your southeast that is steep near the top but then cleanly skis into the southeast gully of the peak. Choose the best line based on coverage and conditions. A few small cliff bands are present part way down the face, but if you stay skiers left they can be avoided, and the gully provides a direct path to the basin below and South Colony Road.

ALTERNATIVES

West Ridge ◆ Ski the west ridge of Humboldt. From 13,750 feet on the west ridge you can stay on the south aspect of the ridge and ski down to the vicinity of Upper South Colony Lake to your southwest. Alternatively, leave the west ridge to the northwest and explore North Colony Basin.

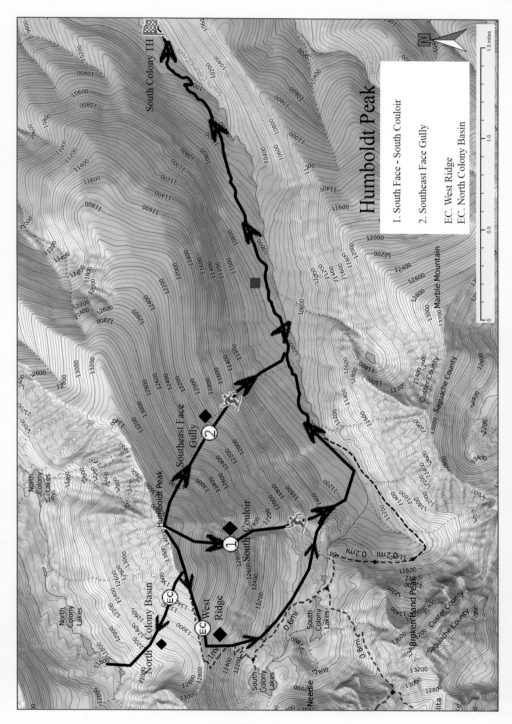

Humboldt Peak

1. South Face - South Couloir

2. Southeast Face Gully

EC. West Ridge
EC. North Colony Basin

HUMBOLDT PEAK

69. Blanca Peak 14,345 feet/4372 meters
70. Ellingwood Point 14,042 feet/4280 meters

SKIABLE VERTICAL:	6345 feet/1934 meters
ROUND-TRIP DISTANCE:	14.5 miles/23.4 kilometers
TRAILHEAD:	Lake Como (8,000 feet)
DIFFICULTY RATINGS:	■ / ◆ / ◆ ◆
SKI TERRAIN:	Four-wheel-drive trail corridor, tree glades, steep faces, and couloirs
OPTIMAL SEASON:	January through May. March, April, and May are ideal.
MAPS:	Trails Illustrated Number 138, Blanca Peak, Twin Peaks, Rio Grande National Forest

COMMENT: Blanca Peak is the sentinel of the Sangre de Cristo Range. The mountain towers over the San Luis Valley and in the right conditions delivers a super long and fun ski descent. Combine both Blanca and Ellingwood to ski two amazing ski lines in one day for nearly 8000 feet of vertical in the early spring.

GETTING THERE
Lake Como Trailhead (8000 feet). From east of Alamosa on US Highway 160, go north on Colorado Highway 150 for 3.2 miles to an unmarked road leading

The summit of Ellingwood Point.

Reaching the summit of Blanca with the South Face of Ellingwood below. Photo by Anne Marie Migl

Ascending the steep Hour Glass Couloir on Little Bear.

Carefully carving turns on the Hour Glass. Photo by Anne Marie Migl

to the northeast. Follow the road for 2 miles as it passes through sandy soils and gets gradually rougher. On rare occasions after a fresh storm you can skin up the road from 8,000 feet. Most of the time, however, you can drive up a fence-line as the road climbs from 8000 feet for several hundred feet more. The road turns left while curving through juniper trees and becomes very rough. Consider parking lower if you value your vehicle, but definitely park before you reach significant switchbacks. The road is generally skiable above 9000 feet if the snow holds. Otherwise, hike up to the snowline, which, during spring, is usually in the basin above.

Ellingwood (center) and Blanca (right) are two fun ski objectives in the upper Como basin.

THE CLIMBS

Blanca Peak, Northwest Face/Ellingwood Point South Face (Class 2+). From 8,000 feet in the San Luis Valley, follow Lake Como Road for 5 miles to Lake Como. The south facing aspects of the road's switchbacks are generally not snowy most of the year, but once you enter Holbrook Basin and travel northeast, the snow conditions always allow skinning toward Lake Como at 11,740 feet. From the east side of Lake Como, follow the four-wheel-drive corridor up through evergreen trees for 0.5 mile to Blue Lakes at 12,100 feet. Above Blue Lakes the pyramid of Ellingwood Point is obvious, while Blanca is blocked by the Little Bear/Blanca connecting ridge to your right (southeast). Climb the basin toward the saddle between Ellingwood and Blanca. After another 0.5 mile above Blue Lakes you will arrive in a bowl below Ellingwood's south face and Blanca's northeast face. In

Descending the lower reaches of the South Face of Ellingwood Point. Little Bear dominates the view into the basin. Photo by Anne Marie Migl

good snow and early morning conditions in April or May climb Ellingwood first to take advantage of the sun angle and avoid warming (if you are doing both peaks). Climb Ellingwood's south face for 0.5 mile to reach the summit ridge and travel west for 200 yards to the true summit. If ascending Blanca, there is a shallow gully/couloir toward the middle third of the west end of the face that can be in excellent booting condition to climb to the top. It is also possible to climb to the connecting saddle between the two peaks at about 13,750 feet and follow Blanca's north ridge to the summit.

DESCENTS

1. ***Blanca Peak Northwest Couloir/Face*** ◆ This descent is straightforward and right off the summit. Drop off from a minor snow roll or cornice on the summit ridge. Skier's left will funnel you toward a minor shallow gully. Ski the gully or chose terrain directly on the face and make your way back toward Ellingwood Point and the bowl near 13,200feet. Ski all the way back to Lake Como and beyond.

2. ***Ellingwood Point South Face*** ◆ / ◆◆ Ski east and southeast along the summit ridge to access the south face, which begins as a small gully but opens up onto the south face. After 400 feet of turns, angle to your southeast to find the best lines that empty into the bowl below Blanca's northwest face.

ALTERNATIVES

Ellingwood Point Southwest Face ◆◆ The southwest face of Ellingwood has plenty of lines, including a main gully and couloir, and in the right conditions is a great challenge. Be aware of the cliff bands on this face and definitely scout well before launching.

Little Bear Peak Hour Glass ◆◆ Instead of climbing Blanca or Ellingwood, ascend Little Bear's west ridge route and climb and ski the infamous Hour Glass.

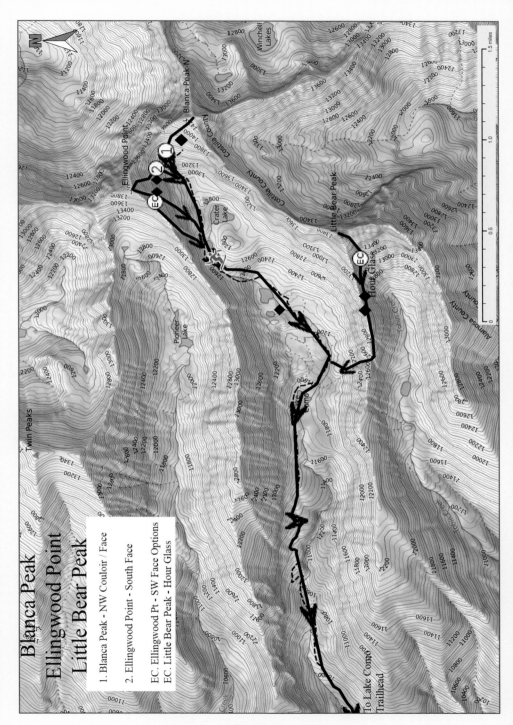

BLANCA PEAK / ELLINGWOOD POINT

Appendix:

AVALANCHE, SNOW PACK, LODGING, AND WEATHER RESOURCES

Colorado Avalanche Information Center: www.avalanche.state.co.us

NOAA: National Oceanic and Atmospheric Administration: www.NOAA.gov

The American Institute for Avalanche Research and Education (AIARE): www.avtraining.org

Crested Butte Avalanche Center: www.cbavalanchecenter.org

American Avalanche Association: www.avalanche.org

American Alpine Club: www.americanalpineclub.org

Colorado Mountain Club: www.cmc.org

10th Mountain Division Hut Association: www.huts.org

San Juan Huts: www.sanjuanhuts.com

Red Mountain Pass Huts: www.skihuts.com

Rocky Mountain National Park: www.nps.gov/romo/index.htm

Great Sand Dunes National Park: www.nps.gov/grsa/planyourvisit

The Author skiing powder in Castle Peak's North Couloir. Photo by Anne Marie Migl

About the Author:

Dr. Jon Kedrowski, author of *Sleeping on the Summits: Colorado 14er High Bivys* and *Skiing and Sleeping on the Summits: Cascade Volcanoes*, grew up in Vail, Colorado. Jon first climbed each of Colorado's 14ers in the late 1990's before he turned 18. Jon went on to complete climbing all 74 named 14,000' peaks in the Lower-48 United States in 2013. Over the years he has skied from every 14er, and in 2016 he skied each Colorado 14er during the same winter season. Jon has skied every peak and ski location in this guidebook.

Jon has climbed and skied on all seven continents and led climbing expeditions to each of the seven summits. In 2012, Jon summited Mt. Everest. He has been featured on several documentaries about his climbing and skiing adventures on the Discovery Channel, Smithsonian, NBC, DatelineNBC, CBS, ABC, FOX, and CNN. He is also a regular contributor to KDVR Fox 31 Denver and KWGN CW2 in Denver for stories about the great outdoors in Colorado.

Jon's favorite hobbies include skiing, mountaineering, and photography. He loves to travel, mountain bike, trail run, river raft, play basketball, and play golf while enjoying the gorgeous summer and fall seasons in Colorado. For more about Dr. Kedrowski, visit www.jonkedrowski.com and @drjonkedski on Instagram and Twitter.

Illustration by Jesse Crock

Join Today.
Adventure Tomorrow.

The Colorado Mountain Club helps you maximize living in an outdoor playground and connects you with other adventure-loving mountaineers. We summit 14ers, climb rock faces, work to protect the mountain experience, and educate generations of Coloradans.